AFRICAN WRITERS SERIES

Editorial Adviser · Chinua Achebe

34

Ten One-Act Plays

D1562275

AWS

Ten One-Act Plays

Edited by

COSMO PIETERSE

HEINEMANN EDUCATIONAL BOOKS LTD

LONDON · IBADAN · NAIROBI

Heinemann Educational Books Ltd
48 Charles Street, London W.1
PMB 5205, Ibadan · POB 25080, Nairobi

MELBOURNE TORONTO AUCKLAND
HONG KONG SINGAPORE

Printed in Malta by
St Paul's Press Ltd

Contents

Acknowledgements

Ganesh Bagchi's play, *The Deviant*, first appeared in *Transition, 2*; Alfred Hutchinson's play, *Fusane's Trial*, first appeared in *The New African*; Athol Fugard's play, *The Occupation*, first appeared in *Contrast*. We are grateful to the respective editors for permission to reproduce these plays.

The Game by Femi Euba, *Yon Kon* by Pat Maddy, *The Opportunity* by Arthur Maimane, *Fusane's Trial* by Alfred Hutchinson and *Blind Cyclos* by Ime Ikiddeh have all been broadcast in the B.B.C. African Service series *African Theatre*, to the producers of which we are grateful.

Introduction

Sometime in 1963 when Richard Rive first suggested the idea of the present anthology, we asked ourselves the question that had often been asked by students of literature and especially by readers of the new writing that was coming from Africa in the early sixties: 'Why is there such a shortage of dramatic writing in Africa: particularly if one considers the wealth of dramatic material in the African situation?'

Today the answer seems clear. The question was being asked too soon! To prove this one need only mention the names of playwrights whose work has come to the notice of theatre-goers and an English drama-reading public: Wole Soyinka, Athol Fugard, John Pepper Clark, Christina Ama Ata Aidoo, Tewfik Al-Hakim, Tsegaye Gabre-Medhin, Duro Ladipo, Alfred Hutchinson, Obotunde Ijimere, Lewis Nkosi, R. Sarif Easmon, Obi Egbuna, J. C. De Graft, James Ene Henshaw. It is a list whose fourteen names cover the continent from Ethiopia to Freetown and from Cape Town to Egypt and includes names of international standing and repute. It covers an output of more than three dozen plays, some of the first order.

And yet when one looks at the section *Drama* in J. A. Ramsaran's *New Approaches to African Literature* (Ibadan University Press, 1965) one finds listed only a handful of original plays published before 1963 – notably Dei

Anang's *Okomfe Anokye's Golden Stool* and Harry Bloom's *King Kong*. A similar pre-1963 dearth of plays prevails in Margaret Amosu's *Creative African Writing – In the European* (University Press, 1965) one finds listed only a handful of *Languages* (special supplement to 'African Notes', University of Ibadan, circa 1964), and this is borne out by a reference to the bibliography in Gerald Moore's *Seven African Writers* (Three Crowns, O.U.P., 1962).

How then do we explain this apparent scarcity of drama in 1963?

First: dramatic *writing*. As with most of the present writing of what appears to be the virtual renaissance of literature from Africa, dramatic writing follows a long, active oral line, not, of course, in English for the most part; and, so far as *published* material is concerned, one *is* thinking chiefly in terms of *English* plays.

Second: the wealth of dramatic *material*. That this was not translated into *drama* for the theatre, was caused by a variety of factors: all over Africa some of these factors operated fairly similarly; in some cases very peculiar conditions determined the 'Silence' of drama.

We shall touch only on the general reasons.

The dramatic material itself is, generally speaking, of two sorts. The political, social and economic situation in a continent full of varieties, tensions and possible solutions supplies one kind. The other consists of the rich resources for excitement and climax to be found in the religions and rituals, the fables and folk tales, the epic poems and praise poems of the African past and present. Why was all this not transformed into plays?

Part of the answer, here, lies in the fact that on both levels this dramatic material was itself quite fully experienced in actual life by the people whose lives *were* these same problems and situations. The energies of men and women, the young and the old, unschooled and formally educated, went into trying to solve the problems of oppression or of achieving recognition, or amenities – including educational theatres. Few theatres and, for many reasons, hardly any 'indigenous' theatre-goers existed.

On the other hand, the manner in which rituals were performed and in which stories were told or poems recited, generally involved the entire group that was concerned. There was no sharp, strict line between spectator and participant in a religious ceremony – whether of prayer or of 'magic' – or in a story-telling session, or in a state ceremony.

Broadly speaking, the dramatic material was the actual, living, communal drama of ordinary people.

This meant that when the theatre as a distinct place of re-creation – for entertainment and instruction – was built in Africa, it took two shapes. One was as an outpost-of-the-Empire story which did not go beyond importing plays and players or styles from 'home' and was fostered chiefly by European expatriate groups. The other started with translations and adaptations of plays from Europe, with adaptations of stories, novels, legends, myths and fables from folk-lore and the Bible, in schools, colleges and churches, in township-halls and in open squares. It went on to deal with the-lives-that-people-lived and life-as-people-see-it and was often characterized by the free audience participation and audience response remarked upon by David Cook (*Transition, 18*) and mentioned by Lewis Nkosi in his essay *Toward A New African Theatre* (in *Home and Exile*, Longmans Forum Series, 1965).

Now, much of the present-day drama from Africa is given body, health, sustenance and beauty by elements that derive from the traditional dramatic forms of ritual, music, praise poems, fable, epic, and re-enacted story.

Once a South African colleague said: 'The theatre is poorly developed amongst the people. There is much virgin soil to be upturned. There is a fine opportunity to build up theatres of the people – theatres that will stage the best plays of the past and present, occidental and oriental, comedy or tragedy, and foster a realist drama that derives from the world in which people live, a drama that will help enrich a people's life and help build a people's destiny.' (F. G. Grammer in a lecture *Drama and Society*, published in a cyclostyled booklet, *Lectures*, by the Cape Flats Educational Fellowship, Athlone, Cape Town.)

Perhaps the implicit hope that Frank Grammer expressed for the South African theatre has been fulfilled in a larger context by some of the plays of the writers mentioned earlier; it has certainly been realized to a large extent by the travelling theatres in West and East Africa (and in some plays in David Cook's *Origin East Africa*, African Writers Series No. 15).

For one feels confident in saying with J. A. Ramsaran ' . . . the modern African theatre is taking shape under the hands of schools of drama, literary and dramatic clubs, radio and television.' It *is* taking very real shape, and its recent and continued fostering through publication is a sign of its phenomenal but sturdy growth.

The present volume, one trusts, will be an added indication of the potential of drama from Africa.

The plays come from Nigeria, South Africa, Kenya and Ghana; their themes range from the domestic and the personal to the social and political and include marriage, war, bribery, deceit, coercion and prison-life. The styles vary from realism and naturalism to the symbolical and poetic, and the treatment covers the media of stage, radio and television.

Our only consideration in the compilation, apart from

choosing plays in the one-act mould originally written in English, was quality. We are sure that the plays will speak for themselves to students, readers, producers, actors and audiences—especially to the last three categories.

To facilitate pleasurable reading, we have tried not to come between the play and its audience; hence the appendices: short biographical notes and editorial comments with glossaries.

The glossaries are to be regarded as no more than indications of the approximate meanings of words from languages other than English, or of references that may be rather local or somewhat remote.

The comments reflect very summarily the opinions formed by the compiler: more often than not they may prove to be controversial. The more discussion, difference and debate they can elicit, the better.

Finally, I must express my indebtedness to all the institutions and individuals who have – through granting manuscripts and copyright, and in various other ways – made this volume possible. There are hosts who do not realize how much inspiring help I have sucked from them!

Especially do I wish to thank Richard Rive, the 'onlie begetter', the nine contributors, Shirley Cordeaux of the B.B.C. (African Theatre) and Judith Verity and Keith Sambrook of H.E.B. for their kind help and patient co-operation.

Cosmo Pieterse

LONDON
NOVEMBER 1967

Encounter

KULDIP SONDHI

CHARACTERS

General Nyati, *African about 40 years old*
Lieutenant John Dewey, *European about 30 years old*
Superintendent Paddy, *European about 40 years old*
Sergeant Kitsao, *African about 50 years old*
2 Trackers, *Africans*
2 Soldiers, *Africans*
Colonel (Terrorist), *African about 45 years old*
Wangai, *African woman about 35 years old*
Terrorist Gangs:
  First gang, *6 men (Africans) seen on stage*
  Second gang, *4 or more seen on stage*
  Bodies, *4 at end of scene 2, increasing to 6 or*
  8 depending on size of stage at end of scene 3

ENCOUNTER

SCENE ONE

Hut on Mount Kenya with view of forests. Assistant Superintendent Paddy (man of about 40) and army Lieutenant John Dewey (a man of about 30) are in heated conversation. Map of Kenya is behind them.

PADDY: The difficulty with you, John, is you're new. This isn't 1945 or the European war, this is 1952 and Africa! The people we're fighting in those forests haven't heard of International law or any other law for that matter.

JOHN: Haven't they?

PADDY: No!

JOHN: Well then I am new.

PADDY: 'Course you are! You've heard all about their oaths I suppose?

JOHN (*lights cigarette*): I have and I know it's pretty grim but –

PADDY: But, but! What's the matter with you, man? You're impossible. How long have you been in Kenya?

JOHN: Two months.

PADDY: Two months! I was born here. That's why I know them so well.

JOHN: Well, that explains it.

PADDY: It does! I know their customs and habits. I know how they think.

JOHN: I dare say I know how they think as well.

PADDY: You do! (*incredulous*) Look man we're up against

people here (*points to forests*) who feel no pain and have no feelings, people who no longer live like human beings, certainly not as we know them. They'd as soon murder a mother or a brother as they would a goat if it came to one of their oaths.

JOHN: Don't be so ridiculous, Paddy.

PADDY: And that's just what I mean. I'm always getting green-horns like you straight out from Home spouting a lot of text-book rot till they've gone in there and seen it for themselves.

JOHN: I'm not making excuses for them, Paddy . . . .

PADDY: Then what the hell are you trying to do?

JOHN: I'm just trying to understand their point of view.

PADDY: Their point of view, are you mad? (*Urgent, as he points finger into forest*) There isn't any point of view in there man. In there there's just death and slaughter. And those aren't men any longer, I tell you. We call them terrorists for want of anything better and we herd them into detention camps when we catch them, but that's only to satisfy some crackpot organization like the United Nations. If I had my way there wouldn't be a single damn terrorist left in Kenya.

JOHN: That would bring back normality and prosperity to the country?

PADDY: The hell with your normality. And how would I know about prosperity? I'm not a ruddy business man.

JOHN (*sighs*): I've heard these arguments before.

PADDY: Then tell us what we should do, Professor. I've only lived 35 years in this country and seen some of my best friends go in there never to come out again! Maybe we're just a set of bungling fools, bringing in civilization, setting up hospitals and schools, teaching them to read and write so that they can turn it all against us. Yes, in that sense we have been fools.

JOHN (*walking slowly up and down while Paddy watches him*):
No, you aren't fools. I wouldn't call you that any more
than I'd call them fools. But that doesn't make you
right either. Or them. You're both wrong in this.

PADDY: Well, now we know. What you want is another
kind of collar, my boy. In that uniform you're all
wrong.

JOHN: I fought in Malaya and Cyprus, Paddy, before
coming out here and in the end it turned out the
guerillas were human after all.

PADDY: Malaya, Cyprus, Korea ... that's what we hear
about now; but these fellows are different, John.

JOHN: That's what they always say.

PADDY: They don't! I was in the last war, and I saw what
the Germans did.

JOHN: Pretty, wasn't it?

PADDY: No. I'm not excusing them. It was hell but let me
tell you, you've got a thing or two coming if you
haven't seen these oaths of theirs. Do you want to
know what they do?

JOHN: Not particularly. With or without oaths the situation would remain the same. Anyway what's this
latest stunt they're up to?

PADDY (*turns to map*): Time we talked of something sensible.
See this area? (*Indicates flagged portion on Mt. Kenya.*)

JOHN: H'mmm yes, can't say it means much to me.

PADDY (*points to scene out of window*): Well, that there is
just a fraction of it. The thickest, most deadly terrain
in Kenya. A hide-out for the two most dangerous
gangs in this country. If we could break them up the
war would be over in a month. In terms of cash alone
it's costing us a cool million a month plus the head-
aches.

JOHN: Then you agree it's a war.

PADDY: Well ... yes; what are you getting at now?

JOHN (*smiling*): Just wondered when you were going to admit the truth to yourself.

PADDY: Truth . . . what do you mean?

JOHN: You're always calling this an Emergency, or a police action or a fight against terrorists when you know darned well it isn't anything of the sort.

PADDY: Then what is it, Mr. Knowall?

JOHN: You just said it . . . a war.

PADDY: Of course, it's a war dammit, between us and the rebels.

JOHN: No, it isn't that simple, Paddy. Let's admit that to ourselves at least. This is a war between us, the privileged few, and the others who won't stand for us any more.

PADDY: God, you're a Bolshie.

JOHN: In Malaya—

PADDY: This is Kenya and I've got a job to do if you don't mind. (*Rings bell.*)

JOHN (*smiling*): Sorry. I'm here to take orders, not to argue.

PADDY: Well, I wish you'd remember that – sir! (*A knock, enter Sgt. Kitsao in uniform*) Are the trackers here, Sergeant?

SGT: Yes sir.

PADDY: Quite ready to leave?

SGT: Yes sir. (*Pause*) Sir, I'd like to make a request.

PADDY: What is it? (*Glances at his watch.*)

SGT: I would like to go with them.

PADDY: Oh, don't you trust them?

SGT: No, it isn't that. But a man who's been a traitor once can be a traitor again.

PADDY: H'mmm, yes . . . that's true of course. (*Turns to John*) That's another thing you don't know. Some of our most valuable trackers and fighters are men who've left the other side and joined us. How'd you explain that – no, never mind. Quite right, Sergeant

Kitsao. You've got a point there. Get ready then and when you're ready report to me again . . . have you got that letter?

SGT: Yes sir, here it is.

PADDY: Good, you can have it back before leaving and I'd like to see the trackers as well.

SGT: Yes, sir, we'll be ready in another ten minutes. (*Leaves room.*)

PADDY: See this? (*Holds out letter.*)

JOHN: I do. What is it?

PADDY: It might not be anything and yet it might prove to be the beginning of the end.

JOHN: For whom?

PADDY: For them, of course!

JOHN: Sorry, I didn't mean to be frivolous.

PADDY: There isn't any time for frivolity here, my boy. This is a small forward post but we are dealing with the future of this country. In fact I'd say we are dealing with the future of Africa here. If we lose this war, we lose Africa – make no mistake about that.

JOHN: Must be an important letter. Is it addressed to the Queen?

PADDY: No, but we've had that as, well for your information. That place (*nods outside*) is full of Knights of the Garter and Field Marshals. Only this one . . . this one . . . isn't from the aristocracy. This is from one of the simple ones . . . someone who's probably sick of fighting and wants peace again.

JOHN: Or his pension, maybe. Hasn't he asked for a reward as well?

PADDY: What! (*Opens letter and reads it again.*) Yes . . . yes he has. Wants safe custody and a thousand pounds.

JOHN: Now that's what I call peace with honour.

PADDY: He might get it too if he delivers the goods.

JOHN: What's that?

PADDY: It's a slim chance ... hardly a chance I'd say
frankly, but we can't afford to let it slip. You see it's
like this. We've been fighting this movement, this war
if you like, for over two years now and the most
dangerous elements in the rebellion exist in those
two gangs. Their leader goes by the name of General
Nyati, and he's the one we really want. Fights with
this. (*Taps head.*) Now if we nabbed him it would be all
over.

JOHN: Is that what this is about? (*Nods at letter.*)

PADDY: Yes. Some member of his gang's told us that they'll
be passing such and such a place tomorrow afternoon,
some fig tree or the other that the trackers know all
about. Fair enough. But before I send out some of our
best boys I'd like to make sure that such and such a
place exists. It might be a plan to ambush us ...
happened before. But on the other hand it mightn't
and I can't afford to let any information slip by now.
We'll never get this bloke unless someone informs
on him.

JOHN: Sounds an unusual fellow.

PADDY: He's a clever terrorist if that's what you mean. No
more.

JOHN: I wonder? He must be more than just a clever
terrorist to lead us such a dance. First it was police
and then it was the Army and now it's the Reserves
with reinforcements coming in from Aden and
Cyprus. No terrorist could do that much.

PADDY: Well, this one's done it.

JOHN: Exactly, and that's because he isn't just a terrorist.

PADDY: He isn't a god either.

JOHN: Nor the devil, however devilish his methods may be.
This one's got that extra bit in him. That's why he's
so dangerous.

PADDY: What extra bit?

JOHN: Some curious humanity that all great leaders possess. They inspire faith in their followers. They can spill blood, commit follies and yet be revered, not from fear but quite literally from a kind of love that's felt right down to the meanest of their followers. Search the history of any nation and you'll find men of that calibre. Cromwell did a thing or two we wouldn't want to discuss now, and old Grivas isn't an old milk-sop either. Such men aren't out for personal gain or even glory. It's more like some universal idea of justice that consumes them. And when that touches people they're ready to march right into the jaws of hell.

PADDY: Wish this one would go there.

JOHN: He probably will but his men will go all the way with him till he loses faith in himself. Then nothing can save him. What do you say he calls himself?

PADDY: General Nyati.

JOHN: Is he a General?

PADDY: Of course not, but he's seen service. By legitimate Army rank he's a Corporal.

JOHN: Another Corporal! The last one wanted to conquer the world.

PADDY: This one isn't in that class, but he's every bit as blood-thirsty.

JOHN: Was he in the last war?

PADDY: Yes, saw service in Burma. Demobbed, travelled a bit in England and on the continent. Bit of an educated bloke, I believe. Came back to Kenya a dissatisfied war veteran and started this racket.

JOHN: H'mmm, that follows a pattern. What does he look like?

PADDY: About forty, medium height, slim, black and incorrigible.

JOHN: Perfect police report. Anything else?

PADDY: Nyati's a sort of forest name he's given himself.
Means 'bull' in their language. That's what everyone
calls him now. We've also got Generals from China
and Field Marshals from Russia, Brigadiers who call
themselves leopards and the lesser fry adorned in
every kind of animal skin that stinks a mile. This
one's real name's Daniel Kamau and he's a Christian.
Also prays to fig trees. Slaughters goats and dabbles
in dreams.

JOHN: Interesting chap. Good speaker?

PADDY: The bloody devil himself.

JOHN: Fearless?

PADDY: Yes and no . . . well, yes, he must be or he couldn't
stand our pressure. Yes, I'll give him that.

JOHN: Plans his campaigns meticulously, I suppose?

PADDY: Don't know about that. But he's a clever fighter
though it's more some kind of sixth sense. 'Course
he knows that damned jungle inside out.

JOHN: I see. And this is the man who's just a clever
terrorist?

PADDY: Well, call him what you want but he's a bloody
nuisance and right now I'd give my right hand to get
him.

JOHN: Mightn't be enough.

PADDY (exasperated): All right then, tell you what, you go
out with my boys this time. It's only a reconnaissance
trip but it'll give you an idea of the kind of country
we fight in.

JOHN: Oh . . . yes . . . yes, I'll do that. Good, I will!

PADDY: I'll have to put you in charge but old Kitsao
knows what to do. Just follow his advice.

JOHN (smiles): But I should give the orders – yes, I understand.

PADDY: I'm afraid you don't understand, John. It's easy
to criticize us when you don't know what we are up

against. These aren't normal people any longer. They're cunning, savage and completely ruthless. Life means nothing to them.

JOHN: Don't they have parents and friends?

PADDY: You don't know what you're talking about. This fellow, the General, he really does pray to a fig tree and plans all his strategy in his dreams. Does that make sense to you?

JOHN: Maybe he's a poet.

PADDY: It's no use arguing with you but remember, in case you come across any terrorists out there, shoot first and talk poetry afterwards. I don't want your scalp on my hands. In any case, are you sure you'd like to go?

JOHN: If you want the truth, Paddy, I don't really want to go, just as I didn't want to come out to Kenya after Malaya and Cyprus. This violence is all wrong. They're silly to have started it no matter how provoked they were, because as rulers we've to be bloody enough to mow them down, however civilized we might be. It's one of the traps of history and it's sprung on every nation that colonizes and I dare say it'll carry on happening till everyone's free. But that's just a personal opinion. With this uniform on I'm in it as much as you are.

PADDY: Glad you realize that. First bit of common sense I've heard from you all morning.

JOHN: And yet in many ways it's all a question of race and prestige.

PADDY: Of course.

JOHN: Exactly and so it must exist for the other side as well.

PADDY: What do you mean?

JOHN: Look, let's face it; this is their war of independence.

PADDY: No, no, that's where you've got it all wrong. This

is just a bloody, dirty, big shauri started by a few hot-heads and once it's over you won't hear a thing about it again. Not from me anyhow.

JOHN: It's fellows like that old Kitsao, the Sergeant, who surprise me. How can he fight against his own people?

PADDY: He's fighting a bunch of terrorists like you are. Nothing surprising about that I hope!

JOHN: Would you shoot at me?

PADDY: Any moment now. Kitsao lost his mother, brother and two sisters when one of these gangs raided his village last year. Don't you think he's human?

JOHN: Sorry, I didn't know that; but that's exactly what I mean. He is human, of course he is – and so are the others.

PADDY: I'm almost hoping you run into some of our friends out there. Teach you a thing or two. You and your history! (*Knock on door.*) Yes, come in.

SGT: We're ready, sir.

PADDY : Lieutenant Dewey will be coming with you, Sergeant. Take two other men as escorts. Where are the trackers?

SGT: At base camp, sir. I thought you could see them there.

PADDY: Good, I will. What's the time now? Nine o'clock, and this place is about eighteen miles west. You may have to spend the night out there, but in any case if you aren't back by evening I'll send someone after you . . . just in case bwana here starts talking poetry to them.

SGT: Pardon, sir?

PADDY: Nothing. I'll come down with you. See you at base camp in fifteen minutes, John.

JOHN: Fine. Fifteen minutes'll be enough to change.

PADDY: The thing's in there. (*Nods significantly and goes out. Lt. John Dewey looks at map of Kenya. Then he stares out of the window. Silence, except for distant clamour of jungle sounds now starting up. Then he opens drawer and takes out sten gun thoughtfully.)*

CURTAIN

SCENE TWO

Trees, firelight, night sounds on Mt. Kenya.

Five terrorists in semi-circle warming their hands: three are dressed in animal skins, two are dressed in torn army tunics; three have woollen caps, two are bare-headed. A woman in army attire tends pot of food under fig tree in corner of stage. When she returns and sits down, one of the men in army tunic puts his arm round her. She leans her head on his shoulder. This man never talks. He is also the most simply dressed of all. His back is to the audience. On the back curtain shadows flit from time to time to indicate rest of gang.

1st TERRORIST: There's a traitor among us.

2nd TERRORIST: There must be. The serkali hunt us like animals now.

1st TERRORIST: When I get my hand on him—(*takes out short, strangling rope and makes significant pull.*)

3rd TERRORIST: That should finish him fast enough. But have you thought, jamaa, why so many of our men should be leaving us?

2nd TERRORIST: These are our own people, black people. That's what I don't understand?

3rd TERRORIST: It's not difficult. What kind of life is this? We live like animals.

2nd TERRORIST: But one day we will be called heroes.

4th TERRORIST: Is that why you're fighting?

3rd TERRORIST: Everyone has his own reasons for fighting.

2nd TERRORIST: Yes, even the traitor among us must have had a reason once.

1st TERRORIST: It will do him no good when I catch him.
He has a lot to pay for! Last week when we ran into a
government ambush we lost five men! The army had
been warned.

4th TERRORIST: Before that two others deserted to the
serkali and now track us like buffaloes. Why do they do
it? Do these people love the white man?

2nd TERRORIST: He is right (*nodding at third*). Not everyone
can stand this life. That is why they desert us and
not because they love the mzungu.

3rd TERRORIST: I wonder if everyone thinks we are heroes?

1st TERRORIST: We are heroes. Our blood will free this
land.

3rd TERRORIST (*laughs*): Dead heroes then. No one will
remember you.

2nd TERRORIST: That's not true. The country below suffers
as much as we do. Look at the way people risk their
lives to bring food and guns to us on the mountain.
We could not fight without their help.

3rd TERRORIST: But will they always supply us with food
and guns? Will they not tire one day and go over to
the serkali like this traitor?

2nd TERRORIST: No, I don't believe that. Some may give in
but now everyone knows this country belongs to the
black man. We will win this war and the traitor among
us must be a fool to think different.

4th TERRORIST: But as long as he does think different our
lives are in danger.

1st TERRORIST: There will be no time for him to think when
I find him out. He has seen me use this on others
(*pulls rope*). Does he think he can escape? Traitors
are cowards . . . let him tremble wherever he is.

4th TERRORIST: If he is one of us he is no coward and will
not tremble.

1st TERRORIST (*springing up*): I say let him tremble!

2nd TERRORIST: I wish he could hear you now but he may not even be among us.

4th TERRORIST: That's right. He may be with the other gang.

3rd TERRORIST: One man among thirty-two. How will we ever find him out?

Sixth terrorist comes on stage. Fourth terrorist rises with a sigh, takes his plate, fills it with food, lifts his gun and leaves.

6th TERRORIST: No one will ever find us here. It is so thick and dark outside. You couldn't recognize your best friend.

2nd TERRORIST (*laughs*): Our best friend is probably here among us.

1st TERRORIST: I say let him tremble wherever he is.

6th TERRORIST: Who?

2nd TERRORIST: The traitor!

3rd TERRORIST: He must know we are all searching for him.

2nd TERRORIST: But since we have changed our tactics he won't be able to do any more harm.

6th TERRORIST: Yes, I hear there has been a change?

2nd TERRORIST: Don't you know? We no longer plan in advance. We change our route from day to day.

Silent man in tunic shrugs, stands up and walks out. The woman goes to her pot of food.

6th TERRORIST: That's a silent one.

1st TERRORIST: Only those who are uncertain or ignorant talk the way we do.

2nd TERRORIST: Or those who are lonely, my friend. So very lonely . . .

6th TERRORIST: The rains are beginning now. In my village they must have planted the wheat.

2nd TERRORIST: This is a time when crops are planted all

over the country. We grow a lot of maize and banana.

3rd TERRORIST: It's the end of the rainy season that I like best, when the maize has ripened and there is plenty of food for everyone.

2nd TERRORIST: Yes, that's when we used to have the dances.

6th TERRORIST: Ah, the dances!

2nd TERRORIST: I remember them so well.

6th TERRORIST: We had music and laughter and girls. What girls!

2nd TERRORIST: Don't talk of it any more. I can see it all so clearly.

6th TERRORIST: So can I.

Fadeout with terrorists all warming their hands and staring at fire. Bright lights come up, on front of stage.

Dance — a gay village dance of Kenya.

Fadeout of lights at end of dance and the forest seen again at the back with the terrorists sitting as they were, staring at fire.

2nd TERRORIST (*sighs*): Yes, I can see it so clearly. But . . . what's the use of dreaming?

1st TERRORIST: No use at all. We are here to fight, not dream. Only one man has real dreams and you will know who he is. (*All nod quietly.*)

6th TERRORIST: You said there had been a change in plan recently.

3rd TERRORIST: Yes, what change is this?

2nd TERRORIST (*turning to 3rd*): You were in the village yesterday when it was discussed.

6th TERRORIST: But what is it?

2nd TERRORIST: Nothing special. If you remember we were supposed to spend two nights at that other fig tree (*points off stage*). Instead we moved off after one night and we move on tomorrow morning again, making our plans at the last moment. The leader saw an attack in his dreams and made this change himself.

1st TERRORIST: He's a cunning one!

3rd TERRORIST: He is!

6th TERRORIST (*to 3rd*): Where were you yesterday?

3rd TERRORIST: I went into the village, the one near the Falls.

6th TERRORIST: But you were away all night. What were you doing?

3rd TERRORIST: What do you think? (*Others laugh.*)

2nd TERRORIST: Yes, sometimes I wish I could get away altogether.

1st TERRORIST (*sighing*): I have an old mother in Nairobi but I haven't seen her in years. I wonder what's happened to her . . . I was her favourite son.

3rd TERRORIST: Where are your other brothers then?

1st TERRORIST: Two in Manyani. The third was caught taking the oath and shot—(*Presses trigger finger.*)

2nd TERRORIST: My wife hadn't given birth to our child when the police found out I had taken the oath. I escaped just in time. Now I wish I had brought her with me.

6th TERRORIST: This is no place for women.

2nd TERRORIST: Nor is the serkali's prison my friend. She was taken away when I escaped. I have made enquiries but no one can tell me where she is.

2nd TERRORIST: I wonder when all this will be over?

3rd TERRORIST: Nothing lasts for ever.

6th TERRORIST: This is going to last for ever. I can't see its end. The serkali have guns and aeroplanes and we . . . what do we have?

2nd TERRORIST: Only our spirit, but God will help us.

3rd TERRORIST: God will also help them. He is not our property.

2nd TERRORIST: No, he can't help them. Even the White

God of the white man knows we are right this time. This is our land and we must get it back. It is ours. The land is ours.

1st TERRORIST: Yes, yes the land is ours! No one can say the land belongs to anyone else but us.

2nd TERRORIST: I remember my father tried to grow coffee but the serkali stopped him. They said coffee could only be grown by white men. And why?

6th TERRORIST: Because it is a good crop and fetches high prices.

2nd TERRORIST: Exactly!

1st TERRORIST: When we go back I'm going to drink a lot of coffee.

6th TERRORIST: We must get the land back. Then we can grow coffee or maize or raise cattle and do as we please. We will live like free men . . . like our fathers did.

2nd TERRORIST: Yet you know, jamaa, it is a strange thing. The man who encouraged and taught my father to grow coffee was a white man. He was our neighbour.

6th TERRORIST: They are strange people. I have never understood how a white man thinks.

3rd TERRORIST: That's what makes them so clever. You can never tell what mzungu will do next.

6th TERRORIST: Many of them are good people. I have always believed that.

2nd TERRORIST: Yes, I agree. When this is over—

1st TERRORIST (*jumping up*): What kind of talk is this! How can they be good people when they rob us, shoot us and hunt us like animals. You are all traitors.

3rd TERRORIST: I only meant—

1st TERRORIST (*whips out panga*): If you say another word I'll kill you.

2nd TERRORIST: Enough . . . enough, jamaa. We are always fighting among ourselves.

1st TERRORIST (*menacing*): Is there anyone who thinks the land should not be ours?

3rd TERRORIST: You will get all the land you want, jamaa. Why are you getting so angry?

6th TERRORIST (*offering his gouri*): Here have some beer, I wish we had coffee for you instead.

WANGAI: Someone brought up a tin yesterday. Shall I open it and make some?

1st TERRORIST (*sits growling*): Give that to the coffee growers. I prefer beer.

3rd TERRORIST: Will you sing for us, Wangai?

2nd TERRORIST: Yes, sing. Then I can think of home again.

6th TERRORIST (*shaking his head*): I had a home once. Now . . . look at us. Sing, Wangai . . . sing so that we can all think of home again.

WANGAI (*takes pot off fire*): Have some food first. Then I will sing.

2nd TERRORIST: When this is all over you know what I will do?

1st TERRORIST: No, what will you do?

2nd TERRORIST: I will become a teacher. I was going to become one before this happened.

6th TERRORIST: And I will become a mechanic. I love machines. I worked on a farm and learned how to repair tractors. The European there said I had magic in my hands. No tractor stayed dead when I touched it. If luck favours me I will go to England and there, maybe, I may even learn how aeroplanes fly. I would love to fly an aeroplane. Imagine me in an aeroplane, jamaa!

3rd TERRORIST: You can have your aeroplanes and farms, I am going to become a tailor. There's a big Indian shop in Nairobi that makes clothes for all the rich people. That's the shop I'm going to take.

1st TERRORIST: You can't have the shop if it's on my land!

B

3rd TERRORIST: But you don't even know where it is!

1st TERRORIST: That doesn't matter, if it is on my land then you can't have it.

2nd TERRORIST: Why, what is your claim?

1st TERRORIST: You do not know the size of my family. I need a lot of land.

2nd TERRORIST: Yes, but how much?

1st TERRORIST: I will need all of Delamare Avenue.

3rd TERRORIST: You're mad, and none of this is possible.

1st TERRORIST (*springing up*): I tell you if your shop is on my land you will have to remove it.

2nd TERRORIST: If you carry on like this the enemy will hear you. And why are we fighting among ourselves? Haven't we enough troubles without that?

6th TERRORIST: They were only wishing. Is that a sin?

2nd TERRORIST: No, that isn't a sin; let every man have his wish, but let's not weaken the cause. What is it that the leader says: 'A twig can be broken by any wind, but the tree will stand a hurricane'? Let our tree remain strong, jamaa.

6th TERRORIST: Our leader is helped by God. Ngai comes to him in his dreams.

3rd TERRORIST: Do you really believe that? How can Ngai come into anyone's dreams?

2nd TERRORIST: That's something I don't understand either, but I have read books of other nations and they too have had men whose spirit took counsel from God. How else do people like us defeat armies and aeroplanes? By ourselves we couldn't do it. It needs a leader. A special man. Our leader is such a man.

6th TERRORIST: His dreams must be real. How many times hasn't he saved us from an enemy ambush when not one of us, (*points at no. 1*) not even him, suspected any danger existed. Yet he lives and suffers like we do.

To look at him no one would think he was any different.

1st TERRORIST: He is different. He is not like us. He understands things that we will never know. We must always obey him.

WANGAI: Yes, we must all obey him. There is a power in him that I have sensed. A power that is in no other man. It must come from Ngai. He says we will win and soon go home again. I believe that to be true.

Sounds of distant thunder.

2nd TERRORIST: If it's not gunfire, it's this thunder. I'm beginning to hate it.

4th TERRORIST: The two sound alike from a distance. And here comes the rain.

Rain outside, increasing in intensity. The terrorists huddle closer to fire.

4th TERRORIST: This mountain is never quiet.

3rd TERRORIST: It won't be till we all go home.

6th TERRORIST: Home . . . you were going to sing, Wangai.

Enter silent terrorist. Sits. Those standing also sit. Wangai looks at silent man who nods and smiles. Wangai sings, accompanied by 3rd terrorist who plays a rimba. (Rimba: A small, hollow wooden musical box, the size of a hand, on top of which are fastened half a dozen flat, sprung wires which resound musically when played with the ends of both thumbs.)

WANGAI'S SONG

1

The deepest pain brings echoes from the past.
All: From the past.
    It burns in every heart,

All: In every heart,
        Trembling in the rain,
        Lighting tapers in the dark.
All: In the dark.
        Ringing bells with the thought:
        This land is ours.
All: Ours!
        This land is ours.
All: Ours, Ours!
        This is our home.
All: Home.

2

        Blow wind,
        Blow in the rain.
        Scatter echoes
        Blind our pain.
All: Blind our pain.
        But blind him too,
        Turn him round,
        Bring him here!
All: Bring him here!
        Turn him round,
        Bring him here!
All: Bring him here!
        The white man, him.
All: Yes, him!
        He stole our home.
All: Home.

3

        Has he no home,
        This red-faced man?
All: Red-faced, whitefaced, deadfaced!
        This deadfaced man

Who comes stealing through the grass,
Dead eyes shod with hate.
All: Hate!
Has he no wife
No children of his own,
No God this man?
All: No God
This deadfaced man
Redfaced, whitefaced, deadfaced!

4

The pain is ours,
The guilt is his.
All: His!
He says the pain is his,
The guilt is ours.
All: Liar!
This redfaced man—
All: Redfaced, whitefaced, deadfaced!
Then let it stop,
Stop this hate.
Let it stop.
All: Let it stop!
Oh God make it stop.
All: Stop!
Stop.
All: Stop!

The silent one springs to his feet. Singing stops. Everyone is on their feet. Backstage there is the sound of muffled machine gun fire. Shadows flee. Sound of bodies crashing through the undergrowth of the forest. Four terrorists from outside rush in and are shot on stage. The five terrorists on stage run from one side to another and find themselves trapped by the Lieutenant and Sergeant in one wing, the soldiers in the other

*wing. They retreat into the centre with hands up . . . the
silent terrorist at one end, Wangai at the other near the fig
tree. Going back she upsets her pot and turns to pick it up.
The Sergeant opens fire. She drops dead. The silent terrorist
makes a move to her while the other exclaim:*

Wangai!

*The Sergeant comes closer and pushes the silent one back, and
doing so, stares into his face. A look of amazement comes
over the Sergeant. The two soldiers are also staring.*

SOLDIERS AND SERGEANT: General . . . General Nyati!

CURTAIN

SCENE THREE

*Night. The same as Scene 2. The stage is darker than before except
where action takes place around the pen. The two soldiers
helped by the Sergeant and Lieutenant are putting last touches
to the pen which is formed by tying lianas around a natural
enclosure of trees. The fig tree stands by itself with the woman's
body behind it. Only part of her body is seen, but unmistakably
so. In the course of this scene a sound of distant thunder is
heard occasionally. The Sergeant and Lieutenant are talking
together as the scene opens.*

JOHN: How many did we get, Sergeant?

SGT: We have counted 26, sir.

JOHN (*nods to darkened corner*): Including that one?

SGT: No, that makes 27. I didn't know it was a woman,
bwana.

JOHN: She had no business being up here. Did any escape?

SGT: I don't think so. We caught them by surprise.

JOHN: If even one gets away it will mean trouble for us.

SGT: In this darkness no one can get far. The other gang's probably far away anyhow.

JOHN: I hope so. We are stuck here for the night. (*Pacing*) But don't you think we should send one of our trackers back to camp to report this capture? It's stopped raining now. He could make it if he knew the way.

SGT: We are in the thickest part of the forest, sir, and there is no moon to show the way.

JOHN: Yes . . . yes, you're quite right. We mustn't lose our heads. Is that other pen ready?

SGT: It is. All the prisoners have been placed in it. The General is with them.

JOHN: General . . . hmmm, you also call him that?

SGT: Everyone calls him that, bwana. He is a most dangerous man. We must keep him separate from the others. While he is with them they will not lose hope.

JOHN: You're right, quite right. But fancy me of all people capturing the most wanted terrorist in Kenya . . . I wonder what Paddy will say to this.

SGT: He won't believe it, sir, till the General is transported away from this mountain to a detention camp. I think some others share that feeling.

JOHN: Then we must make sure the General is provided with transport, Sergeant. Finish this off quickly. I'll just see how those trackers are getting on. (*Goes.*)

SGT: He hasn't yet understood what we've caught.

1st SOLDIER: I can't believe it either.

2nd SOLDIER: Nor can I.

SGT: For months hundreds of men have been trying to catch the General and now suddenly we get him like this.

2nd SOLDIER: I wish we had hundreds with us at this moment.

1st SOLDIER: I wish we hadn't caught him. We came

hunting for rabbits and we've trapped the biggest lion in the forest instead. This is going to be the most difficult night of my life.

SGT: The white man can guard the General himself. That's why I've had this built.

1st SOLDIER: Yes, let him do that. I don't want to be near the General. It is said that he gives the strongest oaths on the mountain.

2nd SOLDIER: I have heard that too!

1st SOLDIER: To break one of his oaths is to go mad and die.

SGT: Is that really true? The traitor hasn't gone mad.

1st SOLDIER: How do we know? Has anyone seen him?

SGT: Not yet.

2nd SOLDIER: We might never see him. He might have been shot with the others.

SGT: No. He would know how to look after himself. Our visit must have been a bit sudden even for him but he must have been prepared.

1st SOLDIER: You believe that he is outside there among those prisoners?

SGT: Yes. And keeping very quiet till he feels safe. That suits us. I don't want anything more to happen till we get out of here.

1st SOLDIER: I wasn't supposed to be coming on this patrol. This is just my luck.

SGT: You came because of the Lieutenant. He wasn't supposed to be coming either. This is really his luck.

1st SOLDIER: If I had even dreamed that we would come face to face with the General I would have resigned from the service. Did you see his eyes?

2nd SOLDIER: Very strong. I couldn't look at his face again.

1st SOLDIER: Can you imagine anyone daring to break one of his oaths?

2nd SOLDIER: No.

SGT: Listen, jamaa, I don't say the General is not all you say he is, but remember if we take him back to camp the war in this forest will probably end and we can all go home.

2nd SOLDIER: Home. How far that seems from here.

1st SOLDIER: I should never have left it. My desire was always to go in for higher learning and become an intellectual. Now I may be lost.

SGT: Shhh! Here comes the white man. Don't let him lose his courage or we will all be lost. (*Lieutenant enters.*)

JOHN: That's a neat job out there. A buffalo couldn't break out of that pen.

SGT: Those trackers deserted from this gang, bwana. They would rather die than let anyone escape from this lot.

JOHN: I hope they don't change their minds again, before the morning. Anyhow we've got to trust them; so tell them to take up positions on the far side of the trees. And let these two guard the prisoners. How's this now – h'm. (*Nods appreciatively.*)

SGT: Alright. Keep your eyes and ears open. (*Nod to both soldiers who leave.*)

JOHN (*as they are leaving*): If I call, answer back only to show that you are present, no more. Understand?

SOLDIERS: Yes, bwana. (*They leave.*)

JOHN (*to Sergeant*): You keep moving around, Sergeant. Keep an eye on everyone – including those trackers.

SGT: Yes, sir. What about these? (*Nods at bodies on stage.*)

JOHN: We can't do anything about them now. It's like a cemetery out there. Leave them where they are. We'll be moving out at the crack of dawn anyway, sooner if possible.

SGT (*looks about*): We must.

JOHN: Well, cheer up, this will be something to write home about, Sergeant. (*Turns away*) I wish I didn't feel so sick.

SGT: It will be a great victory, bwana.

JOHN: Will be? Sergeant, I want you to understand clearly, we are taking this man back alive. If not alive, then in any other way. He is going to make use of the transport that Superintendent Paddy has waiting for him.

SGT (*confused*): That's also what I meant, bwana. Shall I bring him in now?

JOHN (*studies pen*): I think we are ready to receive his lordship. Yes, bring him in (*As Sergeant looks at him a bit sceptically*) He's not a god, you know ... (*Confused suddenly, as he recalls that this is Paddy's phrase*) – or devil. Not at all! He's ... he's just an ordinary person, like you and me. He may have some persuasive powers to rally people around him but no divinity, for God's sake! What are we discussing him for, anyhow? Bring him in! I'll deal with the fellow.

SGT: Yes, Sir. I'll bring the General now. (*Leaves.*)

JOHN: General! (*But there is no joy and little frivolity left in his mood. He lights a cigarette and walks around bodies, pauses at dead woman in corner. On a sudden impulse he rips a cloth off one of the other bodies and covers her face and limbs. The effort has cost him something and it has been observed from the wings by the captive General who pauses with the Sergeant behind him. General, with hands tied in front of him, watches the Lieutenant take out a handkerchief and wipe his face. Lieutenant turns. The two men look at each other for a moment. General walks round the bodies slowly, as though inspecting, watched by the Lieutenant and followed by armed Sergeant. At the pen, the Sergeant stands aside deferentially for him. General slips in with a last look at the shroud.*)

JOHN (*expelling deep lungful of smoke*): Alright, you can go, Sergeant. I'll call if I need you. (*Sergeant leaves with apprehensive glance from wings. John speaks abruptly under strain and with some bravado.*)

JOHN: What's your name?

GENERAL: General Nyati.

JOHN (*startled by the educated voice and accent*): Is that so?

GENERAL: You gave us no time for introductions, I'm afraid.

JOHN: We came by invitation actually.

GENERAL: You didn't use the front door.

JOHN: We found the back one open.

GENERAL: Silly of us. The place is full of bandits.

JOHN: And generals, I'm told. Since when did you get promoted?

GENERAL: Since I accepted command of this forest. You're behind times.

JOHN: Am I? Well let me warn you in time that every prisoner is under strict orders to remain quiet.

GENERAL: I understand. You haven't told me your name as yet.

JOHN: I'm Lieutenant John Dewey, and at the first signs of trickery my men have orders to shoot.

GENERAL: Naturally. There is no better way of instilling respect. And your men know how to shoot. (*Head turns as he looks at bodies.*) Their aim (*gaze stops at shroud*) was perfect.

JOHN: You can't blame us for that. If she'd identified herself we wouldn't have touched her.

GENERAL: We don't carry identity cards in this service.

JOHN: That's not our fault.

GENERAL: In that case I must accept the responsibility. She can't be written off as an accident. Of course . . . she should never have been allowed to join us.

JOHN: Was she . . . I mean, was she your—

GENERAL: My wife, yes. She was. However, you had no way of knowing it.

JOHN: General, provided you behave yourself, I promise you, you'll get a fair trial. I hope you can take my word for it.

GENERAL: An English officer's word?

JOHN: I wouldn't call it worthless.

GENERAL: How could it be . . . backed by tanks and aeroplanes.

JOHN: Backed by British justice, I would prefer to say.

GENERAL: Yes, that sounds much better.

JOHN (*turns away*): Anyhow, I think we understand each other. (*General chuckles. The Lieutenant turns, annoyed.*) What's the matter?

GENERAL: The difficulty I thought was that we didn't understand each other.

JOHN: I've got all the understanding I need for one night, so don't start an argument. I'm quite clear in my mind about everything here. Bloody clear. (*Sits on log.*)

GENERAL: You interest me.

JOHN: It won't change this situation in the slightest.

GENERAL: It will if you keep that up.

JOHN: What? (*Realizing suddenly, holds up cigarette.*) You mean this?

GENERAL: My men are everywhere.

JOHN: Don't fret; we can take care of ourselves.

GENERAL: You certainly can. This will win you a promotion at least.

JOHN: Remember I've warned you.

GENERAL: Don't get nervous, Lieutenant. You've done your bit.

JOHN (*putting out cigarette*): I'm not nervous, damn you. (*Goes backstage and calls.*)
Sergeant! (*Answer from darkness: Sir!*)

Johanna! (*Answer from darkness: Sir!*)
Githaki! (*Answer from darkness: Sir!*)
(*Turns round satisfied and relieved.*)

GENERAL: Good. All's well. Now you can relax.

JOHN (*Points revolver at him*): I'm warning you for the last time, General. Don't try my patience.

GENERAL: Put that away, Lieutenant. I'm your prisoner. (*Holds up hands.*) There isn't any possible harm I could do you.

JOHN (*lowers gun*): Well, I'm glad you understand that. You'll find me fair if you play the game.

GENERAL: You're new to Kenya, aren't you?

JOHN: What's that got to do with it?

GENERAL: A lot, if we're going to play the game. You need my advice before you misunderstand everything.

JOHN: Tell that to the judge. He'll be interested in what you have to say.

GENERAL: I might not be interested in what he has to say.

JOHN: The firing squad won't listen to that one.

GENERAL: In that case you should listen while you have the chance.

JOHN: It's not me who's going. . . (*Takes out cigarette case, shrugs, puts it away and sits on log*) . . . it's you!

GENERAL: You know of course that we are going to win.

JOHN: Don't raise your voice. I'm taking you in, dead or alive; just remember that.

GENERAL: How can I forget? (*Raises bound hands in mock defeat.*) But tell me, Lieutenant, do you feel right in what you've done. Don't you have any qualms about— (*looks around*) all this?

JOHN: Shooting down your bunch of thugs? No! Do it again any time.

GENERAL: You are a good commander. (*Lieutenant looks at him in some surprise.*) I agree: duty demands single-minded devotion, whatever your personal beliefs. That's why we have instilled such a strict code amongst our own people.

JOHN: Code? You mean this 'Oath' of yours?

GENERAL: Yes. The Oath. What do you think of it?

JOHN: It's dirty and shameful . . . Vile!

GENERAL: It upsets you doesn't it?

JOHN: Good God!

GENERAL: Yes, you're right I suppose. Even I who have been through hundreds of such ceremonies haven't quite got used to it. It isn't for the squeamish, I'm afraid.

JOHN: I wonder if you aren't mad?

GENERAL: We may both wonder. Do sane men shoot at each other?

JOHN: There are conventions even in war.

GENERAL: Provided both sides are equally matched.

JOHN: We didn't start this.

GENERAL: I don't think that matters now.

JOHN: Of course it matters. War is war but you can keep it within certain limits. It can still be clean, even civilized. Your oaths and all this other mumbo-jumbo reduce it to the level of animal brutality.

GENERAL : That level? (*Nods at bodies.*)

JOHN: They're dead because we're fighting each other. But they weren't degraded by us in any way. And all those prisoners out there, including you, will be given a fair trial before, well before—

GENERAL: Before we're shot.

JOHN: No, before you get whatever you deserve.

GENERAL: I must admit, Lieutenant, our code doesn't have so many refinements. We don't have the right kind of schools here.

JOHN: I don't know why I should discuss anything with you but you've been abroad and seen a better life. You aren't like the others. Why do you sink to this barbarism?

GENERAL: You're wrong there. I'm just like the others, like all these and the others out there. They wouldn't have accepted me if I was any different. And it's because I've been abroad and seen another life that I've become what I am. I am an idealist at heart.

JOHN: Talk sense, General. It doesn't really make any difference now, but I had hoped for some honesty from you.

GENERAL: Why are you so surprised? To me idealism means a belief in something. That belief we have. We are patriots each one of us, and idealists all.

JOHN: Words, that's all it is! The only reality here is this (*indicates bodies*). But there are other ways of getting what you're after. With force you'll never succeed against us. We're stronger than you are that way. If you shoot at us, we'll shoot back. (*Takes out pack of cigarettes and takes one out of pack.*) How can you expect anything else?

GENERAL: I don't.

JOHN: It's useless talking to you. (*Holds out packet to prisoner who looks at him. He starts, realizing what he is doing and returns cigarette into pack. Gets angry.*) You're doomed and you know it. There isn't a hope in hell for you! (*Turns and goes to wings.*) Sergeant!

SGT: Sir!

GENERAL: I'm sorry if I upset you Lieutenant.

JOHN (*calls*): Here Sergeant! (*Sergeant enters.*) Just keep an eye on him. I'll take a round.

SGT: Everything is quiet outside, sir.

JOHN: Good. I just feel the need for fresh air. (*Goes. Sergeant looks perplexed.*)

GENERAL (*chuckles*): Fresh air. He needs fresh air on the top of Mount Kenya! (*Surveys Sergeant sardonically.*)

Do you also need fresh air, Sergeant?

SGT: What?

GENERAL: No. You need a full stomach.

SGT: What are you saying to me?

GENERAL: I'm saying, what do you live for?

SGT: I'm a soldier.

GENERAL: A soldier who fights against his own people?

SGT: It's my duty to obey orders.

GENERAL (*nods at dead woman*): Who gave you that order?

SGT: She would be alive if she had kept her hands up.

GENERAL: No! She would be alive if you hadn't shot her.

SGT: But if she had—

GENERAL: It doesn't matter now. Do you carry any food on you?

SGT: Food? Yes, yes, I have some food, General. Are you hungry?

GENERAL: You came just before we were about to eat.

SGT: Here. (*Pulls candy bar out of pocket. Looks to wings.*) You can have it General. (*After another glance to wings unwraps bar and takes it to General who stretches out his bound hands. Sergeant hands over the bar, with one hand, keeping his gun away with the other, notices the woman, is embarrassed.*) I've heard who she was General. I am sorry. It was really a mistake.

GENERAL: Untie my hands, Sergeant.

SGT: What?

GENERAL: Be quick about it!

SGT (*frightened*): No, General! (*But unable to retreat*) No!

GENERAL: You will never get out of this forest alive. He doesn't understand that, but you do.

SGT: No . . . no!

GENERAL: This is your only chance to live.

SGT: I can't . . . No . . . I can't . . .

GENERAL: Why not? Do you fear him more than me?

SGT: I don't fear him at all. But I can't desert. (*Sound of thunder: Touches forehead. Looks up fearfully.*)

GENERAL: Yes, it's beginning to rain again. You won't hear them come now. This is your last chance. Untie me at once!

SGT: No! I have twenty years of service. I'm wearing this uniform. How can I throw it all away.

GENERAL: You are throwing your life away, you fool! (*Thrusts hands out.*) Come on or I'll have you shot!

SGT (*retreats*): Your men killed my whole family in one of their raids. Now you are threatening me?

GENERAL (*looks at bodies*): Do you want more revenge than this?

SGT: I don't want any revenge. I'm sick of this war. If you stop fighting we can all go home. It's all your fault!

GENERAL: You think that with me out of the way all this will stop?

SGT: If the head is cut off, the snake dies.

GENERAL: You're an even bigger fool than I thought. Snake! If you wish to call me that, is there only one snake in the forest?

SGT (*raises gun*): I don't want to listen to you anymore. With them I know where I stand; with you no one can be sure of anything. You only think of yourself. You are a devil!

GENERAL (*taking in his hands, knowing his bid has failed*): Now I'm a devil! This is something the white people have always been good at. They not only get us to fight each other but we even get attached to them. (*Bites chocolate.*) Get out and tell your master to return. I prefer his company. (*Sergeant retreats, stumbles over a body and General laughs.*) Just look at you. You're not fighting for him. You're not even fighting for yourself. You're just lost in the woods.

SGT: Keep quiet! You are a prisoner now. (*Sounds of distant thunder.*)

GENERAL (*Looking up*): It won't be long.

(*Sergeant whirls as Lieutenant enters from wings. Lieutenant looks at both men in surprise. General chews chocolate.*)

JOHN: What's happening here, Sergeant? (*Sergeant stands looking shaken.*)

SGT: Nothing, bwana; nothing.

GENERAL: We were discussing the weather. The Sergeant is afraid of thunder.

JOHN: I don't need any opinions from you about my Sergeant. What's that in your hand?

GENERAL: This? This is a bribe.

JOHN: What? (*Advancing urgently*) Give it to me!

GENERAL: Certainly. (*Hands chewed bit to Lieutenant who looks at it in surprise.*) I offered the Sergeant his freedom so he gave me a chocolate in return.

SGT: (*as Lieutenant turns to him*): He was hungry, bwana. That is all. Don't listen to him. He is the devil. (*Turns away.*) Sorry, I . . . I need some fresh air. (*Goes.*)

JOHN: You tried to corrupt him, did you? (*Puts chocolate down on pen for him. General ignores it.*)

GENERAL: He's uncorruptible, your Sergeant. Completely brain-washed.

JOHN: Your tongue's been loosened, it seems.

GENERAL: Bad weather has that effect on me.

JOHN: Don't let it encourage you. This is only a drizzle. The rain has turned off in another direction. My trackers confirmed it for me.

GENERAL: Your trackers? They were trained by us. They are your eyes and ears in this operation, aren't they?

JOHN: This operation is going to succeed, General, with or without trackers. Half the night is over.

GENERAL: So it is. Soon this encounter will pass into history. Do you aim to kill the patient?

JOHN: No. We aim to cure him if only he'll stop struggling so hard.

GENERAL: Has it ever occurred to you that your diagnosis may be wrong. You're operating on a perfectly healthy man.

JOHN: In that case let him not fight so hard. If he does, we have to keep him down.

GENERAL: He wants to stand up, Lieutenant: not be kept down. That's why he has become violent.

JOHN: There isn't a hope in hell, General, unless all this stops.

GENERAL: Are you sure?

JOHN: Well, aren't you by now? This has been going on for two years already. And it's your people who are paying the price. The poor people. The ones who have all this faith in you. With our resources we can keep this up indefinitely, however distasteful it may be.

GENERAL: So can we, with our resources. For every deserter to your side at least ten others join me from the villages below.

JOHN: And the suffering increases.

GENERAL: Does that bother you?

JOHN: It obviously doesn't bother you. You are ready to use your people in any way that suits you. That's the hideous part of this whole thing to me. They trusted you and you have become completely callous.

GENERAL: I am my people's symbol.

JOHN: A symbol can have a heart as well as a head. You know your people are backward. They are unprepared for modern life. Instead of leading them into forests and oaths and all your other bestialities why don't you let them grow into the twentieth century in a reasonable, civilized manner? That's what you really want anyhow.

GENERAL: You mean crawl in through ghettoes and restricted areas?

JOHN: No. I mean grow into it through education. Get used to the twentieth century. You'll only fall flat on your faces if you try leaping into it from these forests. We'll help you if you accept our advice. And for God's sake, what's wrong with accepting the simple fact that you're not ready to rule yourselves as yet!

GENERAL: (*pacing his pen*): Listen! Like all Europeans you understand little about us. You say we are backward, we are unskilled and untrained in modern ways; yes, there's truth in that. But we are a sensitive people. That's the dilemma! My problem has not been how to leap into the twentieth century but how to awaken a sleeping race. Your oppression drugged us. You called us inhuman and under the burden of that inhumanity we refused to think anymore. It was simpler to remain hypnotised. Your lordship over us assumed the proportions of a self-evident truth when it was really a self-evident lie. So it was not easy to break away at first, for I am no different to them. (*Nods at bodies*). But once an outline of prison bars is made clear, freedom becomes a call of nature. Reveal oppression and the people rise up in arms. Spill blood and the crowd grows maddened. That's all I've done. It's quite simple, really. Are you listening, white man?

JOHN: Carry on! This is your last chance anyhow.

GENERAL: Then know this. You accuse me of using force, but force, like peace, is in the very air of our existence. It has existed in our tribes from the earliest days. We loved peace but we often had war. The healthiest nations fall to that disease. But when you came with your new civilization we welcomed you. We hoped finally for the great peace and happiness that is promised by every religion. Instead you broke our tribes and shattered our traditions. You showed us even more force. Force, mark you, is what you used to conquer us. Not love! When we protested you turned to your guns. Now force is everywhere. In the conquerer and the conquered. It touches every idea. So it was a glorious thought when it came to me — this: to grasp the Force of Common Human Brutality and wield it as a Sword! To sharpen its edge with oaths and slay the usurpers who dared trample over our land. To obliterate every resistance from our path. To be free at any cost. You taught me that and even you, white man, stripped of your civilization, could be made to dance like a savage in our moonlight.

JOHN: Paddy was right. You're a fanatic! The head-hunters in Borneo have nothing on you.

GENERAL: Quite so! You left me no choice. The only difference is that I want what's in the head. I planned this rebellion and now our methods have crystallized. Here, in this forest, where we have challenged you, savagery is a premeditated course of action. Our Oath is primitive but without guns and Paddys it's no more bloody than your own brutality. In our hands Force is a flaming sword. In yours, it's a blight on your conscience.

JOHN: That's a lie! We brought light into this darkness of yours. We did! But you want equality before we can give it to you. You're guilty every bit as much as we are. And you will pay the penalty of your crimes. You certainly will.

GENERAL: I am ready for that, Lieutenant, if you do indeed succeed in getting me out of here; but these days, would you believe it, I keep thinking: my God, what if we win!

JOHN: Don't worry, you won't.

GENERAL: We will if this continues. You keep us here with

your threats of law and order, though time is on our side. My work in this forest is now finished. I want this to end. It would be a tragedy putting Africa back a thousand years if this continued much longer. But it must end on our terms, not yours. Our honour and achievement must remain intact.

JOHN: What about ours?

GENERAL: Your pride, not your honour is involved. And your pride has been a false one in this case. It must go, or not just Africa, but the twentieth century itself will soon be in the bonfire.

JOHN: You've turned and twisted every argument in the book, General. Nothing can stand up to this kind of talk. Its reasons supply its own answers. You shoot at us and we shoot back at you. There isn't anything else in this until we stop fighting. You're bitter and we're angry. It'll all be over one day but right now there's one thing I can promise you: We'll finish you and your gangs first!

GENERAL: In our own time, Lieutenant, not before. When we finish from these forests for the last time, the black folk of Africa will have been wholly roused to know that they stand together. Your victory and our victory will be the culmination of my policy. Then by all means we shall need your education and way of life. We no longer have any of our own. You destroyed that. But on this mountain the conscience of the black race is being reborn, white man, and you are its midwife!

JOHN (*bitter*): Conscience is it, you can say that? (*Goes to end of stage, looks into darkness and returns.*) I saw the village you massacred last week. Is that the new conscience?

GENERAL: Many of our people have suffered, it's true. Some fear our approach even more than your bullets.

But what is a village to atone for the birth pangs of a nation? We never pardon traitors.

JOHN: You don't?

GENERAL: No, Lieutenant, we don't. And the one among us will be known before the night is through.

JOHN: That's to be seen. (*Returns to wings and calls softly*) Sergeant! (*Answer from darkness:* Sir!)

Johanna! (*Answer from darkness:* Sir!)

Githaki! (*Answer from darkness:* Sir!)

I suppose you'll sleep over it and see the traitor in your dreams, eh General; your dreams?

GENERAL: So, even my dreams trouble you?

JOHN: In any sane society you'd be locked up. It's that simple.

GENERAL: It's simpler. In any sane society there would be no need for dreams.

JOHN: But aren't you taking a risk in predicting this time? The traitor, if there is one, may not reveal himself by the morning.

GENERAL: The traitor, Lieutenant, will reveal himself before the morning. It is quite logical. When you march us away, if you ever do, he will declare himself to you. And if we take you away instead he will panic, knowing that I will find him. I have my ways.

JOHN: Perhaps. But what about these attacks and ambushes you're supposed to have seen? Were they also dreams on your part?

GENERAL: You forget I'm a veteran at this game and have a certain intuition in these matters. It has proved correct on occasions. Add to this a certain amount of faith and you have the stuff of miracles. It's no lie to call them dreams.

JOHN: Well, they let you down this time.

GENERAL: You have been lucky, that is all. At great cost to me.

JOHN: I agree, we have been lucky, if you can call this luck . . . and at great cost to everyone. (*Turns to General again.*) There, we agreed on something finally.

GENERAL: Have we? On what?

JOHN: On our feelings for life. At this moment, General, in spite of everything, I have a kind of sympathy for you .

GENERAL: I don't need your sympathy.

JOHN: From it can grow understanding.

GENERAL: Will it set me free?

JOHN: In time, it will set us both free.

GENERAL: You are a philosopher. What are you doing in that uniform?

JOHN: You're not the only one who's asked me that. We shouldn't really be enemies at all, General.

GENERAL: We don't want your enmity. We just want to be free of you.

JOHN (*thoughtful, aloud*): I wonder what you'd do if you did manage to escape?

GENERAL: There is an easy way of finding out. (*Holds out bound hands challengingly*) Here!

JOHN (*startled*): What! (*Recovering*) Can it be that simple?

GENERAL: Between us it could be.

JOHN: What about the others?

GENERAL: Leave that to me.

JOHN: But how can I be sure you'd put an end to all this if I let you go?

GENERAL: By letting me go .

JOHN: But how could I be sure? You make your own laws.

GENERAL: That's why I can be sure.

JOHN: But what about me? For me it would be an act of faith.

GENERAL: In yourself.

JOHN: And in you. Without you it wouldn't work.

GENERAL: If you can trust yourself you can trust me.

JOHN: No . . . no, this is crazy. What are we talking about?

You've had hundreds killed. And you'll go on doing it till you get what you want. You've just been telling me about that!

GENERAL: For a moment I thought we understood each other.

JOHN: For a moment, so did I. God, you almost had me! (*Incredulous laugh.*) You are dangerous!

GENERAL (*withdrawing his hands like a man withdrawing an offer*): I'm only dangerous to those who resist me.

JOHN: There you go again, the Messiah, or is it the devil! You're never wrong. You're never in any doubt.

GENERAL: And you're always in doubt. If you were one of my soldiers I would never trust you.

JOHN: I'm sorry, General, I shouldn't have started this. I don't know what came over me. (*Sergeant enters from wings.*) Yes, Sergeant?

SGT: Did you call me, bwana?

JOHN: No, I didn't call you.

SGT: I thought your voice . . .

JOHN (*small laugh*): Oh yes, you probably did. We've been talking a bit. But . . . it's all over.

SGT: (*perplexed*): What is?

JOHN: Oh . . . nothing. I cracked a little joke which the General couldn't see. Or maybe it was the other way round. Anyhow, how are the prisoners?

SGT (*perplexed*): What is?

JOHN: Well, I don't suppose they'll sleep if they can't be sure of waking up again. (*Looks at watch.*) It's almost daybreak. Doesn't this damned night ever lift?

SGT: It's full of dark clouds, that's why. But have you noticed, sir, the rain has stopped completely?

JOHN: So it has, yes, it's not even drizzling. Couldn't we send one of our trackers off to base camp now?

SGT: I've already done it, sir. He left over an hour back.

JOHN: Good, good; I like a man who makes up his mind.

He should meet our relief patrol somewhere in the forest. I know Paddy will have sent others after us by now. We're overdue.

SGT: They won't find us unless the tracker guides them here, Sir.

JOHN: Why not? The Superintendent knows where we are, the exact spot. (*After short silence*) What's the matter Sergeant? Are you hiding something from me?

SGT: I'm not hiding anything from you, sir, but I have just learnt something from the other trackers, about this place.

JOHN: What thing?

SGT: They only told it to me just now.

JOHN: You've already said that.

SGT: They must both have known it, of course, but I don't think they were sure of it themselves till a little while back.

JOHN: Look, come out with it, will you?

SGT: We came to the wrong place, bwana.

JOHN: The wrong place?

SGT: Yes. This is not the spot mentioned in that letter. This is another fig tree. There are many of them in this forest and many places look alike. Where we were supposed to go is about ten miles from here.

JOHN: Then . . . how?

SGT: This is a mistake. A lucky mistake. We missed the real place and found them here.

JOHN: But if we were supposed to see these chaps there and instead meet them here, then it means—(*throws up hands*) well, either the information was all wrong or there's something completely cock-eyed about this whole operation.

SGT: We have got the General, sir.

JOHN: Yes, so we have. (*Turns to look at impassive General.*) I won't get any more out of him (*to Sgt.*) Do you think we might have walked into a trap at the other place?

SGT: Bwana Paddy did warn us about it, sir.

JOHN: True he did. In that case we've got to make sure the other patrol doesn't go there. They'll be ambushed.

SGT: That is what I fear too, bwana. And they will be going there unless someone warns them.

JOHN: Christ, what a mess! (*In low voice*) Does that also mean there is no informer among those prisoners after all? No one we can talk to?

SGT: I have been thinking about it ever since I heard this news, bwana ... and I can no longer be sure of anything. Only (*indicates General*) he knows what's really happened.

JOHN: And he's not telling! Look, I tell you what, Sergeant; tie all the prisoners together, gag them and let's get the hell out of here. It's not quite so pitch dark now. We'll make some progress.

SGT: Yes, sir, let's get out of here. We have stayed too long already. (*A significant birdcall from the darkness of the forest, heard over and above the other night sounds. Both men freeze, listening.*)

JOHN: Our tracker's signal?

SGT: Could be.

JOHN: Maybe he's made contact with the other patrol?

SGT: So soon?

JOHN: It's impossible.

SGT: I will find out. (*Goes.*)

JOHN: Anything's possible. (*Draws gun. In his pen, General is looking around with quiet expectation. Lieutenant looks all around across back curtain. Lieutenant sees them, understands.*)

JOHN: Christ! (*Rushes to one wing*) Sergeant! (*There is immediately a sound of muffled machine-gun fire. General crouches in his pen. One of the soldiers comes rushing through, pursued by three terrorists from the new gang. Soldier is shot*) *down on the stage. Lieutenant whirls and shoots all three terrorists, then he aims to fire at General who immediately throws himself down. There is a shot and the Lieutenant falls to the ground as two more terrorists rush in, one with a revolver and one with a panga. The one with revolver rushes to pen and frees General. The other kicks revolver away from Lieutenant, who is crawling to retrieve it and stands over him menacingly with a foot on his back forcing him to remain down.)*

COLONEL (*leader of new terrorist gang, as he frees General*): Are you alright, General?

GENERAL: Yes, I'm alright, Colonel. You came just in time.

COLONEL: I suspected something when no one appeared at the other place. We were waiting for them.

GENERAL: They were going there. The warning I had received in my dream was correct. Someone had informed them where we were. This was an accident. They lost their way in the rain and found us here by chance.

COLONEL: We would have come sooner if the night had not been so dark and wet.

GENERAL: It rained everywhere. We never heard them come.

COLONEL (*grimly looking around*): I can see that. (*Sees shroud.*) Is that—

GENERAL: Yes, it's her.

COLONEL: They will pay for this; (*nods to Lieutenant*) he will. (*Terrorist with panga, who has been listening, lifts his weapon in sudden rage over Lieutenant. General stops him.*)

GENERAL: No! Not yet. Tie him to this tree. (*Two more terrorists from new gang enter. With their help the Lieutenant is dragged to tree and tied. General talks with Colonel while this is going on.*) I want my men brought in here, Colonel. There is some business to finish before we leave.

COLONEL: Oh? (*Nods in sudden understanding, with glance at*

Lieutenant.) Oh, I, see; yes they should all watch it. (*As the Colonel exits through one wing, the 1st and 2nd terrorists enter from the other wing. The 1st terrorist is flexing his strangling cord.*)

1st TERRORIST: I got him with this. These askaris die like rats.

2nd TERRORIST: The other one is also finished. General, are you safe?

GENERAL: Yes. You see me. Here I am. (*Holds out hands to indicate invulnerability.*)

1st TERRORIST: Truly, this is a miracle. No one can touch the General.

2nd TERRORIST (*in wonder*): In the middle of it all he remained standing.

GENERAL: I have been chosen for this work. Those who fight me will die.

1st TERRORIST: You have shown that to be true again and again, General. There is only one leader for us.

2nd TERRORIST: Only one.

CHORUS (*others on stage*): Yes, only one. General Nyati!

GENERAL (*who has accepted all this calmly as his right, now becomes businesslike*): Those responsible for this treachery will pay the price. But first, where is the Sergeant and that other tracker?

1st TERRORIST: The Sergeant is out there, General. That other one I don't know.

2nd TERRORIST: I haven't seen him either.

Colonel returns with remaining four terrorists from General's gang. All the terrorists from scene 1 are now back on the stage together with some of the new arrivals.

GENERAL (*to Colonel*): One of them's escaped, an old deserter of ours.

COLONEL: They are always the worst and most dangerous.

1st TERRORIST: He won't get away. (*Walks over to Lieutenant and flexes his cord menacingly.*) Nor will you.

Other terrorists start rifling the Lieutenant's pockets, finding

*a fountain pen, a purse, with money and a small family picture.
They start passing all this around themselves – first with amusement, then with intent to keep. They are excitable and there is
something innocent about them but it turns into a killer's vicious-
ness as soon as they are thwarted. The Colonel and General talk in
front of stage.*

GENERAL: He's gone to meet a government patrol.

COLONEL: We can trap them all if we catch him before they
    meet.

GENERAL: Exactly!

COLONEL: Do you know which way he went.

GENERAL: That Sergeant should know. How many men did
    you bring with you?

COLONEL: Twenty. They are spread out to keep a watch till
    you leave from here. Shall I call them?

GENERAL: No. The one I'm after is in my own gang. But
    I want this finished quickly. It is dangerous for so
    many of us to be assembled in one spot. Our enemy
    grows more cunning every day. They found us here
    today. What will they do tomorrow? Bring in the
    Sergeant. (*Colonel goes; General turns with speculative look
    to Lieutenant.*) You were going to shoot me, weren't
    you? (*Terrorists squabbling over possessions.*)

1st TERRORIST: That's mine, give it to me! (*Snatches at purse
from 2nd – who has just taken it from someone else. The others
are squabbling over the pen. The photographs have been torn and
thrown aside.*)

2nd TERRORIST: No, I claimed it first. You'll have enough
    when you get Delamere Avenue!

ANOTHER: But I wanted that!

GENERAL: Stop it, you fools! (*Terrorists are immediately
    quiet though the 1st Terrorist tries to sneak purse into his
    pocket. This is quietly but firmly resisted by others.*) You'll
    end up nothing but thieves at this rate. (*Sergeant is led
    in by the Colonel. He walks erect without defiance or fear.*)

GENERAL: I'll give you a chance to live. Which way did he go?

SGT: Who?

GENERAL: Don't waste time. You know who I mean.

SGT: You won't catch our tracker. And I don't know which way he went.

1st TERRORIST: Give him to me. If I can't have any of this (*indicates loot on floor*) let me take him!

GENERAL: You hear that? (*He is answered by silence. Turns impatiently to Colonel*) We are wasting time. It will take too long to make him talk.

COLONEL: Let me try.

GENERAL: Do you think you can do more than me?

COLONEL (*confused*): No, of course not, General. It was only an idea.

GENERAL: Ideas can be dangerous. Take your men and disperse quickly. The serkali will be sending their aeroplanes here within a few hours.

COLONEL: I am going at once General.

GENERAL: Leave these (*gesturing to those on stage*) with me till I get a few more recruits of my own. In a few days I will send a message where we are to meet again. This fight goes on.

COLONEL: Yes, General. (*Turns to go.*)

GENERAL: Colonel! (*The Colonel turns.*) I think you had better take him with you. He's useless to me.

1st TERRORIST: Oh no! (*Stamps foot in frustration as Sgt. is led away.*)

JOHN: Sergeant! (*Sergeant turns. John is suddenly at a loss for words. Shakes his head weakly.*) I . . . I'm sorry!

SGT: Kwa-heri, bwana. (*Goes out with Colonel and one terrorist.*)

1st TERRORIST: (*spreads out empty hands*): We have nothing now.

2nd TERRORIST: We have him (*Nods to Lieutenant.*)

GENERAL: We also have a traitor.

(*Everyone falls silent and becomes wary of his neighbour. General grows thoughtful. Surveys the massacre dispassionately. Looks up at fig tree. As he speaks the terrorists become reverent, bowing their heads till they are in an attitude of prayer.*)

GENERAL: This was sacred ground. This was where I came to pray. Some go into stone buildings to be alone with God. Others search the sky and hear his voice in the sound of bells. For me the secrets of the heart have found their echo in the fig tree. This is our altar.

ALL: Amen!

GENERAL: This is where I have prayed.

ALL: Amen!

GENERAL: In the shadow of the holy fig, wherever it be, my dreams have taken shape.

ALL: Amen!

GENERAL: Here Ngai speaks.

ALL (*very reverent*): Amen!

GENERAL: And yet it is near a fig tree that I have been betrayed. While I prayed Judas plotted. The greatest treacheries on the mountain have taken place in the shadow of these altars. For how long can this continue? For how long, oh Ngai! Give me an answer. Your servant listens! (*Sound of single shot is heard outside. In the stunned silence the Lieutenant starts sobbing quietly. General turns to his awed followers. As he speaks now his voice continues to rise till it ends in its final terrible warning.*) Thus die all traitors to the race. And so too shall die the traitor among us. I have seen him. Yes, I know him. He stood before me in my dreams. I knew we were going to be betrayed. That is why we moved. This was an accident. But he cannot escape. I know him. He has taken the Oath. Let him confess! (*Silence.*) If I name him his spirit will go mad and wander like a hyena for all eternity. Let him confess! (*Silence.*) No one can escape the Oath. Let no one try. The Oath goes beyond the grave. It is the Oath that curses, not I. Now I am going to name him—

3rd TERRORIST: No! (*Claps hand to mouth. Looks round terrified and breaks into run. Is immediately seized. 1st terrorist leads him out.*)

1st TERRORIST: You . . . lying tailor!

4th TERRORIST: He can make clothes up there now. (*Points upwards*) It must be cold.

GENERAL (*looks at massacre*): My men cannot be brought back to life nor my wife resurrected. So be it. The fight goes on. (*Turns to terrorists*) Every second here increases our danger. Our enemies are everywhere. We do not even have time to bury our dead. (*To one group*) Alright, go. I will meet you at the high stream where we were last week, near the snow line.

5th TERRORIST: What about him? (*Nods at Lieutenant.*)

GENERAL: Leave him there. He'll probably die. The animals in this forest are as ferocious as its men.

5th TERRORIST: It won't take me a minute, general.

GENERAL: No! If the serkali find him alive he can tell them whom they deal with on this mountain. They still do not understand. That is why he is being spared.

5th TERRORIST: But, General—

GENERAL (*calmly*): We go now. (*All terrorists leave quickly behind the General. The 5th terrorist is the last to leave. As he is going out the 1st terrorist comes in. He points incredulously at the Lieutenant. The 5th shrugs.*)

5th TERRORIST: It is the General's wish. (*As he is leaving*) Don't try anything. You might appear in one of his dreams. (*Goes. 1st terrorist inspects the Lieutenant contemptuously, rifles his pockets, sees half-finished candy bar on pen and chews it. Tilts Lieutenant's chin, looks longingly at his neck. Makes him open his mouth at a sudden thought and shakes his head.*)

1st TERRORIST: Useless! (*Sees purse behind him and retrieves it eagerly. Rifles it. Throws it down in disgust. Mutters aloud)* Thieves! (*Goes to one wing; then turns round slowly and, with a nod to Lieutenant, flexes strangling cord, vanishes. Silence on stage. Light begins to dawn revealing a leg of dead woman. The Lieutenant begins struggling with his ropes. Starts panting and gasping.*)

LIEUTENANT: Oh God! (*Sound of distant thunder. A monkey chatters and laughs in a nearby tree. A shadow flits across the screen. The Lieutenant sees it and stops struggling. Shadow goes behind him. He starts shouting.*)

Oh God! Get it over with . . . what are you waiting for . . . Oh God, he's mad. Mad! (*Sobs. General now materializes, goes to body of wife, bends, lifts it and walks out unseen by Lieutenant who cannot turn to look and starts shouting again.*) Oh God, no . . . no . . . Oh God . . . No!

CURTAIN

Yon Kon

PAT MADDY

CHARACTERS

Yon Kon
Pagu   } *Prisoners in the jail*
Gbaratae

4 Other Prisoners
Warder 99991
Prison Officer

Agba Saiteiny
Salu   *Friends of Yon Kon*
Bobor

YON KON

SCENE ONE

The Prison Yard

YON KON (*shouting*): Right, left, left, right, right, left. Keep
marching. Why do you stop?

PAGU: This is stupid. I'm tired.

YON KON: Don't argue, keep marching. Right, left, left,
right. Hey, hey, hey.

PAGU: We are not in the army. I can't do right, left,
left, left, right. It's wrong.

YON KON: In this prison yard, you do as I say. If I, Yon
Kon, say right, left, left, right, then you march:
right, left, left, right. Right?

PAGU: You are just a prisoner like me, Yon Kon. All
of us here are prisoners. (*Prisoners murmur.*)

YON KON: You are all different prisoners from me . . . I
know everything about this prison yard. I have
been here – on and off – since I was sixteen. I come
in when I like, and I discharge myself when my
time is over. (*Shouting*) Right, left, left, right.

PAGU: That's all you know about here, right, left, left,
right. I am not here for physical exercise. I've never
been in prison before, and I'm only here for two
weeks.

YON KON (*jovially*): We'll make it two weeks' hard labour
then. March. Right, left . . .

61

PAGU: I'm not taking any more orders from you, Yon
Kon.

YON KON: No! Don't be too sure. What's your name?

PAGU: I have no name.

YON KON: Don't play tough with me, boy! You think
that because you are six feet tall, with a broad chest,
big fists and hair like Samson, you are almighty.
(*He laughs and prisoners join in.*)

YON KON: Now, speak! (*Twisting Pagu's arm*) What is your
name?

PAGU (*gasping with pain*): Ai! Ai! You're breaking
my arm! P-Pagu. My name's Pagu.

YON KON (*still holding*): Pagu? Is it? Well, now you
are talking – better and clearly too. (*Laughs.*) You
will answer me some more questions.

PAGU: Let go my arm ... I will tell you anything you
want to know. Please let go my arm.

YON KON: No! I will not. You ask for it ... rough.
(*Laughs.*) I like it rough too, with people like you who
like to be tough.

PAGU: I'm not being tough. I was only joking.

YON KON: Yah, joking, eh? Tell me more! (*Shouting*)
What's your name? Your full name?

PAGU (*still groaning*): Pagu Ekele.

YON KON: Who is your mother?

PAGU: My mother is a trader, she is in Yaba – Ai! (*Prisoners.
laugh.*)

YON KON: Who is your father?

PAGU: My father is a sailor, I don't know where he is.
We've never met.

YON KON: What is your profession?

PAGU: I used to work as a storekeeper.

YON KON: Where? For who?

PAGU: At Kissy Town, for Ali Zasso, the Syrian merchant.

YON KON: What is your nationality?

PAGU: I am of mixed blood . . . half Creole, half Syrian.

YON KON: Are you married?

PAGU: No! No! I'm not.

YON KON: How did you manage to get involved with the police?

PAGU (*shouting*): Stealing . . . oh, my arm . . . I stole a pair of shoes.

YON KON: Is this your first offence?

PAGU: Yes! Yes!

YON KON: Do you like it here? Would you like to come back here? (*Pause – then shouts*) Answer!

PAGU (*yelps with pain*): Yes . . . NO . . . NO . . . Yes. (*Prisoners laugh.*)

YON KON: You are not certain . . . O.K. Now we will do some more routine exercises and marching as well.

PAGU (*groans*): Oh – Oh! You have blistered my arm, Yon Kon.

YON KON: You should be glad I handled you myself. If I had taken you down to the quarter deck, you would have had twelve lashes on your bare back – your hair shaved off your head – you would have had to go around bare-foot – no meals – and sleep on a bare concrete floor, possibly a wet one too, and for seven days.

PRISONER 1: You should thank Yon Kon.

PRISONER 2: He is a good man.

PRISONER 3: He is boss around here.

PRISONER 4: Everybody respects him.

PRISONER 1: Everybody likes him.

PRISONERS: Yeh – everybody likes him.

YON KON (*commandingly*): Up on your feet . . . Come on Pagu! Leave your arm alone; you over there, hey Pa Gbaratae, come on. Routine exercises, come on, after two. You all know the words, one, two.

PRISONERS 1 & 2: We must not steal.

PRISONERS 3 & 4: We must not steal.

PRISONERS 1 & 2: We must not kill.

PRISONERS 3 & 4: We must not kill.

PRISONERS 1 & 2: We must not fight.

PRISONERS 3 & 4: We must not fight.

PRISONERS 1 & 2: We must not lie.

PRISONERS 3 & 4: We must not lie.

PRISONERS 1 & 2: We must obey the laws.

PRISONERS 3 & 4: We must obey the laws.

PRISONERS 1 & 2: We must behave —

PRISONERS 3 & 4: —as good citizens should.

YON KON: Right! Stand easy! Now, what are the things necessary?

PRISONER 1: Work hard from Monday to Saturday, if possible Sunday.

PRISONER 2: Be responsible and respectable to yourself, your family, your neighbours.

PRISONER 3: Pay your debts, and be at enmity with no-one.

PRISONER 4: Be honest, faithful, true and sincere with yourself in whatever you do.

YON KON: What do you promise to do when you leave here?

PRISONER 1: The things we used to do that are wrong —

ALL PRISONERS: We will do them no more.

PRISONER 2: The places we used to go that are bad —

ALL PRISONERS: We will go there no more.

PRISONER 3: The words we used to curse and swear —

ALL PRISONERS: We will use them no more.

YON KON: O.K. ... Good ... It's twelve o'clock. Time for lunch. Line up. Ready? Right, left, left, right, right, left ...

PRISONERS: We will be good ... we will be good.

YON KON: Pa Gbaratae, reserve my chair for me ... I just want to send a quick message.

PRISONERS (*voices fade as they go off*): We will be good . . . we will be good . . .

YON KON (*on telephone, muttering*): Just a quick message. Come on, come on! Answer! Ah! (*Shouting*) Is that the orderly room? Er, let me talk to warder nine-nine-double-nine-one . . . It's me, Yon Kon, chief prisoner . . . Ah, nine-nine-double-nine-one! (*laughs*) What's cooking . . . I got a bit rough today, with a new recruit; but I handled him very well. Yeh, Yeh, he knows me now, very well too. But eh, that's not what I wanted to talk to you about. I'm just going for my lunch. You know I discharge tomorrow, yeh, well, I want you to take a message for me to Agba, you know, Agba Saiteiny. Tell him to send a taxi to collect me tomorrow morning at 6.30. Yes, I want to travel in style. I want to leave this yard and forget all about it tomorrow. In and out of this prison yard for forty years is enough for me . . . I mean it. When I leave tomorrow I will never come back. Not as a prisoner, anyway. (*Laughs*.) Tell Agba that . . . and tell him to come in the taxi himself, tell him not to be late. O.K. Bye.

SCENE TWO

The Mess Hall

GBARATAE (*angry tone*): I tell you, Pagu, don't sit on this chair!

PAGU: Why not! I will eat my dinner where I like! And I like this chair.

PRISONERS (*murmuring*): You looking for more trouble, eh? You going to get it tough with Yon Kon. You look out for Yon Kon. Yon Kon won't like this.

PAGU: Why the hell are you all afraid of Yon Kon? He's no demi-god!

PRISONERS: I'm not afraid of Yon Kon. I'm not scared of no-one. But Yon Kon's the boss.

PAGU: Ah, yes ... you all tremble before him! You're all scared to speak in front of him! You all worship him like he is a blasted ...

GBARATAE: Get off this chair! I warned you, Pagu. Cheeky little upstart. (*Slap.*) Untrained ... Uncultured ... (*Prisoners laugh and murmur encouragement.*)

GBARATAE: I will give you the training your silly lazy mother did not give you.

PAGU (*panting*): You keep your filthy tongue off my mother ... you ... you ... (*Pagu grabs hold of Gbaratae: they grapple. Gbaratae is brought to the ground, Pagu on top of him.*)

PRISONER 1: Help him up! Help Pa Gbaratae to his feet!

PRISONER 2: Yon Kon, Yon Kon, come!

PRISONER 3: Pagu, get away from him! Don't kill Pa Gbaratae.

YON KON (*approaches out of breath*): Stop! What's going on here? Who's that on the floor?

PAGU: Yon Kon ... I didn't mean it ... He abused my mother. He refused to let me sit on the chair. (*Crying*) He hit me ... I was only trying to defend myself. I ... I ...

YON KON: You break the man's head with a chair, and you say in self-defence? What are you all standing here gaping at? Ring the alarm bells, call the Governor, get the Doctor. You, Pagu, get some water.

WARDER (*approaching, out of breath*): What's been going on here, Yon Kon?

YON KON: I was not here, Sir. I was on the telephone . . .

WARDER: What happened to him, lying on the ground?

PAGU (*approaching*): Here is the water, Yon Kon.

YON KON: We don't need water. He is dead.

PAGU: Dead . . . Dead . . . but how could he . . .

WARDER: No, no. He's still breathing. Get some prisoners to take him to the hospital . . . You come with me to the Governor's office, Pagu. Get all the other prisoners to come with you to the Governor's office when you've finished, Yon Kon. Come on now! Get a move on!

SCENE THREE

Agba Saiteiny's. Evening – same day. Drum music, singing, shouting

AGBA (*shouting*): Stop! We must finish the sharing first before gumbay practice. (*Shouting, music stops.*) O.K. right. You boys done good boy yeternight. Here, Salu, take this . . . plenty good lappa for you wife an' mother.

SALU: I want no lappa – I like that cotton bale!

AGBA: Take what I give you – right?

BOBOR: Right, Agba you are boss of the gumbay – but remember, this night we got big job to do.

AGBA: Salu, take this clock . . . plenty money when you sell it.

SALU (*mutters*): All right.

AGBA: Bobor, you take the cotton bale.

Knock at door – hard and repeated.

AGBA (*quietly*): Put all the stuff in the room – lock the door. Quick, now! Bobor, Salu, Amadu – crack the gumbay, while we get these things hidden.

Bobor, Salu and Amadu rush off with bale, clock etc. Immediately after gumbay beating, loud.

99991: (*from outside*): Agba Saiteiny! Is Agba Saiteiny there?

AGBA: Coming, coming! Don't break the door. This is not the prison gate!

AGBA (*into wings*): Oh! What brings you here, nine-nine-double-nine-one? Stop the gumbay, boys. It's a visitor from the prison.

99991: You always pull a long face on me, why?

AGBA: Uniform men and me don't get on.

99991: Why?

AGBA: I got work to do. You got any message, out with it.

99991: Are you not going to ask me in?

AGBA: For what? When I next come to prison deal with me accordingly.

99991: It's a long time you have not been in.

AGBA: Is that why you come to visit me?

99991: No. No. I have a message for you from Yon Kon. He is discharged tomorrow. He wants you to meet him in the morning. The usual time – 6.30. Oh, eh, he says you should come in a taxi, because he is not going to cross the prison gates any more. Not as a prisoner, anyway.

AGBA: Is that all?

99991: Yes . . . he says I should tell you not to forget, and not to be late.

AGBA: Goodbye. (*Turning back to the others who have singly reappeared on stage*) You hear? Yon Kon is coming out in the morning. Salu, you go out and rent a taxi. No job tonight. We must pick him up in the mornin'. Bobor, Amadu, you clean the house. I am going out to buy some agbakra and knick-knacks. (*Laughs.*) The gumbay set will be just right now for any engagement . . . Christmas just round the corner! Boy, boy, we will swing left, right and centre. Without Yon Kon, the group is not complete. (*Gaily*) We need him, we want him, everyone miss him when he away.

SALU: I hope this time he will keep his promise and keep away from stealing fowls.

AGBA: I will talk to him when he come home tomorrow. Give me my hat, Salu, I'm going out to buy the knick-knacks. Get busy, Amadu, Bobor.

SCENE FOUR

Prison Cell

PAGU (*shouting*): I don't like the way that clock is ticking. Be quiet! Yon Kon . . . Yon kon, are you there? Can you hear me? Get me out of this cell. Yon Kon, Mr Yon Kon.

YON KON (*approaching*): Why are you screaming like that?

PAGU (*hysterical*): Yon Kon, is he dead? What did the doctor say this afternoon? Are you sure he is dead? Are they going to hang me? Are you going to help me?

YON KON: I can't help you, I am just a prisoner like you.

PAGU: But you are a different prisoner, you said that this morning.

YON KON: That is true. But in a situation like this, that difference holds no water.

PAGU: Listen to that clock ticking. It is driving me insane. I feel as if I am in a condemned cell, counting my last minutes. What do you call this cell? It is so damp – there is no bed. How long will they keep me here?

YON KON: I don't know.

PAGU: Don't go, Yon Kon. You are a man of experience. Talk to me, stay here with me.

YON KON: I have to pack. I discharge in the morning. Whether I stay or not it makes no difference.

PAGU: It was self-defence. I didn't mean it. I haven't got the mind to kill a fly.

YON KON: Don't try to convince me, Pagu. Keep your pleas for the judge and jury, they will understand you better.

PAGU: You are hard, Yon Kon. You don't want to help me. You don't want to understand me.

YON KON: Prison life, Pagu, is a different life, a different world, with strange stories. You never know what to understand and who to help.

PAGU: What do you mean?

YON KON: The understanding and help you want from me should have come from your home, or among your friends.

PAGU: But I have no friends. Those who used to help me spend my money deserted me when they knew I was in trouble.

YON KON: You see. That's the secret. Everything you do with your life must be very well planned and well done. The law is made by man for man to obey and observe. The moment you slip, you are in the net.

PAGU: How old are you, Yon Kon?

YON KON: Fifty-six.

PAGU: How long have you been in prison?

YON KON (*laughing*): This time I was sent in for nine months.

But I have been in and out of the Pademba prison gates for forty years. I got my first lock-up when I was sixteen.

PAGU: What did you do?

YON KON: I stole a cock. (*Imitates a cock crowing.*)

PAGU: A fowl? But what did you want to do with it?

YON KON: I like playing with them. The same way people like dogs and cats.

PAGU: Do you always steal a cock and get sent to prison for that? Why not rob the bank, or something valuable?

YON KON: I don't believe in robbing banks or breaking into houses. I don't steal fowls because I want to sell them.

PAGU: Do you eat them?

YON KON: No! You see, as a child, I spent all my time with fowls, breeding them, even sleeping with them . . .

PAGU: You can't sleep with fowls.

YON KON: Oh yes, I slept in the barn where the fowls were kept.

PAGU: Why?

YON KON: You ask too many questions.

PAGU: It sounds funny that your parents should allow you to sleep . . .

YON KON: No. No. It wasn't my parents . . . as a kid I lived with a foster-mother. My father died before I was born. My mother died two days after I was born.

PAGU: I'm sorry, Yon Kon.

YON KON: Sorry for what? I used to take good care of these fowls. And they knew me like any dog or cat knows its master. The cocks used to wake me up in the mornings (*imitates cock crowing*). Six o'clock to the dot. The hens and chickens would always follow me about for their feed of rice and corn. One day I killed a dog that tried to frighten the chickens. So my foster-mother turned me out of the house. I tried to get a job (*Laughs*.) It was impossible. I have no education, no skill in any job.

PAGU: But you . . .

YON KON: Wait – don't interrupt. I have a great liking for fowls. I always want to collect them. Being jobless and homeless is bad enough for me, but seeing fowls straying about in the streets infuriates me, because they can easily get killed. The first fowl I took I didn't mean to steal. I thought it was stray.

PAGU: That's how you got your first lock-up?

YON KON: Yah. And so it continues. I pick up a fowl, get arrested, judged, sent in for six or nine months every year. And for the past forty years I've always spent my Christmas in here for the same crime.

PAGU: And you like it here?

YON KON: Yes, I like it. The way I do it. Half of the year I'm out, the other half I'm in here. I'd hate to spend six, seven years in here.

PAGU: I will never get out of here, any more. (*Cries*.) I am a murderer, a criminal, good for nothing.

YON KON: No. No, you're not. But you shouldn't have been so hasty. You should try to control your temper. Gbaratae did not die on the spot.

PAGU: Go on.

YON KON: They will charge you with manslaughter, I should think. If the other prisoners like you they will speak in your favour.

PAGU: What did they say to the Governor?

YON KON: I don't know, but I wouldn't trust prisoners.

PAGU: Yon Kon, you can help me. You can get them to tell the truth. It wasn't my fault; he abused my mother, he slapped me on the face. He was humiliating me . . .

YON KON: And you didn't like it.

PAGU: Anyone who abuses my mother never gets away with it.

YON KON: But he is old enough to be your father, and your father can do the same.

PAGU: I have no father. I've never known my father. I don't know what a father's love is.

YON KON: Don't worry. I will do some routine check before I go to sleep.

PAGU: What kind of routine check? (*Clock ticks.*) Yon Kon, what are you thinking about?

YON KON: I'm a bit puzzled.

PAGU: About what?

YON KON: Many things.

PAGU: Like what?

YON KON: Things like the doctor.

PAGU: What about him?

YON KON: He saw old Gbaratae before he died this afternoon.

PAGU (*eagerly*): Well?

YON KON: It's not only the Doc I'm thinking about . . . things like, eh . . . what happened between you and me this morning.

PAGU: But how do you connect the doctor, you, me and Gbaratae? How?

YON KON: Tell me, have you got a good bank savings?

PAGU: Why?

YON KON (*shouts*): I want to help you. How much have you got in the bank?

PAGU: Not much . . . only . . . well . . .

YON KON: Speak up, boy! Speak up. How many figures, two, three, four . . . ?

PAGU: Two . . . two hundred and something, I can't remember. My book is with my mother.

YON KON: Not bad, not bad. Is your mother well off?

PAGU: How do you mean?

YON KON: Has she got money? Will she be prepared to help you?

PAGU: Leave my mother out of this. If you want to help me you can. Without asking me about my mother and my savings. Can't we help each other out of human kindness and sympathy? I did not kill Gbaratae because I hated him. I only tried to defend myself, and here I am accused of murder. I'm not a murderer!

YON KON: You are a coward, you are frightened. Ever since you started bragging this morning I knew the type of boy you are.

Roll of thunder.

YON KON: I was like you – thunder, it is a sign – I was like you when I first came to prison. Talk, brag, fight.

PAGU: I am not like you. No two people are the same. No two circumstances are the same. And you didn't kill a man the first time you were imprisoned.

YON KON: No. I didn't kill a man. I stabbed three men – two prisoners and a warder.

PAGU: Did they die?

YON KON: No. They survive with indelible scars . . .

PAGU: Why did you stab them?

YON KON: They hurt my pride.

PAGU: What did they do to you? I mean the law?

YON KON (*laughs*): Nothing. I got away with it. By spending the last penny I had. 'See to see' boy, '*See to see*'.

PAGU (*puzzled*): I see.

YON KON: Can you hear the rain? It's a full moon, that's why it is raining . . . Tomorrow I will be out of here . . . It is late now, I must go to my block. You don't need my help, do you?

PAGU: No! Not the way you want to help me.

YON KON: You see, it's no good to put sense into people's heads. I'm only advising you. You can take it or leave it. All I'm suggesting is that I can see Doc and talk to him, because he is a good man. That's if you are prepared to spend your £200, of course. What cannot money do? I know!

PAGU: And how can my £200 get me free?

YON KON: That's easy, Pagu, easy. Doc is a clever man. One, as I see it, Gbaratae was a dying man. He always had strokes and heart trouble. Two, you were, at the time trying to defend yourself and under great emotional strain, and the balance of your mind was disturbed, due to reasons which the Doc can analyse. Three, Gbaratae, according to Doc, was still alive when we took him to hospital. He died fifteen minutes later ... um ... according to the fracture Gbaratae had on the skull, it is obvious that it was not a blow inflicted by you, from you, or any object handled by you.

PAGU: Who do you suggest inflicted the blow that fractured his skull?

YON KON: The pavement, man. He had a stroke. He fell and hit his skull on the pavement.

PAGU: So that is your defence for me ... What about the prisoners?

YON KON: They didn't see you hit him.

PAGU (repeating): They didn't ... Do you want me to believe you can arrange all this? So that I give you my life savings to get me free?

YON KON: Oh no! You don't have to believe me or give me the money either. Remember, I said earlier, it's just advice. Take it or leave it. But think about it. And remember this, there are times when we pay for our innocence. It's not too dear a price.

PAGU: Listen, Yon Kon, I come from a good home. I don't believe in any form of bribery, deceit, lie or injustice. I'd rather die an undeserved death. I asked you to help, because I looked upon you as an older man full of experiences – prison experiences, I suppose. Why should I bribe you or anyone else? I know I'm not guilty.

YON KON: There is a lot you've got to learn. (*Pause.*) Pagu, listen. The rain has stopped. I've got to go and pack now. Goodnight. (*Walking away*) But think of my advice and forget your pride. A prisoner hasn't got any. And stop being a coward.

SCENE FIVE

Agba's new place—on the hill. It is about six months later

99991: (*shouting*): Agba . . . Agba . . . Agba Saiteiny!

AGBA: You want to talk to me, warder, you come over here, don't shout my name.

99991: Hello, Agba. I've been trying to trace Yon Kon for over three weeks. I didn't know you had moved from your old residence.

AGBA: Ah, we moved six months ago.

99991: Why?

AGBA: People complain that we make too much noise with the gumbay drums.

99991: How is Yon Kon? I haven't seen him. He seems to be keeping his promise.

AGBA: Nine-nine-double-nine-one – Yon Kon is not changed. He still steal fowls. But lucky for him they don't catch him. Yes, the other day he nearly get trouble. That is why we move up to the hill.

99991: But he promised not to steal fowls any more.

AGBA: He will never stop. I can't stop him. You can't stop him. Nobody can. He is made that way.

99991: Where is he now? I have an important message for him from Pagu.

AGBA: We had small palava. Small quarrel. I don't know where he is gone.

99991: I thought you were very good friends, and you were getting on well with the gumbay business?

AGBA: Yon Kon don't like it here with me again. He don't want any more business with the gumbay. He say we lazy, idle, free . . . but that's all I can do and nothing more. Gumbay is my life.

99991: I am sure you will make it up. I must go now—I'm going on duty.

AGBA: What is the message?

99991: Oh yes; well, you know about Pagu Ekele? He was sentenced to seven years imprisonment for manslaughter . . . while he was serving two weeks hard labour for stealing . . . you remember the case? Well, his mother died some months ago in a road accident. Since then he has been sort of going out of his head . . . mad . . . he is in hospital, very ill, not eating, he talks to no one. Three weeks ago he asked me to tell Yon Kon he wants to see him. I think he wants to tell him something. So if Yon Kon could come down to the prison tomorrow morning, I think Pagu needs him greatly.

AGBA: I will tell him when he comes back tonight.

99991: Well, goodbye, Agba. Thank heavens you don't pull a long face at me any more.

AGBA: There is a time for everything, nine-nine-double-nine-one, a time for everything . . .

Pause. Blackout.

SCENE SIX

Agba's old place

AGBA (*approaching*): Bobor . . . Salu . . . Amadu . . . Yon Kon. Anyone at home?

YON KON: Ai.

AGBA: When did you come back, Yon Kon?

YON KON: Can't remember. But I'm kicking out again.

AGBA: This evening, now?

YON KON: Yeah.

AGBA: Where to?

YON KON: Land of no return. Prison, maybe.

AGBA: Prison! You talk like you going out of your mind.

YON KON: Hah, so you think I am.

AGBA: Well, if the only place you think about is prison, there must be something wrong with you.

YON KON: There are many things wrong with me . . . for a start I am not happy with you here and your gumbay set.

AGBA: That's no reason why you should be proud of going back to prison.

YON KON: It is the only place I can be proud of. I feel happy and content there.

AGBA: But you promised not to go there again.

YON KON: I did . . . six months ago . . . that's a long time now . . . and what have I got being out of jail? No friends, no job of any good standing . . . no nothing. In prison I enjoy the rice, ginger beer, cakes, band entertainment, important visitors, discussions and many other things.

AGBA: I used to enjoy all those things too. We both used to. And we can enjoy them still better outside where we are free.

YON KON: I don't feel free outside. I will never feel free or enjoy anything outside prison. Prison was built for people like me. I will always make new friends there. I will have people to command. It is the only life I understand, and the place I know best.

AGBA: Nine-nine-double-nine-one was here to see you.

YON KON: Yes, he still remembers me. I know they miss me very much – warders as well as prisoners.

AGBA: They don't miss you. They respect you; they respect you, because they think you are keeping your promise

YON KON: Ha! Promise. Well, they will soon welcome me in again . . . maybe tomorrow.

AGBA: Yon Kon, you are not going . . .

YON KON: Yes, I am. I go in when I want to . . . Christmas is round the corner, I must not miss a Christmas in prison.

AGBA: I have a message for you.

YON KON: Yes? What is it – who from?

AGBA: Pagu. Nine-nine-double-nine-one says he wants to see you desperately . . .

YON KON: For what? He never took my advice – he was too big-mannish, too proud . . . too good to listen to me.

AGBA: Don't you think you are like that?

YON KON (laughs scornfully): You're kidding – I'm not.

AGBA: If you knew yourself you wouldn't be so sure. Anyway, according to nine-nine-double-nine-one Pagu's mother is dead, and he is very ill, going mad, not eating, talks to no one.

YON KON: You see, they need me! Well, when I get in he will do routine exercises for me, sick or well, sane or insane.

AGBA: You bet he will.

YON KON: Go find me a taxi. I'm going to confess my crimes and get back to prison.

SCENE SEVEN

Warder's Office

WARDER: Who've you got for us today, constable?

OFFICER: Only one prisoner, sir. Yon Kon.

WARDER: What! Well, Yon Kon. You haven't kept your promise, then?

YON KON: No sir, you see —

WARDER: What's the offence. Fowl stealing again!

YON KON: Yes sir. You see I found I couldn't be happy . . .

WARDER: Take him to his usual block. Oh, yes. We kept it for you, safe. We thought you might come back some day.

YON KON: Thanks, sir. How are things, eh? Still the same routine?

WARDER: Still the same.

YON KON: And the prisoners? How are they making out? How's . . . er . . . Pagu?

WARDER: All right, Yon Kon. You go and find out. They're all yours again, now. You're back in charge.

SCENE EIGHT

Prison Yard

YON KON (shouting): Right, left, left, right, right, left, left, right. Pagu, Pagu. Come over here.

PAGU: Yes, Yon Kon. Yon Kon, I want to talk . . .

YON KON: For the past two weeks, I hear you have been dodging exercises, why?

PAGU: On doctor's orders. I must . . .

YON KON: Join the rank . . . doctor's orders or not – fall in. Yap, yap, don't argue.

PAGU: I can't . . . I must talk to you. It's very important.

YON KON: Later.

PAGU: Yon Kon, did you know that my mother is dead? Did you get my message? I was not present to give my mother a burial . . . I don't know what has happened to my money, my savings, she had everything, my last penny. You must help me, Yon Kon. Where will I go when I leave here? I must talk to you, Yon Kon, I must.

YON KON: Later. We will talk about everything later. There's plenty of time. (*Shouting*) Right, left, left, right. (*To Pagu*) Don't stand there gaping and wailing, Pagu, fall into line.

PAGU: I . . . I . . . I . . .

YON KON: Yap yap, don't argue. You are wasting my time. Come on, you prisoners, routine exercises, come on Pagu. Hey, you over there! Come on, after two. You know all the words. One, two.

PRISONERS 1 & 2: We must not steal.

PRISONERS 3 & 4: We must not steal.

PRISONERS 1 & 2: We must not kill.

PRISONERS 3 & 4: We must not kill.

PRISONERS 1 & 2: We must not fight.

PRISONERS 3 & 4: We must not fight.

PRISONERS 1 & 2: We must not lie.

PRISONERS 3 & 4: We must not lie.

PRISONERS 1 & 2: We must obey the laws.

PRISONERS 3 & 4: We must obey the laws.

PRISONERS 1 & 2: We must behave —

PRISONERS 3 & 4: – as good citizens should.

YON KON: That's right. Right, left, left, right, right, left, left, right, right, left.

The Game

FEMI EUBA

CHARACTERS

Baba Tunde, *A rich businessman*
Awero ⎫
       ⎬ *His wives*
Aduke ⎭
Idikoko, *A poor beggar*
Blindman
Yakubu, *Baba Tunde's Taxi-driver*

THE GAME

SCENE ONE

AWERO (*low voice*): Idikoko! ... Idikoko, wake up! ...
Idikoko! ...

IDIKOKO (*jerking from sleep*): H'm? ... (*Whines*) Can a poor
beggar not even sleep peaceably out here – on the
common pavement? ...

AWERO (*giggles*): It's me, silly fool.

IDIKOKO: H'm? Awero! Where are you going, so early
in the morning?

AWERO: Shhh! ... Don't wake my husband up ... Here,
here ...

AWERO: Take two shillings. ...

IDIKOKO: H'm? ...two shillings? ... Ah, I dreamt it was
my lucky day today! (*Yawns*) ... but I thought it began
with two *pounds*! ...

AWERO: Sh! ... Do the job well, and I'll reward you
greatly in the evening ...

IDIKOKO: Job? ... What job's this?

AWERO: I want you to watch my husband's movements,
like a cat does a rat. And if he asks anything of you,
throw him off the track as much as possible!

IDIKOKO: You can count on me, my precious jewel!
But ...

AWERO (*giggling*): Use your tricks well on him ...

IDIKOKO: That shouldn't be difficult ... You know I'm
the cleverest scoundrel in town!

AWERO: Good, good!

IDIKOKO (*reproachfully*): But two shillings . . . !

AWERO: I said I'd reward you . . .

(*The town clock starts to chime seven.*)

AWERO: I must be off . . . (*Going*) You know where to find me, don't you? (*Goes.*)

IDIKOKO (*sighs, amusedly*): She hasn't told me what it's all about! But never mind! Idikoko's equal to any game! So, I'll camp myself here, until that rich devil, her husband, wakes up . . . (*Yawns contentment.*) Ah, what a beautiful day it's going to be. (*Settles to sleep.*) . . .

BABA TUNDE (*savouring the air*): Ah, what a lovely morning. Hey, you, Idikoko. (*Hissed*) Get off! (*Idikoko pretends to snore.*) I know you're not asleep. Get off my pavement! you heard me!

SCENE TWO

IDIKOKO (*as if from sleep*): H'm? Hum?

BABA TUNDE: Get off! Find other pavements in town!

IDIKOKO (*pretends to be dumb*): Awooh! Awooh!

BABA TUNDE: Dumb, eh? Good! May you be dumb forever!

IDIKOKO: Have mercy on a deaf . . .

BABA TUNDE: That's right!

IDIKOKO: – who's also blind!

BABA TUNDE: And lame, and one-armed! But your tricks can't sell here. So be off, before I lose my temper.

IDIKOKO: Baba Tunde, have mercy on a poor soul!

BABA TUNDE: My house is out of mercy! Go and work!

IDIKOKO: You're the kindest man about the town, Baba!

BABA TUNDE (*sharply*): I'm not kind! Look, do you want me to come out there and kick you away?

IDIKOKO: The richest man, too!

BABA TUNDE: Thank you. I sweated for my money. You go and do the same.

IDIKOKO: Penny for a poor man, Baba Tunde!

BABA TUNDE: I have none, I have none! Scamp!

IDIKOKO: Bless your children!

BABA TUNDE: Your blessing is a disease in my house!

IDIKOKO: Bless your wives and concubines!

BABA TUNDE (*raising his voice in anger*): Clear away I say! Just you wait till I come round to you! Pig!

IDIKOKO (*getting up*): All right, all right! I'm going. (*Goes off a little way.*)

BABA TUNDE: Aha! Why didn't you wait for me?

IDIKOKO: I go, I go. (*He gradually gets more distant during this exchange.*)

BABA TUNDE: Vagabond! Pest!

IDIKOKO: You'll regret this, Baba Tunde . . .

BABA TUNDE: Jobless creature!

IDIKOKO: For the sleep you forbade me.

BABA TUNDE: You're healthy, like anybody else!

IDIKOKO: For the names you call me . . .

BABA TUNDE: I'll call you a thousand more!

IDIKOKO: And the woman you took from me!

BABA TUNDE (*raising his voice*): Wait for me! Just you wait and let me get hold of you!

IDIKOKO: Miserable miser! I shall be revenged! And today!

BABA TUNDE (*raising his voice to him*): Don't let me find you here again, do you hear me? Keep out of my way, if you don't want yourself cudgelled!

(*Idikoko laughs jeeringly from a distance.*)

ADUKE: Come in Baba Tunde . . . (*soft caressing voice.*) Leave him alone for now.

BABA TUNDE: Oh, Aduke . . . I'll deal with that – that s-son of, son of—

ADUKE: Let him be for now, Baba Tunde. You'll get him some other time.

BABA TUNDE: Fancy th-that Idikoko accusing me of taking his woman! The g-goat!

ADUKE: It's all right, my lord. Come in. Breakfast is ready.

BABA TUNDE: Ah, thank you, Aduke. You're a good wife to me! I'll come with you . . .

SCENE THREE

BLINDMAN (*almost singing tone*): Blind that I am . . . Blind that I am . . . Penny for a blindman. Penny for a blindman.

IDIKOKO (*approaching*): All right, all right! Here is—

BLINDMAN (*shakes container eagerly*): Thank you, sir!

IDIKOKO: – a stone for you. Hello, old friend!

BLINDMAN (*hisses with contempt*): It's you! The one and only Idikoko! The one that begs sloth to brand him as his child. Taught by hunger, he knows all the arts of contortion! As swift as lightning, he deceives no one but himself!

IDIKOKO: What a thing to say to an old friend!

BLINDMAN: I'm not your friend! Don't come here and bring me bad luck!

IDIKOKO: How much have you made this morning?

BLINDMAN: Thief, thief! Leave my money alone!

IDIKOKO: All right, all right! I wasn't going to do anything.

BLINDMAN: Liar, liar! What do you want here?

IDIKOKO: To say hello to an old friend.

BLINDMAN: Yes, hello! Goodbye!

IDIKOKO: All right, all right! If that's how you want it. I've got myself a job anyway.

BLINDMAN: A likely story! But keep it to yourself, do you hear?

IDIKOKO: A first-class job, actually.

BLINDMAN: Tell me another!

IDIKOKO: Nothing like the begging game I'm used to. A *real* game this. And *I* make the rules!

BLINDMAN: Good for you. But leave me alone in peace, I beg of you.

IDIKOKO (*continues regardless*): A mature game of hide and seek! A husband dissatisfied! Jealous wives! The adulterer and the adulteress! All are in this game. Everybody in it schemes not to be found out. The winner, the most successful may claim so much.

BLINDMAN (*intrigued*): And the loser?

IDIKOKO: Well, it's hard to say just yet.

BLINDMAN: Whatever happens, may *you* be the loser!

IDIKOKO: Just you wait till I've done with them all! I'll be so rich! You'll come begging for bread from Idikoko.

BLINDMAN: Heaven forbid such a day!

IDIKOKO: Will you join in this game of mine?

BLINDMAN: Go away from here, I don't want anything of yours. You've robbed me of my alms already, these past few minutes you've been here.

IDIKOKO: All right, have it your own way. Duty calls me presently to the market, anyway. To see my employer.

BLINDMAN (*with an air of disbelief*): Employer?

IDIKOKO: Yes. And if she's *not* in the market, I think I know where I will find her. Oh yes, I know all right . . .

SCENE FOUR

YAKUBU (*fussily delighted*): Awero!

YAKUBU: Come in, come in! I thought you wouldn't make it! I thought . . .

AWERO (*giggles flirtatiously*): Good morning, Yakubu!

AWERO (*giggling*): I promised, didn't I?

YAKUBU: Tell me, tell me, is it all right? He – I mean – your husband?

AWERO: Of course. He was still asleep when I left for the market.

YAKUBU: Good! Good! And your co-wife, Aduke?

AWERO: She's helping me by getting his breakfast.

YAKUBU (*a bit frantic*): You mean – you mean she knew? About us? (*Awero giggles.*) Did she know that you were coming here? Awero, stop laughing! Did she?

AWERO: Of course not!

YAKUBU (*sighs with relief*): Good! You almost frightened me, you know. Ah, Awero, my sweet . . . (*Awero giggles. Uneasily still*) But she – she saw us together the other day in the taxi. Could she have suspected?

AWERO (*giggling*): What if she does?

YAKUBU (*thrown, he is again a bit frantic*): Awero, that's bad! She might tell Baba Tunde, mightn't she? You know she's jealous! About you! And she thinks he loves you more than her!

AWERO (*giggling*): And what's bad about that?

YAKUBU: But Awero, do you want him to find us out?

AWERO: You could find him out with one of his many concubines any day. You know about this, don't you?

YAKUBU: Yes, yes, but . . .

AWERO: Well then, if *he* finds *us* out . . .

YAKUBU: Not yet, not yet, Awero! We must keep it secret for the moment. You know I'm still his taxi-driver. You know he owns this house too. L-let's fool him yet longer.

AWERO: And then? And then you'll marry me?

YAKUBU: You know I'll marry you, Awero. In the end.

AWERO (*flippant*): In the end? When is the end? Five years, five weeks, five days? Today?

YAKUBU: No, no! Not today, Awero. Soon, soon!

AWERO: How soon?

YAKUBU: Very soon.

AWERO: Promise?

YAKUBU: Promise! But seriously, Awero. Will Aduke suspect, and tell him?

AWERO: Really! (*Giggling*) What does it matter, to be offered a lift in my husband's taxi?

YAKUBU (*relieved*): Nothing, of course! Ah, Awero, my love! Awero, my sweet!

AWERO (*giggling*): Stop it, Yakubu! Behave yourself, now! Anyway, there's plenty of time.

YAKUBU (*delighted*): You mean, you mean you'll stay the whole day?

AWERO: Umhum?

YAKUBU: Ah, my treasure! We'll have the whole day to ourselves. Tell me, who keeps your market stall for you?

AWERO: My apprentice, of course.

YAKUBU: It's all right, then. As long as it's not that idle, good-for-nothing Idikoko. (*Awero giggles.*) Really, I don't know why you sometimes ask that scoundrel to do things for you.

AWERO: Well, we must help the poor.

YAKUBU: Poor, indeed! He's just a parasite!

AWERO: Leave him alone! He does a good job for a fair sum, anyway.

YAKUBU: That's it! You go on encouraging him! One of these days he's going to play out with his tricks. Take all your money and run away. I warn you.

AWERO (*giggling*): It's all right, Yakubu.

YAKUBU: Damn him! He doesn't come *my* way! He knows me. (*Suddenly overcome*) Ah, Awero, my sweet! Awero, my love! Treasure of my heart!

AWERO (*giggling*): Stop it, Yakubu. Stop it!

YAKUBU: Come and sit over here, Awero. Ah, Awero, my treasure, my bliss—

SCENE FIVE

BABA TUNDE (*breathes contentment*): Ah, Aduke, my sweet. This is a good breakfast. It's a long time since I've tasted your breakfast.

ADUKE (*meaningful tenderness*): The old skilful hand will yet know how to please its lord best.

BABA TUNDE: Then the old hand must resume its past skill.

ADUKE (*politic*): Thank you, my lord! It is only too willing, but . . . I fear this will hurt Awero's feelings.

BABA TUNDE (*touchy, prickly*): It's nobody's fault but her own. I can't understand her any more.

ADUKE: Isn't it wise, my lord, to find out a reason for this?

BABA TUNDE: Reason! Going off to the market, just like that . . . not minding my meals . . . What reason could she give for such behaviour? Tell me.

ADUKE: She . . . she said she had an urgent sewing to do, my lord.

BABA TUNDE: Urgent my foot! A wife's first duty is to her husband.

(*Slight pause.*)

ADUKE (*musing*): Hmm, a wife you love so much . . . who makes you even want, nearly, to forget your first wife . . . and your children . . .

BABA TUNDE: And yet she has no child of her own, for me . . . ?

ADUKE: I do not mean that, my lord!

BABA TUNDE: You implied it! But no matter. You're right, I loved Awero so much. (*Slight pause then affectionately*) Um, Aduke, my love, I must let you into a secret . . . It has been in my mind for some time now, and it's only fair to tell you.

ADUKE: What, my lord?

BABA TUNDE: I'm thinking of taking in another wife!

ADUKE (*after a short pause, with concern*): Is . . . is two not enough, my lord?

BABA TUNDE: I've let myself into it already. It's too late to change. Are you hurt, Aduke?

ADUKE (*stiffly*): Do what pleases you best, my lord.

BABA TUNDE (*breathes relief*): That's settled then. I must go presently.

ADUKE: Where, my lord?

BABA TUNDE: End of the month, Aduke. I must go round to collect the rents. Yakubu is not here today. Otherwise he could have done it for me.

ADUKE: Of course, his day off! One of your other drivers might as well do it, my lord.

BABA TUNDE: No, Aduke, I trust none other than Yakubu. He's an old hand I'm used to.

ADUKE: My lord means wisely. (*Pause, then brightly*) Is my lord going by chance near the market? . . . But it does not matter?

BABA TUNDE: But say what you will, Aduke! I may pass by the market. What do you wish?

ADUKE: Well, my lord, just to give a minor message to Awero . . .

BABA TUNDE: Awero! No matter, what is it?

ADUKE (*hesitantly*): W-well, if you will please give her this material? For the children's school uniform. I forgot to give it to her this morning. If you *should* be passing by her stall . . .

SCENE SIX

BLINDMAN: Blind that I am! Blind that I am! Penny for the blindman! Penny for the blindman!

IDIKOKO: All right, all right, that's enough.

BLINDMAN (*hisses*): It's you again. What do you want now?

IDIKOKO: To save you from moaning a bit. You like wailing, don't you?

BLINDMAN: You're not in gaol yet, then?

IDIKOKO: Ha, ha! Not until I've had my fun, full circle . . . You haven't seen a fat, rich man pass this way, have you?

BLINDMAN: How could I?

IDIKOKO: Oh, I forgot.

BLINDMAN (*mocking*): You couldn't find your 'employer' then?

IDIKOKO: Don't worry, I know where she is right now! Don't you worry! She's with my counterpart!

BLINDMAN: Your counterpart? What are you talking about?

IDIKOKO: We have affection for the same woman, you see!

BLINDMAN (*mocking*): You fancy yourself doing many things you're incapable of, don't you!

IDIKOKO (*almost to himself*): He's at the moment having his share. But my turn will come. Fair is fair.

BLINDMAN (*more mocking still*): You! A woman? . . . And who is this woman, that is the curse of all women?

IDIKOKO: Awero! The only one that will stand by her rights. The only one daring to set an example to her female tribe, married and unmarried alike! Who'll go from one man to another, and set the world free – and full of jobs for people like me. Awero, the cat

by night! Jewelled eyes and full of wit. Who knows
what she schemes overnight . . .

BLINDMAN (*completely bewildered*): You've been talking in
riddles since you came here, Idikoko. Can't you make
yourself more clear?

IDIKOKO: Never mind. Don't bother me now. For we are
going to begin the game proper! Here comes one of
the players. But no words from you, do you hear me?
This is all my job, no concern of yours.

BLINDMAN: Well, don't play any of your tricks here.

IDIKOKO (*disregarding him*): Here he comes, and what a
rage he's in! Because he couldn't find Awero at her
stall, I expect! Anyway we shall soon find out . . .
because he obviously wants to speak to me.

BABA TUNDE (*approaching*): You there! Look here, you! I'm
talking to you, Idikoko! Scoundrel!

IDIKOKO: That's right, Baba Tunde, go on! As though I
was still on your pavement.

BABA TUNDE: H'm, I may forgive you for all you said this
morning if you will answer me.

IDIKOKO: Go on, we shall see who forgives who (*to himself*) . . . in this game.

BABA TUNDE: What did you say? No matter. Have you
seen my wife anywhere this morning?

IDIKOKO (*pretending to grumble*): First it was abuse . . . And
now he makes the abused thing the watchdog of his . . .

BABA TUNDE: Answer my questions, and don't be insolent!
Have you seen my wife or not?

IDIKOKO (*again grumbling*): Anyone would think he was
a king this morning! Calling me names my mother
daren't call me. Swearing and cursing. Not even a
king has the liberty, do you hear me? Not even a king!

BABA TUNDE: All right, all right! I take back all I said
about you!

IDIKOKO: Just like that! Not even a king would escape

compensation, do you hear me?

BABA TUNDE: All right, I know what you want. Here, take sixpence.

IDIKOKO: Agh!

BABA TUNDE: What is the matter with you? Here, I make it threepence more.

IDIKOKO: Don't think I want your money sir. But if *you* want to give it to me – then, that's not enough!

BABA TUNDE (*sternly*): Thief! You might as well take all my house! Scoundrel!

IDIKOKO: Watch your language, sir.

BABA TUNDE: Agh! Look, take one and six, or nothing!

IDIKOKO: I'll take nothing sir. Go your way and I'll go mine. I don't know why you came to me anyway.

BABA TUNDE: You know why, damn you, you know why! You sometimes keep Awero's stall for her, don't you?

IDIKOKO: Maybe, maybe. But I still don't know what you're talking about . . .

BABA TUNDE: Here, here. Two shillings!

IDIKOKO: I'm not the only one that knows things about your wife. Find the other people, and ask them.

BABA TUNDE: You know more than anybody. Take two shillings!

IDIKOKO: All right, if I must name my bid, sir, and only because it's you, I shall take nothing less than five shillings.

BABA TUNDE: Thief! Vagabond!

BLINDMAN: Penny for a blindman, sir! Penny for a—

IDIKOKO (*severely*): Shut your trap, will you, you blind fellow!

BLINDMAN (*protestingly*): This is *my* station!

IDIKOKO: Find another one, and shut up!

BABA TUNDE: Now there's a reasonable man! Content with small things! You, you! Take threepence.

BLINDMAN: Thank you, sir! Thank you sir!

IDIKOKO: And be off, will you? (*To himself*) Spoiling my game!

BLINDMAN (*into distance*): Thank you, sir! Thank you sir!

BABA TUNDE (*calling*): You wouldn't know where my wife is, would you?

IDIKOKO (*shouting after him*): Yes, go on, tell him all you know!

BLINDMAN (*shouting back*): I wish I did know, sir.

BABA TUNDE: Oh, well, never mind. Thank you all the same. Now look here, Idikoko, take three shillings or forever be damned!

IDIKOKO: You'll learn a lot about your wife that way.

BABA TUNDE: Thief! You shall pay for this. (*Reluctantly*) Here, here ... five shillings, then. May it be lost in your pocket!

IDIKOKO: Thank you.

BABA TUNDE: Now then. Did you see my wife, this morning?

IDIKOKO: Yes, I saw your wife this morning.

BABA TUNDE: Where, where, fool?

IDIKOKO (*pretends to think*): Where did I see your wife ... Somewhere around, of course!

BABA TUNDE (*irritated*): Heaven and earth! Doing what, goat?

IDIKOKO: That's another matter. Do you think you could buy *all* my news with five shillings?

BABA TUNDE (*shouting*): You, you son of a –

IDIKOKO: Ah!

BABA TUNDE: You shall get nothing more from me, do you hear? And I shall take back all I gave you.

IDIKOKO: Good day sir. No wonder you deserve all your wife has done to you. Here, your money.

BABA TUNDE: What has my wife done to me?

IDIKOKO: If you heard sir, you would go and – kill yourself.

BABA TUNDE (*frantic*): Tell me!

IDIKOKO: Aren't you forgetting something . . .?

BABA TUNDE: All right, take a shilling . . . I beg of you, take it and tell me!

IDIKOKO: You'll not abuse me again, will you?

BABA TUNDE: No, I won't.

IDIKOKO: I'll strike a bargain with you. Make it two shillings, and I'll tell you all.

BABA TUNDE: Oh, you're incorrigible! Anyway, here!

IDIKOKO: Alas! (*Feigning sympathy*) To think Awero, sweet Awero, could leave her husband, and run away – with another man.

BABA TUNDE: Impossible! Why should she do such a thing – to me!

IDIKOKO (*teasing*): I have heard that you – ill-treat her.

BABA TUNDE: Don't be silly! Anyway, whom did she run away with, and where to?

IDIKOKO: I only saw them go into a lorry . . . and off they went! How do I know where?

BABA TUNDE: But who's this man?

IDIKOKO (*outraged*): You can't get that from me!

BABA TUNDE (*in a rage*): After giving you so much? What more do you want? Tell me!

IDIKOKO: I don't know him, I say. Never seen him before in my life.

BABA TUNDE: Liar!

IDIKOKO (*cunningly*): But I can find out!

BABA TUNDE: You'd better, or I'll—

IDIKOKO: Well, this is business you know (*meaningfully*). Nothing is done without money.

BABA TUNDE: What about all I've given you?

IDIKOKO: For the news. That's for the news.

BABA TUNDE: Thief! (*checking himself*) All right, all right, I'll reward you handsomely – when you've done it.

IDIKOKO: Oh no you won't! It might involve some travelling expenses, you know.

BABA TUNDE (*grumbling*): Awero shall suffer for this ...
Here ... and you'd better return with something
worthwhile!

IDIKOKO: Trust me! I don't think it'll take me long to find
your man for you!

BABA TUNDE: It had better not!

IDIKOKO: So long!

BABA TUNDE (*to himself*): Ass! Scoundrel! (*Walking away*)
You drained my pocket – but no matter. Awero is to
blame! It crazes me to think of her, deceiving me with
some other man! ...

(*Pause.*)

SCENE SEVEN

YAKUBU (*urgent whisper*): Awero! Awero, get up!

AWERO (*sleepily*): Hum? Hum?

YAKUBU: Awero, get up! Get up!

AWERO: Hum? What is it?

YAKUBU: I – I've suddenly remembered!

AWERO: What, Yakubu, my love?

YAKUBU: It's the end of the month today. You must go
away at once!

AWERO (*laughing*): What are you talking about?

YAKUBU: Awero, have you forgotten? Baba Tunde collects
his rent today.

AWERO: Forget about that for now. Come. Settle down
my love.

YAKUBU: N-no, Awero! C-can't you see? I collect his rents
for him?

AWERO: Umhum?

YAKUBU: Well, I'm off duty today, so he'll collect them
himself.

AWERO (*calm*): So what?

YAKUBU (*more agitated*): You can't have forgotten that this is one of his houses: *he'll come here*! Please, hurry, Awero, and get up!

AWERO: K-e-e-p c-a-l-m! He won't come here. He knows you'll collect for this house and give it to him to-morrow.

YAKUBU: W-we can't take chances, Awero.

AWERO (*mothering him*): Come and sit down. Nothing will happen. Anyway, it won't happen without our knowing.

YAKUBU: How? How?

AWERO (*giggling*): He's being watched and followed. I tipped Idikoko—

YAKUBU (*annoyed*): Idikoko! So you did bring him into this, after all! And if *he* knows, the whole world will know!

YAKUBU (*more to himself*): God of my forefathers! (*Raising his voice*) Awero, please get up and go! Before I get angry!

AWERO (*huffy*): What a thing to say to me, Yakubu! I come to spend the whole day with you, and . . .

(*A knock on the door.*)

YAKUBU (*frightened low voice*): Who's that?

AWERO (*expectantly*): Idikoko at last!

YAKUBU (*unsure*): How do you know?

AWERO: It's Idikoko, I'm sure.

YAKUBU: Here, your blouse! Please hurry!

AWERO: I say it's Idikoko. Go on and open the door.

YAKUBU: Take your wrapper . . .l-look, you must get out – through the window, i-into the backyard.

AWERO (*giggling*): It's Idikoko!

(*Harder knock.*)

AWERO: Yakubu, go and open up!

YAKUBU (*confusedly*): A-all right, all right! G-get behind that cupboard, will you!

AWERO (*huffy, going off*): Very well. But it's quite un-
necessary.

(*Slight pause.*)

IDIKOKO: Are you all deaf in this house?

YAKUBU (*with relief*): Idikoko. (*Tough*) All right, big-
mouth, what do you want here?

IDIKOKO: Is our wife here?

YAKUBU (*confused*): Whose wife?

AWERO (*approaching*): Idikoko! I knew it was you. What
news, Idikoko, tell me!

IDIKOKO: Everything's gone according to plan.

AWERO: Oh, good! Do you hear that, Yakubu?

YAKUBU: W-what plan? You can't come in here, and you
know it, fat-face!

AWERO: Yakubu, do let him come in. You can see, he's
on our side. Let's hear the news he's brought us.

YAKUBU: Awero, this is all your doing. You didn't have
to bring him into this.

IDIKOKO (*chuckling*): Who told you I knew nothing about
it before?

YAKUBU: Say what you want to say here, at the door, and
go away.

IDIKOKO: Even a stranger deserves a seat when he brings
good news!

AWERO: Yakubu, let him come in.

YAKUBU: B-but Baba Tunde—

AWERO: Idikoko, is Baba Tunde coming this way?

IDIKOKO: Of course not.

AWERO: You hear that Yakubu?

YAKUBU: How do we know Idikoko's speaking the truth?

AWERO: Yakubu, please.

YAKUBU: All right then. Two minutes! I give you two
minutes, do you hear?

IDIKOKO: You'll change your mind, I assure you.

YAKUBU: We shall see about that!

AWERO: Idikoko, tell me, tell me how's it going?

IDIKOKO: Everything's according to plan. Your husband's fuming with rage now – as jealous as ever – looking for you.

YAKUBU (*panicky*): Looking for her! What do you mean?

IDIKOKO: Keep calm, keep calm! It doesn't concern you.

AWERO: Tell me from the beginning, Idikoko. What happened?

IDIKOKO: Well, you left me on the pavement this morning, didn't you?

AWERO: Yes, yes? You saw him then?

IDIKOKO: If you call it seeing – he greeted the morning with abuses hurled at me. Then Aduke, the jealous one, came out to rescue me from his caustic tongue, and I watched them disappear into the house.

AWERO: Continue, Idikoko.

IDIKOKO: I wanted to report this little incident to you, but of course, you weren't in the market.

AWERO: Yes?

IDIKOKO: As I was just talking to an old friend there —

YAKUBU: Another thief, I don't doubt.

IDIKOKO: Up came your husband in a fearful rage – looking for you. It was a surprise. I don't know who tipped him off you weren't there . . .

AWERO: I'll bet it was that old cat, Aduke!

IDIKOKO: Anyway, for about half an hour, I left him to shout without a word from me. Then, seeing that he couldn't move me that way, down he went on his knees and started to implore me! Heaven and earth he used to beg me. Then he started dealing out money, to win me over.

AWERO: Never! The miser that he is!

IDIKOKO: He certainly did, I assure you. Couldn't believe my eyes!

YAKUBU: Well and good. What did you tell him – with your many-sided mouth?

IDIKOKO: Ah, you want to know now, don't you? You were going to push me out a moment ago.

YAKUBU: I will yet, if you don't—

AWERO: Keep calm, Yakubu. What did you tell him, Idikoko?

IDIKOKO (*simply*): I told him you'd gone off with another man.

YAKUBU (*furious*): You did what?

(*Knock at the door.*)

YAKUBU (*whispering, agitated*): God of my forefathers! Get out, get out of here, both of you!

IDIKOKO (*lowered voice*): What's he talking about? Expecting another girl?

YAKUBU: Get out, I say.

IDIKOKO: How?

YAKUBU: Through the window, into the backyard.

IDIKOKO: Thank you very much, I'm not a robber.

AWERO (*concerned*): Idikoko, we must hide somewhere! It might be my husband!

IDIKOKO: Never! I didn't tell him where you were.

AWERO: Yes, yes, but . . .

(*Again knock on the door.*)

YAKUBU: Please go, both of you! You've caused enough trouble already!

AWERO: Come, Idikoko. Do as he says! I'll hide behind the cupboard here.

IDIKOKO: Me, too.

YAKUBU (*snaps, but without shouting*): No! The window! Out!

IDIKOKO: All right, all right! (*Into distance*) But I'm not through with you yet!

(*Knock again.*)

AWERO (*hisses*): Go and open up, Yakubu.

YAKUBU (*exasperated, confused*): Agh! (*Petulant*) Oh!

BABA TUNDE (*friendly*): Hello, Yakubu! I thought you were not in.

YAKUBU: Good afternoon, Baba Tunde! (*Yawns*) Oh, I'm sorry!

BABA TUNDE: Oh, did I interrupt your afternoon sleep?

YAKUBU: Mm. Well . . .

BABA TUNDE: Well, well, I won't keep you! No – I only came to remind you that it's the end of the month.

YAKUBU: Oh yes, yes, of course. You want me to collect the rents?

BABA TUNDE: Well, I've collected some of them already, actually. The rest I can do this evening. I'd better leave the ones here for you to collect.

YAKUBU: Yes, I'll do that, and give them to you tomorrow. (*Expectant pause.*)

BABA TUNDE: Ah, well, I'd better be getting along then . . . (*Turns away.*)

YAKUBU (*with relief*): So long, Baba Tunde!

BABA TUNDE (*turning back*): Oh, by the way, Yakubu, you haven't seen Awero, by any chance, today, have you?

YAKUBU (*gulping*): A-Awero? I-isn't she in the market?

BABA TUNDE: Well, she's supposed to be there. I went there this morning, but she was nowhere to be seen.

YAKUBU (*a sudden thought*): C-could she have taken a dress to a customer?

BABA TUNDE: Well, that's what her apprentice suggested. (*Puzzled*) But then, Idikoko saw her running away with another man this morning.

YAKUBU: B-but Idikoko! He's a blasted liar, Baba Tunde, you ought to know that!

BABA TUNDE: Yes, yes!

YAKUBU (*gathering courage*): Idikoko would enlarge on anything at all – anything that would delight him, and earn him a few coppers. Naturally, he might have seen her with a man–(*Nervous laugh*) He might even have seen her talking to *me* for instance! But that's enough for him to play on. He has no heart, that vagabond!

BABA TUNDE: I know. (*Musing*) I wonder if he was playing a trick on me?

YAKUBU: I'm *sure* he was, Baba Tunde.

BABA TUNDE (*grinding his teeth at the thought*): He got more than ten shillings off me!

YAKUBU: He ought to be sent to gaol!

BABA TUNDE (*pathetic*): I don't even know who's fooling me now – Aduke, or Awero, or this scoundrel, Idikoko!

YAKUBU: I shouldn't worry t-too much about Awero. I'm sure she's in the market – right now. (*A noise off.*)

BABA TUNDE: What's that? You'd better see to it, Yakubu.

YAKUBU: Oh, it's all right, I-I think it's the saucepan and things I stack on the table! It's nothing!

BABA TUNDE: Oh well. I'd better be going now. I shall see you tomorrow morning.

YAKUBU: Yes, Baba Tunde. So long! E-excuse my not escorting you . . .

BABA TUNDE (*paternally*): Go and rest, Yakubu. Go and have your rest. A hardworking man needs his day of rest. Goodbye.

YAKUBU (*huge sigh of relief*): Awero! Awero! Awero! Where are you? She was behind this cupboard just now!

IDIKOKO: All right, all right!

YAKUBU: Idikoko! Don't you jump in again!

IDIKOKO: Prevent me if you can.

YAKUBU: Well, then, now you're in, perhaps you can tell me what happened to Awero?

IDIKOKO: She's gone.

YAKUBU: Gone! Gone where?

IDIKOKO: She took the hint. To the market, of course!

YAKUBU: And what's *your* business?

IDIKOKO: Well, we still have matters to settle, haven't we? This is where you start paying for the fun. You enjoyed the game didn't you?

YAKUBU (*irritated*): What are you talking about?

IDIKOKO: The game! Which you played on Awero –which she played on her husband – which you enjoyed, but must lose, – which her husband lost, but must win – which I might even now win or lose . . .

YAKUBU (*puzzled and angry*): Get – out – of – my – house!

IDIKOKO: Oh, no! Not until I've won my share of the proceeds! You've had yours, haven't you?

YAKUBU (*puzzled*): What?

IDIKOKO: Awero!

YAKUBU (*furious*): Why you . . .

IDIKOKO: By the way, imagine you telling all those lies to her husband! At least I'm not alone in that sort of thing now!

YAKUBU: Get out I say!

IDIKOKO: Look – catch my meaning once and for all. I know all that's gone on between you and Awero – today, before today, all the time. And I shall not be silent.

YAKUBU: Nobody will believe you.

IDIKOKO: A-ha! But Aduke, the jealous one, could be brought to speak out. What she knows, and –er –what she doesn't know – yet.

YAKUBU: Blackmailer!

IDIKOKO (*pleased*): That's right!

YAKUBU: You wait until I've got the police on to you!

IDIKOKO: You can do that –if you want everybody to know.

YAKUBU: You'd talk?

IDIKOKO: You yourself called me 'big-mouth'. But – er – the mouth could be brought to shut, and make all others shut, too, if you wish.

YAKUBU: What do you want?

IDIKOKO: A-ha, we're talking business.

YAKUBU (*confused*): Take – a pound, and get out of my house!

IDIKOKO (*outraged*): *One* pound! I want five at least!

YAKUBU: Thief! Jailbird!

IDIKOKO: Watch your tongue! Five is the smallest sum I could think of accepting ... with your abusive language, the fee could go up.

YAKUBU: You'll regret this!

IDIKOKO: I know, I know ...(*counting*) one, two, ...

YAKUBU: You'll pay for this!

IDIKOKO: Sure, sure ... three, four ...

YAKUBU: May you be cursed again and again!

IDIKOKO: Five! I am cursed already. Thank you!

YAKUBU: Now, get out of my house!

IDIKOKO (*laughing*): All right, I'll go! But I'll be back! It's only fair ...only fair ...

YAKUBU (*shouting after him from door: the voice gets fainter as Idikoko walks off*): Heartless parasite! Insolent pig! Insolent ass! Incorrigible jailbird! You'll pay for this! Just you wait until I run you over!

IDIKOKO (*laughing*): A very fair game this! Not bad for a single day ... not bad at all ... Awero greeting me with a little something in the morning ... that rich fool, Baba Tunde, playing into my hands, throughout the day ... then this! An evening meal every day, a constant source of cash, if I so wish ... (*Sighs contentedly*) Ah, what a beautiful evening!

BLINDMAN (*distant*): Blind that I am! Blind that I am! Penny for the blindman!

IDIKOKO (*mimics*): 'Penny for the blindman'. I wonder how much *he* has made today? Er ... no, I'll not go to him now ...I've got bigger fish to fry. I must see Awero in the market ... might even see Aduke, too ... and then there's that rich devil, Baba Tunde ... Hm, when I see him again ... well, I'll think up a story that'll keep him paying me well. It's a great life! It's part of the game!

Blind Cyclos

IME IKIDDEH

CHARACTERS

Olemu   Nkem
Elisa   Amos
Samuel   Medicine Man (Akonnedi)
V.I.V.

BLIND CYCLOS

AKONNEDI: I am Akonnedi the medicine man. My knowledge comes from the Seven Stars. Confined to this shrine I move with the winds. Flit thro' swamps, in and out with tides at sea. Blind, I have the habit of sight. An owl by night, a crow by day. As now, from my hut, I well can see Chairman Olemu beginning his rounds. And, people of our land, this is Round One.

Knocking, becoming progressively more violent.

OLEMU: Open! Open! I say open this door! Amos, do you hear me? You want me to break your jaw when you open it? You know I can do it! What devil is making a tool of you, you fool? Where's your rent? Pay up at once! No excuses this time! Everybody else has paid. Don't waste my time, I still have other houses to visit this evening.

AMOS: Please, sir, as I said last week ... I haven't ...

OLEMU: Nonsense. You're just fooling. I've said there's no excuse. You were paid only yesterday.

AMOS: My mother is sick, sir.

OLEMU: Rubbish. Your mother doesn't come in here. You are keeping the money to spend on a girl.

AMOS: I have no girl, sir. I swear to God, my mother is in hospital.

OLEMU: *You* should be sent there, if they could cure people of telling lies. Look at the shirt you put on –

111

Triple Three! It costs *four pounds* and is brand new! Now look at mine: *fifteen shillings* I paid for it. And you come with your usual tale of mother sick, father dead.

AMOS: I will try on Monday sir, I swear to God. How can I lie to you? I beg you, Chairman, I won't find another house if you push me out!

OLEMU: So you know that? Listen, Amos, you have been wasting my precious time. You know how much work I left in the office, don't you?

AMOS: I know, sir.

OLEMU: The three files brought in before we closed, I didn't touch. *Three files*!

AMOS: It is true, Chairman, I remember.

OLEMU: Right, I had to leave the office two hours before time, to catch those boys living in the house along Jakande Street. They haven't paid their rent for two months – *two months*! And they were receiving their pay today. Can you imagine that?

AMOS: Yes, sir, I know. It is very bad of them.

OLEMU: Listen, you know nothing. I have thrown them out. I shouldn't have to go around collecting rents; I have caretakers. But you people are too difficult for them to handle.

AMOS: Mine is only one month, sir, and it is because of my mother . . .

OLEMU: Now look, Amos. I like you very much, because you're the best messenger I've had in that office – that's why I brought you to live here. You know all other tenants have to buy me drinks when they come in, or pay five pounds Agreement Fee. You, I charged you nothing.

AMOS: I know, sir, and God will bless you.

OLEMU: Forget about God. What I am saying is, you earn five pounds a month, and you can manage well with it, if you are sensible. You must bring the money to the office on Monday. Is that clear?

AMOS: Yes, Chairman, but . . . but, sir . . .

OLEMU: There's no but. You can go to your brother and borrow the money. I mean the taxi-driver. What's his name?

AMOS: Samuel, sir.

OLEMU: Yes, Samuel. He makes a lot of money. What's the time? Good gracious! He's bringing Elisa back from Ibadan this evening. And it's already half-past six!

Pause.

*

AKONNEDI : I'm no hunting dog, but by my eyes
The track I sniff is of a car
Whining in speed; in it a tall lad, and
A wench come back from a father
Whose bones lie in red-earth topped by an anthill.

Car approaches and stops.

ELISA (*yawning*): Honestly, Samuel, I'm so tired – like a goat that has dysentery.

SAMUEL: Am sorry, Miss Elisa. But if Chairman comes, he will give you drink to cool down, and you will rest plenty in the night.

ELISA (*amused*): Ha! Samuel, you don't know. How can I rest when he is here? He is a leopard!

SAMUEL: Well, if the leopard gives the goat plenty money, why worry?

ELISA: Oh, as for money, he gives me that. And he gives me this house free. Have you seen the double-bed and radiogram he bought me last month? £150 both of them.

SAMUEL: You see now? You have nothing to complain! It's we who suffer in this world. What is £3 or £4 a day, when the sun digs into your flesh like this?

ELISA: £4 a day is a lot of money. And you work by hours.

SAMUEL: You won't understand, Miss. You think I get all that? Not so. Look at my body. It used to be smooth like polished floor, now it is like tarred road. (*Pause.*) I must go; am smelling with sweat; am suffering, but God's time is the best.

ELISA: I am suffering too.

SAMUEL: With all the money he gives you? You are laughing at me. Oh, pay me fare; I must go.

ELISA: Look, Samuel, money is not everything in this world. I am not happy.

SAMUEL: You don't work for anything – you have it free, and you talk of suffering! I can't understand you women, truly I can't.

ELISA: I am afraid! You know I have other men apart from Chairman. But he gives me the most money, that's why I can't leave him.

SAMUEL: Why leave him if he gives you plenty money?

ELISA: I don't love him Samuel. Can't you see, he's too old for me? The man I love is the one I went to see in Ibadan. Only he doesn't care for me, and is not rich. So, what can I do, when I have to take care of my mother and brothers and sisters?

SAMUEL: The one in Ibadan, has he no job?

ELISA: He is in the Police.

SAMUEL: Police? Let him stay where he is! I don't like cops – they sniff round too much for money.

ELISA: Austin doesn't keep his money – he drinks like a gutter. When I arrived, he was broke, and I had to give him two pounds.

SAMUEL: Does Chairman know about him?

ELISA: Chairman thinks I go to Ibadan to see my father;

the poor man died four years ago, and I had to leave the Convent School. But one day, Chairman may find out. Oh, I'm so worried!

SAMUEL: That's no trouble, Miss. There are many ways of catching a rat. I can take you to a medicine man seven miles from here. He can make proper medicine and close the eyes of both men, so they won't worry.

ELISA (*doubtfully*): I have heard such stories before.

SAMUEL: I have seen it many times. Chairman will sprinkle money on you like rain water, and the other one will love you more than fresh fish.

ELISA: Are you sure, Sammy? You taxi-drivers play a lot of ways.

SAMUEL: Well, if you think it is tricks, you can leave it. The man is the brother of the husband of my wife's sister. I am not telling you story; I know him, I have taken people there before; bishops, ministers and so on, and they all come back to thank me.

ELISA: Oh, if he can do it, I should be so happy. Look at me – am not slimming; it's because I can't eat.

SAMUEL: You wait. After we see this man, you'll eat like a man just come from jail. But you will give me a small commission, Miss.

ELISA: I will give you ... I will come and visit you Sammy, if your wife doesn't fight me.

SAMUEL: We can arrange that ... There's one thing – the medicine will go deep if Chairman goes there in person. As for the other man, if you have his photo, that's enough.

ELISA: I can manage that. Chairman will go anywhere there's hope of more money, and now he's worried about the elections too. He's ready to do what I tell him, provided I have no other man.

SAMUEL: Then push him there, after we have been.

ELISA: When can we go, Sammy? Tomorrow?

SAMUEL: We can see the blind man today, if I lick my hand first.

ELISA: Blind? How does he see what he is doing?

SAMUEL: That's not your business or mine. Pay me for today, Miss. I must go – my wife and children must eat.

ELISA (*fondly*): How much is it, Sammy boy?

SAMUEL: You know it is three pounds; for another person it should be four pounds.

ELISA: You didn't charge me so much last time!

SAMUEL: Things have changed since Austerity Budget.

ELISA: I'll pay one pound, Sammy!

SAMUEL: Not even for you, Miss Elisa. Two pounds is the least.

ELISA: All right, I'll pay you. Here.

SAMUEL: No worry, Miss! You will get the money from the Chairman. I am off.

*

AKONNEDI: A man whose soul grinds with power engines,
Is wrapped in soft sheets, and hung to house gables –
Where won't he go?
But first he's to receive in office
A Very Important Visitor

VIV: Is this Mr Olemu's Office?

AMOS: You mean Chairman?

VIV: Yes – the Chairman of the Housing Committee.

AMOS: Chairman is very busy. You can't see him. Who are you?

VIV: Just a visitor. He knows I'm coming to see him this morning. Are you his messenger?

AMOS (*stiffly*): I'm his clerk. I have told you, you can't see him, sir. Come back at one o'clock!

VIV: That's his lunchtime, I think, and I'm catching a train then. Just go in and tell him a visitor is here. Here's sixpence for you.

AMOS (*hurt*): Two shillings, sir! (*Pause – nothing happens.*) Oh, all right, I shall see what I can do for you.

AMOS: Visitor to see you, Chairman!

OLEMU (*sternly*): Send him in!

AMOS (*to Viv*): Chairman will see you now.

VIV: Good morning, sir!

OLEMU: Good morning. What can I do for you? Sit down. No, the other chair.

VIV: It's about the plot of land in Victoria Square, sir . . .

OLEMU: Wait a minute! Are you the one looking for a plot?

VIV: Yes.

OLEMU: Right. You can get it today or next year, or not at all. Depends how you play your cards.

VIV: I understand sir. Only I'm spending too much on a court case now . . . thieves broke into my largest shop along Commercial Avenue and carried away everything.

OLEMU: Misfortune is everywhere. Three of my lorries have broken down; four houses need repairs, and my cook ran away with five pounds the other day . . . I can hardly concentrate on what I'm doing here.

VIV: I see I'm not alone. Has my brother whispered to you? I mean the Minister.

OLEMU: Yes, the Honourable Minister phoned up just before you came. He has gone through this himself and he knows the risk involved. The land is Crown land now acquired by the Town Council, and you know what that means. I assured the Minister, though, that I was going to treat you as a Very Important Visitor.

VIV (*hushed tone*): Try and manage it for me, sir – there'll be small kola.

OLEMU: Well, for the sake of your brother, it will be seventy-five pounds; other people pay as much as one hundred and fifty pounds. You can see, it's a risk. If you go out now and bla-bla-bla, I'm finished.

VIV: I can't do that, Chairman ... I've done business before. Let it be thirty pounds, please.

OLEMU: Then you haven't done good business before. You know there are six other members of the Committee, and they must have their share of the kola?

VIV: I understand. I shall give fifty pounds, it's here. Let it stand at that, I beg you.

OLEMU: Well, there's no need continuing the argument. Give what you have to my messenger; there's no fear about him.

VIV: Er – there's another matter, Chairman. It's about my house along Oluwa Crescent. The Council want to pull it down; they say I didn't keep to dimensions.

OLEMU: Hm. How large are the rooms?

VIV: Eight feet by six.

OLEMU: That's rather small. Why didn't you make them larger?

VIV: The land was small, sir, so I had to use economy. The kitchen is large and there's a European lavatory.

OLEMU: In the kitchen?

VIV: Well, not exactly. I gave the tenants a curtain to separate it with.

OLEMU: That's a tricky point, my friend. We don't allow such houses now that we want to introduce rent control. Our policy is to have a standard for all houses.

VIV: You should see this one I'm talking of. It's a modern house: the plan was drawn by A. Carpenter & Sons.

OLEMU: Well, time is going. We'll see what we can do. Of course if we can manage it, you'll give some kola to the Committee.

VIV: Oh, I know that.

OLEMU: Good morning, then. Ring me up some time and we'll settle it. Bye-bye . . . remember the messenger outside.

VIV: I won't forget. Thank you very much, sir. You'll hear from me.

OLEMU: Good heavens, that foolish fellow has taken twenty minutes of my time!
(*Telephone rings.*)

OLEMU: Hello!–Oh, . . . Elisa, . . . What a surprise! Where are you phoning from? . . . Mogambo Club? What are you doing there? . . . Your brother, I see . . . Yes, I've been thinking of it, darling; you're such an angel . . . yes . . . yes . . . especially my new fleet of transport . . . and of course the elections next month . . . Yes, he may be useful, but am still wondering, Liz . . . most of these medicine men are out to make money . . . Yes, I agree this one may have something useful to offer . . . Yes, I have an idea of the place . . . I can go there this evening, O.K.? I'm longing to have you in my arms, dear . . . haven't done a thing today . . . Right then, don't let any man touch you there . . . Yes, you're always a good girl, I know. See you then, dear . . . bye, bye . . . (*Puts down receiver.*) Amos! Amos!

AMOS: Yes sir, yes sir!

OLEMU: Where are you, you fool?

AMOS: Please sir, I was . . .

OLEMU: Your lies again! (*Less loudly*) What did that idiot give you?

AMOS (*counting*): Sir, forty-nine, no forty-nine pounds, ten.

OLEMU: Lower your voice, you stupid thing!

AMOS (*almost whispering*): Sorry, sir.

OLEMU: Wasn't it fifty? Fifty pounds! Come on, don't
waste my time!

AMOS: Yes, sir, but ten shillings for the duster you said
I should buy for the office.

OLEMU: You're an incurable liar. Amos, put it here and
get out! Take these files away first! If anyone rings
tell him I've gone out on business.

*

AKONNEDI: When my left eye twitches
A great visit is round the corner,
For here at last, approaching my abode,
Comes His Eminence, Chairman Olemu.
And, people of our land,
We are set for Round Two.

OLEMU: Is this the shrine of Akonnedi, please?

AKONNEDI: It's the holy place of my son, and
Welcome to our hut.

OLEMU: Well, I want to be quick, so I shall tell you my
business. I've come to ask for help.

AKONNEDI: Don't talk, my son.
I know your troubles.
The gods revealed them all to me,
Before you set out from the town.

OLEMU: You mean you know what I've come for?

AKONNEDI: Aye, and much besides:
You're the first son of Chief Olemu
Whose power is great in Ijebu.
You have Oyinbo post in the town
But enemies are jealous of your power;
Your lorries break down; your houses
Don't yield:

White ants have bored into your life.

OLEMU (*taken aback*): Yes, you're right! I wonder how you know? I'm extremely surprised! Look, do you think you can help to give a push to my business, and assure me of victory in next month's town council elections?

AKONNEDI: Success, prosperity . . . they're what you want;
 The gods give these to whom they please.
 But mark, the earth, that takes round ours and us,
 Is deep and unclean as a refuse pit.
 Success may lie at failure's door.
 So, poverty and plenty are coughed
 From one and the same stomach.

OLEMU: These are great words of wisdom!

AKONNEDI: Don't be the hawk swooping on the chick,
 Not minding the wails of mother hen;
 Trusting too much the people you love
 Can be the beginning of the end.
 The tortoise knew this, and confided
 In himself alone. Thus has
 Wisdom guided him through
 A world of self and guile.

OLEMU: Thanks very much for the advice.

AKONNEDI: And now the time of offering is up!
 Step out with this red rag
 Round your eyes. It's strange how well
 A man can see
 Without the aid of mortal eyes.
 Before my fathers called me
 And took away my eyes,
 I saw the world in one straight line.
 Now I see it whole.

OLEMU: I have tied the rag. Good God, I can't see anything! What am I to do next?

AKONNEDI: Sharpen the eyes that are within

E

And run round where you are;
Go on and on until you see
How everything goes round.

OLEMU (*exasperated and panicky*): I'm tired – I'm dizzy –
I'm falling down! Can't I stop now? I must have gone
round seven times! Are you there?

AKONNEDI: It can be seventy times seven times,
According to how well or ill you run.
Now take off the rag
And take your seat. Rub that oil
On your left big toe,
It's the oil of the Seven Stars.

OLEMU (*still panting*): Thank you, but I am sweating
badly. I must be going soon; I have an appointment.

AKONNEDI: And now for your fee,
It's up to the gods
To say how much they want.
Look behind and read whate'er is
The writing on the wall.

OLEMU (*jerkily, terrified*): Someone is writing, but who?

VOICES (*slow, measured chant*):
Seven cowries, seven manillas,
Seven farthings, seven pence,
Seven toròs, the same of sisi,
Seven shillings, seven pounds,
Seven guineas in seven places . . .

*

Large excited crowd at election meeting.

FIRST VOICE: Hey, who's speaking next?

SECOND VOICE: Chief Olemu, I think.

THIRD VOICE: Oh, is he a chief?

FIRST VOICE: My friend, you can become one for two
pounds, a goat and whiskey! Are you going to vote for
him?

THIRD VOICE: Depends if he's a chief.

SECOND VOICE: Oh, not that! Think of the rents, the rents, the rents . . .

VOICES: Ssh! Ssh! He's going to speak!

OLEMU: Now the time of reckoning has come, and I am appealing to you to judge each man according to his record (*roar of applause*). The burden of my speech is: Respect for Human Divinity (*greater applause*). Gone are the days when our illustrious town, and indeed the entire country and continent suffered under the insidious yoke of economic, social, and moral strangulation at the hand of the imperialistic . . . (*even greater applause*). My party is committed to the total eradication of the exploitation of man by man (*roar*). To this end, and having the interest of our people at heart, we have set up a high-powered committee to work towards better housing conditions, a strict control of rents, and the greater happiness of all . . . (*Deafening roar and fade out.*)

*

ELISA: Your speech tonight was very good. I'm sure many people will vote for you.

OLEMU: I've done my bit – it's their business if they allow themselves to be fooled when they vote tomorrow. Give me a warm embrace for that, Liz.

ELISA: Wait a moment. Let me turn the radiogram off.

OLEMU: Working well, I hear.

ELISA: Mm. You must be tired, Chairman.

OLEMU: Yes, I am. But there's no rest. When I leave you, I am going to examine the plot of land I bought yesterday.

ELISA: A new one? You never told me. Who sold it?

OLEMU: Oh, well, actually it's Crown land – it comes through special arrangement. Don't tell anyone.

ELISA: But you know I can't, Chairman.

OLEMU: Close the window – we must hurry, Elisa. I have to collect rents today, too.

ELISA: Let us rest a little – you can come back after you've done all that.

OLEMU (*angry*): What rest are you talking of, when my head is swimming and dizzy with so many things to do! Do you know, at seven am attending a naming ceremony with my wife? Am taking the chair, which means I can't be late. Then . . .

ELISA: Your wife is lucky. You only remember *me* when you want the window shut.

OLEMU: Don't be impossible, Liz! You know how many nights I've spent here. But these two weeks . . . (*Softening*) But I can't help it! You're so sweet!

ELISA (*flattered*): Then call me honey.

OLEMU: No, you're sweeter. Simply overwhelming! Like some unexpected money. Won't you close the window now?

ELISA (*sharp again*): Yes, am fit for that only.

OLEMU: Oh, come on, you've been very useful during these campaigns.

ELISA: Are you going to give me something for the weekend, or not?

OLEMU: How much do you want? Lock the door first.

ELISA: Only seven pounds.

OLEMU: All right, when we finish. You know I can't deny you anything! But I must keep five pounds for the naming ceremony.

ELISA: *Five pounds*? That's too much at once!

OLEMU: You know these things, Liz; if I don't give so much, my election chances are ruined. I have to go round and round, and my money goes with me. That's what the world is.

ELISA: Other people don't run round like you.

OLEMU: You can't help it in politics and business – it even nags into your ordinary life, like a bad woman.

ELISA: Even when people are making love?

OLEMU: If they're unfaithful, yes. Won't you stop these questions now? The room is so dark, oh! Come, come . . .

*

AKONNEDI: One full moon it is to a day
Since that taxi brought the young woman
To my door, now it's at hers; so,
Good people, the cycle is worked, and
It cannot but be the final round.

Knock at the door.

ELISA: Samuel!

SAMUEL: How now, Miss Elisa? Is the rat caught in the trap?

ELISA: Which rat?

SAMUEL: The big rat who digs holes all over the land and wants to eat up all the corn in town.

ELISA: You mean Chairman? Oh, a clever rat can always escape.

SAMUEL: Ha! Ha! Cunny man die, cunny man bury!

ELISA (*confidentially*): He says the blind man charged him heavily. He's been so annoyed ever since!

SAMUEL: Why should he worry? Every month he collects pay enough to fill a hat, not to talk of the houses and lorries and tractors.

ELISA: He's broke!

SAMUEL: That's what he tells you; it's a trick. I shall go and ask the medicine man for my commission.

ELISA: You know, since he returned from the medicine man, he's been quarrelling with his wife nearly every day?

SAMUEL: Good for you! That's how it works.

ELISA: If only he didn't have to spend so many nights here! (*Yawning*) He doesn't let me sleep.

SAMUEL: Well, lie down and take your rest. Am going to the blind man, now.

ELISA: Oh! Let me come with you.

SAMUEL: If you like. The day fish die at sea may start with a little rain – you never know!

ELISA: Yes, it's raining outside.

SAMUEL: Hurry up then, I don't want your Chairman to come and find me here.

ELISA: He doesn't come this hour. Let's go. Bring that umbrella, Sammy . . .

*

AKONNEDI: I hear booted steps approach that office,
I smell gin from breath that traps sandflies;
Those eyes are of a vulture drawn by law
To a feast that starts before the law. See,
He stops, he knocks; can this be all for nought?

Knock on the door.

NKEM (*drunk*): Mr Olemu: Chairman of the Housing Committee – this is his office, surely . . . Where's the bastard, then? Damn it, I could have had another bottle at the club . . . Oh, what the hell! (*Telephone rings.*) Hello . . . yes, the Chairman's office . . . yes . . . What kola? Oh, in connection with my help over your house! . . . Thirty pounds, I see . . . to bring it here? No . . . now look, can you come round to Mogambo Club at eleven? . . . Fine . . . I may be there with a cousin of mine, don't be afraid . . . yes, I know you're the Minister's brother . . . Yes, we're

trying our best for you . . . Eleven p.m. prompt.
Okay . . . What, my voice? . . . Oh! Just a little tired,
that's all . . . right . . . fine . . . bye-bye.

OLEMU (*approaching*): Ah, you're the police Inspector,
I guess? Sorry to keep you waiting. I went out on
urgent business.

NKEM: That's all right, Mr Olemu. I've found out the
damn place, and I thought I should have a chat with
you before settling to work.

OLEMU: Well, as you know, it's about this clever rogue
of a medicine man. I've made a statement already.

NKEM: Yes, sir. Headquarters brought me all the way
from Ibadan, following your report.

OLEMU: Well, and you *will* do all you can for me to recover
the money, Mr . . . sorry, what name is it?

NKEM: Nkem, Austin Nkem.

OLEMU: You're a brother to me, Mr Nkem! Let me tell
you, I've been living on an overdraft for months.
That's why I can't afford to bury sixty pounds in the
drain.

NKEM: You're lucky you continue to get overdraft! They
won't even advance me beer-money!

OLEMU: Er . . . of course Inspector, if I get back this
money, we shall drink together. And there will be
some kola for you, as you know.

NKEM: Well, we can talk about the kola later. As for
drinks, we needn't wait for eternity! Can you manage
it at Mogambo Club tonight, say, ten-thirty?

OLEMU: Yes, why not?

NKEM: Right, I should be through with the next part of my
investigations by then. But just one question before I
go: how did you first come into contact with this
medicine man bloke?

OLEMU: Well, you know the way these things go: some

stupid fellow talks about him excitedly to a woman of mine, and she tells me. I know I was a fool to be taken in, but . . . well.

NKEM: I see. You think this fellow and this woman will come forward and give evidence if invited?

OLEMU: I don't know about one, but the other wouldn't refuse. As I said, she's very close to me – almost a second wife, in fact. I can take you across to see her now.

NKEM: No, not now.

OLEMU: Well, surely you would like me to go to the shrine with you, then?

NKEM: I have been a detective for five years – I can do my job, without your help, Mr Olemu. See you at Mogambo tonight. Bye bye!

OLEMU: What effrontery! (*Shouting*) Amos! Where were you when the visitor arrived? And where's your rent?

AMOS: Please sir, I went to see Samuel!

OLEMU: Your brother? During office hours?

AMOS: About the rent, sir. You said I must pay in two hours.

OLEMU: What's he muttering? Come here, I am going to teach you sense, you famished chicken!

AMOS: Oh, sir, sorry, sir! You have hurt yourself!

OLEMU (*spluttering and cursing*): My head, my head! You little devil! You'll regret it!

VOICES (*echo*): Well, stand up! Be a man!

OLEMU: I'm blind! I can't see!

VOICES (*echo*): It's only a little cut above your eye. It was all your fault.

AMOS: Am sorry sir. Let me get some water for you.

OLEMU (*muttering*): There's blood all over my eyes – so much blood . . . I called him a chicken . . . yes, I did . . . Why did he tell me: 'Don't go after the chick like a hawk'? (*Louder and faster*) That blind fool, why did he say that? But who is a hawk, me or him?

VOICES (*echo*): You're delirious, Mr Olemu. Why not leave the boy alone? Shall we call an ambulance, or send you to a medicine man?

OLEMU (*muttering*): What did he know of this chicken, this boy, playing truant instead of paying my money? (*Loudly*) What does *he* know! (*Muttering again*) Tied a bloody rag over my eyes . . . set me running round a vicious circle . . . (*louder*) and robbed me of my money! The crook! I will fight him like a bull! Wring his neck like a chicken! My money! I must go for it *now*! I must get it *today*!

VOICES (*echo*): Mr Olemu; why not wait? Mr Olemu, why not think?

AMOS (*approaching*): I have brought the water, sir.

OLEMU (*furiously*): And the rent as well?

AMOS: N-no, Chairman.

OLEMU: I give you till eight tonight, and you'll have to find where I'm going.

*

In the background there are sounds of music and muttering: Mogambo Club. Nearer there is darkness and night sounds.

ELISA (*subdued*): Tell me, Sammy. The blind man, does he always hide away in that cage?

SAMUEL: For ever he doesn't leave it – he eats there, sleeps there, does everything there.

ELISA: Thank God we're out of his terrible shrine! I wouldn't come here alone – he doesn't seem to belong to this world.

SAMUEL: His world is round the full moon. But he knows our own better than we . . . He says we may meet some trouble today, Miss. We must try to reach the town in daylight.

ELISA: How much did he give you, Sammy?

SAMUEL: That's my business.

ELISA (*offended*): What's your business? Aren't you giving me some?

SAMUEL (*shouting*): You women, I say I can't understand you. I bring you luck and you don't even thank me. Don't you know your Chairman is going to push my brother Amos from his room unless I pay rent for him today?

ELISA (*shouting back*): So what! I came here with you and ... Mother of God! –That's Chairman's car! Sammy, why didn't we go?

OLEMU (*approaching*): Hey! What monkey business are you two up to? Elisa, who sent you here?

ELISA (*evasively*): Oh, Chairman, your eye! What's wrong?

OLEMU (*ignoring this*): I'm asking – what are you doing here?

ELISA: We came to ... em ... I mean, Sammy brought me ...

OLEMU: What are you muttering! Who is Sammy? I have come to demand the money I lost in this cursed shrine, and here you are flirting with a taxi-driver at the very spot!

ELISA (*hurt*): Who is flirting?

SAMUEL: Nothing like that, sir. Just to greet the blind man.

OLEMU (*furious*): Shut up! Why with Elisa? I am going to knock sense into both of you, you wait.

SAMUEL: I won't move, sir – I haven't done wrong.

ELISA (*frantically, to herself*): That's Austin! Holy Mother!

NKEM (*approaching*): Mr Olemu, why? I told you not to bother! Oh, a plaster on your eyes! An accident! How did it happen?

OLEMU (*indifferently*): Don't bother, Mr Nkem.

NKEM: Well, what's happening? Why, Lizzy, what are you doing here?

ELISA (*paralysed with guilt*): Oh, Austin, I came ... I ...

NKEM: O.K. Lizzy, bring out your wallet. (*Intimately*) I'm in town again on some investigation – just had a few bottles at Mogambo, and seems am running dry and out already. I'm leaving you three bob. All right?

OLEMU (*painfully*): Do you know her, Mr Nkem?

NKEM (*casually*): Lizzy? Yah! She's my fiancée – my wife, if you like. Can't get her a decent job in Ibadan, so she has to manage here with some firm of rotten bed-makers. But why are you here, Mr Olemu? You may spoil my job, you know.

OLEMU (*shouting*): Why am I here! What a question! When I've just discovered that much of my money comes round to you! That this woman has been flirting with you, and even that taxi-driver! And you ask why I am . . .

NKEM: Hey! You there! Stay where you are! You are inviting trouble!

SAMUEL (*from a distance*): I am a taxi-driver, sir! That's my business!

ELISA (*sobbing and calling*): Sammy! Sammy please don't leave me! Sammy!

NKEM (*to Elisa*): Keep quiet, will you? (*To Olemu*) Sorry, Mr Chairman, I can't understand anything happening in this meeting. Maybe the world has been spinning too fast today. Or else *everybody* has been drinking.

OLEMU (*deeply hurt*): Look here, you must learn to size up the tree you plant your yam to! I don't take such cheek! This woman lives on *my* money, and . . .

NKEM (*incredulously*): *Your* money? Elisa?

OLEMU (*storming*): Yes, and on top of that, she drove me into running in a blind man's circle and losing my money. Now I can see how I lose it all round – even to you, far away in Ibadan! (*To Elisa*) You slut!

ELISA (*screaming*): Austin! Austin!

NKEM (*commandingly*): Hands off the girl at once, Olemu!

She's *my* girl. And remember, I'm here on duty as well.

OLEMU: Duty! I found you in my office, *drunk*, Nkem, and I knew at once you wouldn't bring my money back.

NKEM: I say I know my duty, and I'm going to perform it.

OLEMU: What duty? I tell you, I am throwing this bitch out of the house I pay for tonight!

ELISA (*weeping*): Who's a bitch! Your wife! Your mother! Who's a . . .

NKEM: My dear fellow, you are only complicating your case by such offensive language. I wish you knew what you are already in for. If you're wise, don't try to resist!

OLEMU (*undaunted*): Nonsense! Leave my hand! She *is* a bitch!

ELISA (*still weeping*): I shall get out of the house. What of all the bribes you give and take? What of the Crown land you said you stole? Ole! Ole!

NKEM: Lizzy, you shut up and get into that car!

AMOS (*approaching, out of breath*): Sir, please, sir, I've brought my rent. Samuel told me the way.

NKEM: Boy, what's your trouble?

AMOS (*shaken*): Sir, my name is Amos . . . Chairman said I must pay him before eight o'clock tonight . . . I . . .

NKEM: All right, stand aside – your Chairman's head is swollen with too much money already. Mr Olemu, I must ask you to come with me. Your behaviour has been so outrageous, you deserve no mercy.

OLEMU: But who is at your mercy? Who wants it?

NKEM: You will soon find out that I know more about you than you realise. Keep going, man!

OLEMU: What do you know? Rubbish. I challenge her to prove anything she has said, anything at all.

NKEM: No, not your car. Get into mine, quick! You are under arrest.

OLEMU: What arrest?

NKEM: The proof to convict you will come from Mogambo
　　　Club tonight.

OLEMU: What proof?

NKEM: It shows how little you know, Mr Olemu. Surely
　　　you don't forget a Very Important Visitor you received
　　　about a month ago? Yes? And you helped him to get
　　　approval for a building of his?

OLEMU (*blustering*): And what about him?

NKEM: Well, he's waiting now at Mogambo with a little
　　　something for you. At *my* invitation. You found me
　　　drunk in your office, but not too drunk to answer a
　　　phone call in your absence.

OLEMU: I'm saying nothing – nothing!

NKEM: Let's be going, man.

VOICE (*echo*): White ants have bored into your life . . .

VOICE (*echo*): Don't be the hawk swooping on the chick . . .

VOICE (*echo*): Don't be the hawk swooping on the chick

VOICE (*echo*): The World, that takes round ours and us,
　　　Is deep and unclean as a refuse pit.

CURTAIN

With Strings

KULDIP SONDHI

CHARACTERS

Dev (D), *Retired Indian Engineer, in 50's*
Savitri (S), *His wife, in 40's*
Mohan (M), *Dev's son, late 20's*
Njeroge (N), *Retired African administrator, in 50's*
Cynthia (C), *African girl, early 20's*

WITH STRINGS

SCENE ONE

Living room. Dev is reading letter. Wife Savitri enters with small picture in frame. Puts it down after looking at it and looks at Dev who is lost in meditative gaze at letter in hand. Savitri is amused.

s.: Don't you believe it?

d.: Frankly, no.

s.: No? (*Takes letter. Scans it briefly.*) Why not? There's his signature. There's the stamp from America. And here he says clearly: 'I will give £10,000 to the family if your son Mohan gets married and produces an heir within the next twelve months.'

d.: Produce an heir! Who does he think he is – God?

s.: Don't be silly. How many times haven't we said ourselves that it's time the boy got married. He's doing it for Mohan's own good.

d.: Mohan's own good! He hasn't even met our boy yet. Do you know what this is?

s.: What?

d.: This – (*grimaces at letter*) – this is aid with strings!

s.: Is it? Well, no one's forcing you to accept it. If you don't want the aid, just say so.

d.: You can't 'just say so' about something so big. It's been offered to us and whether we accept it or not now our lives will never be the same again. Whatever happens to us from now on will be his responsibility.

s.: Your pride's been touched, so you're thoroughly

prejudiced against him now; but if Mohan turns out to be like cousin Sobod I'll be proud of the boy.

D.: Nonsense. The two can never be alike. Mohan's a chemist, and an educated man. Your cousin is just a fruit-picker – made good. He's even given us his telephone number in case we want to show our appreciation!

S.: Let's not argue any more, Dev. You are giving me a headache with your talk. We have been offered a very generous gift and it's up to us to take it or leave it. To me it's like a dream come true. It no longer matters if Mohan gets a dowry with his marriage or not. All he needs is an educated girl with the right background. How much easier that makes everything.

D.: It doesn't. We will have sold ourselves into the bargain. Don't forget that. Your soul will no longer be your own.

S.: I don't think cousin Sobod buys souls.

D.: This is a different kind of soul.

S.: The difficulty with you is, you read too many books. That's why you get confused so easily. But wait till Mohan hears the news. He will be delighted.

D.: Of course. Who wouldn't be at the thought of getting so much money. He may not want to pay the price for it though.

S.: Pay the price! – (*Telephone rings. Picks up the receiver.*) Hallo. Oh, Mohan, is that you – where are you speaking from? Back at your flat – good! Well, you must be tired after that long drive from Mombasa. No, don't take a taxi, I'll come over. (*Pause.*) In about 15 minutes. I have some exciting news for you, Mohan. No, not on the phone. I'll tell you as soon as we meet. Goodbye. – (*To Dev*) He's given his car for washing.

D.: Has he? The difficulty with your son is he doesn't take life seriously enough. He has a nice little shop

in the centre of Nairobi but half the time he's out
of it. I'm sure he could increase his trade if he paid
as much attention to his customers as he does to his
own pleasures. Last year he must have made at least
ten trips to the coast.

s.: He has business down there.

d.: What business? Have you ever asked him?

s.: Yes. He told me that as a chemist he deals in every
branch of chemistry, or whatever he calls . . .

d. (*looks doubtfully at his wife*): He probably meant
anatomy. Well, never mind, you're his mother. If
this money does tempt him to get married, it will
at least have done some good. Actually there are
a few good families from our community on the
coast and if he has his eyes on someone suitable in
Mombasa there is no harm in it.

s.: I wish he would choose Laxman's daughter. They
are big people and Veena is a beautiful girl.

d.: Yes, it would be an ideal match. He used to be very
friendly with her once, I remember. Perhaps he
still is. But you can never tell what that boy is up
to from day to day. (*Looks at watch.*) Now don't be
long, you know I expect Njeroge this evening. If he
brings his niece with him you should be here to
meet her.

s.: The one who's just returned from England, is it?

d.: I believe so, though I haven't met her, they're good
people; and Njeroge is a sound man. I like him.
(*Becomes reflective.*) You know, Savitri, I have great
hopes about this new business I'm after.

s.: The one with Mr Njeroge?

d.: Yes. (*Pause.*) You have some doubts about it, don't
you? Why?

s.: Not about the business.

d.: I see.

s.: I know you like Mr Njeroge, Dev, but are you sure you can trust him?

D.: You can't forget that he's an African, can you?

s.: That's true, I can't. And why should I? Do you think he forgets that you are an Indian, or an Asian as he probably calls you?

D.: He doesn't call me anything but Dev.

s.: I'm not criticising him. I'm wondering how well you know him.

D. (*shrugs and paces as he thinks aloud and talks*): As well as I know any other man. Better I'd say. We worked in the same department for fifteen years. He also retired as a superintendent in the Post and Telegraphs. We are about the same age and citizens of the same country. How much closer can I get to Njeroge without one of us changing colour?

s.: No one's asking you to change your colour. All I'm saying is do you trust him? Do you know how he thinks?

D.: Sometimes, Savitri, I don't even know how you think. When Njeroge and I are together we forget our racial differences. Isn't that a sign of trust?

s.: No, that's only a sign of your thinking. Do you realise, Dev, that you are going to risk a part of our life savings in this new business.

D.: I do, yes I do, Savitri, but I'm sure I'm doing the right thing. Njeroge is an African and if I am to make a proper start in business, I want an African with me. Don't forget this is his country.

s.: It's also supposed to be our country. Mohan was born in Kenya, and everything we have is here now. But none of that will help if you lose your money simply because you want to trust Njeroge.

D.: But I do trust him, Savitri. I couldn't trust him any more if he were an Indian. And the business is a very

simple one really. All we need are a few touring cars.
With a good contract from the Tourists' Association
to start us off, we are in. Anyhow, aren't we soon
going to have another £10,000.

s.: We haven't got it yet, and have you forgotten you're
sour? (*Starts bustling in her bag and looking for keys.*) Now,
enough of this. Mohan's waiting.

d.: You are in a difficult mood. (*Bell. Dev opens door.
Njeroge enters with niece.*) Come in Njeroge, come in.
So this is your niece.

n.: Yes, this is Cynthia. She arrived from London last
night. (*Shakes hands. Cynthia is pretty, refined, self-
assured but quiet.*)

d.: How do you do, Cynthia. I'm glad he brought you
along. This is my wife.

c. (*shaking hands*): How do you do.

n.: I'm a bit early, Dev, but I've brought some news for
you.

d.: Good news I hope.

n.: Judge for yourself. I found out that one of the directors
of the Tourists' Association is an old school friend of
mine. I rang him up just before I came and he asked
me to come over to his house, straightaway, for a
chat. Will you come with me?

d.: Of course. This is good news. Now maybe things will
start moving. But sit down for a few minutes. Let's
have a drink to celebrate Cynthia's arrival while
Savitri fetches Mohan from his flat. We can leave
after that.

s.: I'd better bring Mohan now if you're in a hurry.

d.: Yes, all right. He must be ready by this time.

Leaves. Dev pours out drinks standing on tray.

n.: Mohan lives nearby, doesn't he?

d.: Not far away. At the end of this road, actually.

c.: Is he all right?

d. (*surprised*): Yes, I think so.

n. (*to niece*): Do you know Mohan?

c.: I met him last year before I left for England. Didn't I tell you at the time?

n.: Not that I remember.

c.: Well, I met him when I was working at the General Hospital in Mombasa. He used to come there to sell his drugs.

d. (*smiles*): Ah, so he was at work on those trips.

c.: I don't know what you mean, but the hospital did place orders with him.

n. (*chuckles*): That boy you know . . . the stories I hear of him! But take it from me, Mohan is a very bright, enterprising young man. There's no harm if he gets around a bit. I wish I had a son like him.

d. (*pleased*): Do you, really?

n.: Well, yes . . . What does he lack!

d.: A wife.

n. (*laughs*): True, though I'm sure he could remedy that easily enough if he wanted to.

d.: If he wanted to – exactly.

n.: You're behind the times, Dev. These days young people only marry if they have something to gain by it. I shouldn't be saying this in front of Cynthia of course.

c.: Why not? As a rule I think that what you say is correct. There is no point in marrying if you get nothing from it.

d.: You can take it from me that Mohan has quite a lot to lose if he doesn't get married within the next twelve months. (*Thoughtful momentarily.*) No, in the next three months.

n.: What's this, you planning the boy's future for him or something?

D.: Not me, but I'll tell you about it later. Well, Cynthia, how does it feel to be back in Kenya?

C.: Wonderful. I will not want to go back, but I'll have to, of course.

N.: Cynthia is studying to become a midwife. She has another year to go for her degree.

D.: Really, that's wonderful. Well, we must see more of you while you're here.

C.: You probably will. One month's a long time.

Laughter in corridor. Door opens. Mohan and mother enter.

M.: Good evening, Mr Njeroge. Hello, Cynthia. (*Holds out hand to her. Their eyes meet for a moment.*) You've told them that we know each other, haven't you?

C.: I have.

D.: What will you have, Mohan?

M.: I would prefer tea, actually.

S.: I'll make some for you just now.

M.: No hurry, mother. So you're back, Cynthia?

C. (*smiling*): Yes, here I am, Mohan.

Savitri glances from one to the other with perplexed smile.

D. (*amiable and relaxed, lighting cigarette for Njeroge and himself*): England must have been a change after this country, eh, Cynthia?

C.: In some ways, though in my work there are few surprises. Babies and mothers act the same everywhere. (*All laugh.*)

N.: But the people are different surely, Cynthia.

C.: Under their reserve I don't think they are so different to us. I don't mean their customs and habits now. These come from the environment, not the heart.

S.: It's a comfortable theory.

N.: I agree with you, Mrs Dev. Of course, people are different, Cynthia. We are all friends here but look at us, aren't we different?

C.: Aside from our colours I don't see any difference.

D. (*smiles*): But you admit then there are some differences.

C.: Of course. How boring it would be if we all looked and thought exactly alike! See how different Mohan is to you.

M.: I'm glad you learnt so much during one year. You must have been working hard in England.

C.: I was. Your father's also been telling us how hard you work. (*All laugh.*)

D.: Be careful what you say to this young lady, Mohan. I think you've met your match.

S.: The only difficulty with a woman going in for a profession is that it usually goes to waste after she gets married. And if it doesn't, she hardly remains a woman at all.

C.: I think it's better to take that risk than becoming a cabbage at home.

D. (*laughs*): Yes . . . yes, quite right! Well, Mohan, when you choose you had better be careful what you get. We don't want a cabbage or a woman who wears pants.

M.: I don't think you'll get either.

D.: Well, the quicker we know the better! Now if you'll excuse us.

N.: Can I leave Cynthia with you till we return, Mrs Dev?

S.: Of course. You carry on now. I'll look after her.

N.: Thank you. (*Goes out with Dev.*)

S.: How would you like to try some Indian masala tea, Cynthia? It's Mohan's favourite.

C.: Oh, I'd love some of that, Mrs Dev. I've had it before.

S.: Well, just sit down then and make yourself comfortable while I prepare it. I won't take long.

C. sits and S. leaves through inside door. Then C. rises swiftly and M. turns to her, crushing out his cigarette.

M.: At last! I thought we would never be alone.

c.: Nor did I. It's been a whole year, Mohan.

M.: The longest year of my life.

c.: Really? I missed the sound of your voice. You used to phone me every weekend at the hospital, remember?

M.: I remember everything.

c.: Everything?

M. (*uncertainly*): Yes, why?

c.: What about Mr Laxman's daughter!

M.: What about her?

c.: You liked Veena once, didn't you?

M.: That was before I met you.

c.: I know, and I'm just being jealous. From now on I'll believe everything you say and refuse to listen to gossip. But Mohan . . . have you really been behaving yourself?

M.: No one believes it, but I have. My trip to Mombasa this time was the first one since you left and it was a genuine business trip. But all the time I kept thinking of you and what you've done to my life.

c.: Tell me what I've done, Mohan.

M.: Don't you know? Because of you I'm going to break from convention. Because of you I no longer see life constricted in narrow bands of colour and feeling. I am possessed by a new sense of freedom and sometimes it is like walking on air. I warn you, I've changed this past year and hold you responsible for any transformation. You realise you are guilty, don't you?

c.: Yes!

M.: All right then, you stand paroled for the rest of your life in my custody.

c.: Mohan, you don't talk like this to other girls, do you?

M.: No, I don't, and there aren't any other girls, not now.

c.: In that case I won't appeal against your sentence, but, Mohan . . . do your parents know anything about us?

M.: I haven't told them yet.

C.: I think we'll have to soon. This isn't really fair on them or on us.

M.: Cynthia, there's something I must tell you.

C.: Yes?

M.: I want you to stay. I can't bear the thought of you going back.

C.: I'm here a whole month, Mohan. We can meet every day.

M.: Yes of course we will, but ... this is ridiculous.

C.: What is?

M.: This secrecy. We love each other. It's not a sin. I want you to marry me immediately.

C. (*happy*): You mean now, just like that?

M.: Yes.

C.: Oh, this is the happiest day of my life! Let me confess it, Mohan, I've always been a bit doubtful about you, but now it's all blown away. No one can really separate us again. But for the sake of the others, let's just wait a little longer. There's no harm done by it.

M.: But there is! Why should we wait? I'm going to tell my parents everything tonight. They'll have to agree.

C.: They may not if you go at them like that.

M.: You take care of your side and I'll take care of mine. I tell you, there is no time to be lost!

C. (*laughs*): I must say you are in a hurry. I'm not running away tomorrow morning, Mohan.

M.: You're not, but time is.

C.: Mohan, is there something that I should know?

M. (*cautious*): How do you mean?

C.: Shall I tell you what I really think?

M.: Of course.

C.: I believe your parents have someone else in view for you and to beat them at their own game you're in this hurry to marry me. Isn't that so? Why are you laughing?

M.: At you because you may be right too. That's why I say let's get married before you return to England. What's wrong with it anyway?

C.: Nothing's wrong when you're with me, Mohan. But I want our marriage to meet with their approval. Especially uncle's approval. He's been so good to me. My parents died when I was very young, but he's never allowed me to feel an orphan. Now I must take his feelings into account.

M.: Your uncle is as conventional and old fashioned as my parents are, even if he doesn't know it, Cynthia.

C.: I know and that's what I'm afraid of. Uncle's got a minister in my future.

M.: A minister?

C.: Yes.

M.: Which one?

C.: Oh, any one of them will do. It's just some sort of dream he has.

M.: Well, he can stop dreaming. No minister's getting you, unless I become one. (*Glances at photo.*) Anyhow, I'll soon be as rich as one.

C. (*catches his glance*): What do you mean?

M.: Oh, nothing.

C.: I'd still like to know, Mohan. Your father was mysterious about something and so are you now. Does it concern us in any way?

M.: It's a silly whim this old uncle of mine's suddenly got. I've never met the old boy, but he's written a letter to say that if I get married and have an heir within 12 months the family gets £10,000.

C.: What . . . I see . . . Why didn't you tell me this before?

M.: I haven't had time to. We've hardly been alone ten minutes. You know that!

C.: I don't know anything. So that's why you're in such a hurry to marry me?

M.: Of course not. I want to –

C.: You mean you want the money!

M.: I want you, I said. But if the money's also thrown in, what's the harm?

C.: What's the harm? You can get someone else for this kind of bargaining. My God, to drag me into something so wicked!

M.: But what's so wicked about it, Cynthia? I knew you wouldn't understand.

C.: It was agreed between us some time back that we'd not think of marriage for some time yet. Now you no sooner see me than you can talk of nothing else. And I was fool enough to think it was all for my sake.

M.: But it is, Cynthia. Don't you see—

C.: No, that's just what I don't see. I don't want to have anything to do with that money.

M.: But it's stupid to throw it away. It's a fortune, Cynthia.

C.: I'm not for sale.

M.: Look, if you think I'm only after the money, I could easily get someone in a matter of days.

C.: You mean Veena; well, why don't you?

M.: Because I don't want to. I want you.

C.: But only on condition I help you to get the money, isn't that so?

M.: Of course not, but I don't want to lose a fortune either.

C.: Well, for God's sake don't. Get your saried beauty.

M.: No, no Cynthia, this is all wrong. You are making it sound crude.

C.: I am making it sound crude? You have the cheek to tell me that?

M.: I'm sorry, I didn't mean it that way.

C.: That's enough now. I won't hear any more of this.

Thank God I've found out in time. I'm not a breeding machine that I can guarantee to produce heirs for your family. Get someone else for that kind of nonsense.

M.: Calm down Cynthia; just listen to me.

C.: No, never! If we get married it's after my studies in a year's time or not at all. But I think it's better if you find someone else. Your money can buy her. Not me. Goodbye.

M.: Cynthia, wait.

Cynthia runs out. Mohan stands frowning. Savitri enters silently from back, tray in hand.

CURTAIN

SCENE TWO

A week later. Evening. Dev and Mohan arguing in living room

D. (*shouting*): I'm your father and I tell you I won't agree to this.

M.: I'm not a child any longer, so why not be reasonable about it.

D.: Reasonable? You mean we've been unreasonable to you all your life? Your upbringing, your education, setting you up in business! You call it unreasonable?

M.: No, I didn't say that —

D.: Of course you did. You're ungrateful like all young people are these days. You have no respect for age or tradition.

M.: I —

D.: Is that the only girl in the world you can find?

M.: But —

D.: Isn't there any Indian girl that you can choose for a wife?

M.: No, there isn't. That's what I'm trying to tell you. I love —

D.: Love! I'm talking about marriage. You've loved many women, young as you are; but you haven't married them all, have you?

M.: This is different.

D.: It's always different.

M.: You're being unnecessarily obstinate about this, father. I've come to get your approval —

D.: Well, I don't approve. With this kind of union you are breaking the laws of society. You will never be happy. You are an Indian and you must marry an Indian.

M.: Is there any law that says I must?

D.: Society says you must. And that's the law for us. We must obey it.

M.: Well, then I won't live in such a society.

D.: I see. So now you are going to form your own society as well. Where is it to be? Half way between Mombasa and Nairobi, or in the middle of the Indian Ocean?

M.: Now you're being ridiculous, father.

D.: Am I? Do you know what society is?

M.: Whatever it is I'll find my place in it.

D.: It won't be an honoured one if you carry on like this. Society isn't a figment of anyone's imagination. It's real, more than you or me. It's the only thing in the world that never sleeps and it has a million eyes to search you out. But once it doubts you there is no appeal against its sentence. Are you going to battle with this sphinx?

M.: I don't want to battle with anyone. And it's time you realised that we are living in a multi-racial country. Things are changing.

D.: Not as fast as you are. The multi-racialism you talk of exists only in clubs. In real life the Indians, the Africans and Europeans are three different races.

God made them so. Not me; God! Let us live as equals and be fair to each other, but keep marriage out of it, for God's sake.

M.: I'm sure God never said that.

Savitri enters; sits quietly.

D.: Leave God alone! You've come to ask my opinion about marrying this girl and your mother's answer and mine are the same – no! You talk to him, Savitri, I've got a headache listening to his talk. He's going on like they do in the cinema. Does Njeroge know of this?

M.: I suppose so, by now. In any case, he's your friend.

D.: He won't be after this.

S.: Mohan, you misunderstand us. I have nothing against that girl as a person. It's the whole idea that's wrong.

M.: It's the girl I want to marry, not the idea, mother. That's the whole difference in our reasoning.

D.: Stop trying to be so clever, Mohan. You know your mother and I can never agree to such a marriage. You've been thinking only of yourself, but do you realise what this could do to our lives?

M.: To your lives?

D.: Yes, to ours! You don't think we can escape the consequences of your actions, do you? We would be ruined. Completely ruined. How can I show my face in the samaj after such a union. I occupy a position of dignity and respect. Do you want to destroy it?

M.: I don't want to destroy anything, father, and I don't think we had better argue any more now. You're right in one thing, we don't understand one another any longer. I had hoped we would, but we don't. Well, that's my bad luck I suppose.

s.: Your mother understands you, son. Tomorrow we are both going to take a plane and fly to India.

d.: Yes, that's it! In eight hours you will be there and away from all this.

m.: I see. And in eight hours after that I can be happily married off, you mean? Let's not argue, mother. My mind's made up.

d.: Don't talk to him any more, Savitri. He has made up his mind that he is in love and now he is going to fight the whole world to show how strong he is.

m.: I don't want to fight anyone, least of all you. Well, I'm going. I hope you'll feel different about it soon. (*Leaves by back door.*)

d.: The boy's gone mad. I've never seen him like this before.

s.: That girl's got him round her little finger.

d.: But, oh God, why did she have to pick on our son? This is going to finish us.

s.: Our fate won't make any difference. She is out to test Mohan's love for her. The greater his sacrifice, the greater will be her victory. In the end she will either win Mohan over completely or turn her back on him for ever. We don't really come into it at all.

d.: My God, what sins have we committed to deserve this? So we either lose our son or we lose the money if he refuses to marry anyone else. That's what it boils down to, isn't it?

s.: It's quite possible that we may lose both our son and the money, but if we have a choice, let's drop the money. Let it go, Dev.

d.: Let it go? You can't be serious. I've already made plans about how every cent of it is to be invested. Our whole future depends on it!

s.: It doesn't. Till the letter came our future depended only on your savings and pension.

D.: But the letter did come. And the money is there for us to use. Oh, this is maddening. Mohan must be made to see sense.

S.: If you press the boy too much at this stage he will only grow more obstinate, Dev. Just wait a few days and let's see what happens.

D.: How can we wait with so much at stake? Can no one shake that boy?

S.: She can. That girl is the only one who can. And she may shake him so hard that he might awake and realise suddenly what a mistake he's making. That's out only hope. (*Bell rings.*) Have you called someone? Are you expecting . . .

D.: No, but it may be Njeroge.

S.: I don't want to see that man now. Ah, what misfortunes have fallen on our house! (*Leaves. Dev opens door. Njeroge appears.*)

D.: Come in, Njeroge.

N.: I suppose you know why I've come.

D.: I think so.

N.: Well, it's terrible. Let me tell you that straightaway – it's terrible. I won't allow it. I have other plans for my niece.

D.: Then you don't approve either?

N.: Certainly I don't. Cynthia is an educated African girl. She has a brilliant future.

D.: I'm glad to hear that. My son also has a brilliant future.

N.: But I forbid him to marry my niece! I have nothing against Mohan, but he is not the right man.

D.: I don't think there is any need for us to argue, Njeroge. You are obviously as against this affair as I am.

N.: I am absolutely against it. For an Asian to marry Cynthia – why that's out of the question. Your son has bewitched her. You must talk to him.

D.: I have, and the impression I got was that it was your

F

niece who has bewitched Mohan. Anyhow, this is getting us nowhere. Can you tell me exactly what Cynthia's told yc ..

N.: She just said, 'I'm getting engaged to Mohan,' and kept repeating it in spite of all my protests. I haven't been able to think of anything else ever since. Your son must leave her alone, Dev. I'm sorry to say it, but I don't think that he's acted like a gentleman. . .

D.: I don't know what you mean by that. Do you think Cynthia's acted like a lady, keeping it from you all this time?

N. (*sitting down, banging fists in despair*): No, no, this has got to stop, Dev. I had planned on the girl entering high government circles.

D.: It's no use getting excited with me, Njeroge. I've just had a row with my son over this. And I can tell you that if we continue shouting and threatening each other all that will happen is that those two will go off somewhere and get married secretly rather than openly. Isn't that what you would do?

N.: No, but I can see Mohan doing a thing like that.

D.: With Cynthia's help, of course.

N.: All right, all right; so they're both of the same colour – right? No I mean they aren't, and . . . damn it! Everything's becoming confused. You know what I mean, don't you?

D.: I do and if you can think of one single way of stopping them I'll listen to you, otherwise you listen to me. There is more to this than two people wanting to marry against their parents' wishes.

N.: What do you mean?

D.: Tell me first, do you really think you can stop your niece from doing what she wants to?

N.: If you want me to be frank, no, I don't think I can. I don't seem to have any more influence on her, and it worries me, worries me sick.

D.: You're right. It should worry you but I don't agree that you have no more influence on her, or I on my son for that matter. If we insist, absolutely insist, they will both delay things for a while.

N.: Can we do that much even?

D.: Yes, that much we can do. We can take the wind out of their sails by granting them a year in which to see for themselves how real their feelings are for each other. It will not be an engagement – we can insist on that. It will simply be a waiting period accepted by us, during which they can sober up to the realities of life around them.

N.: H'm, that's possible.

D.: More than possible. I'm sure they have already had some argument. Haven't you noticed how much on the defensive they are in spite of all their talk? (*Pause*.)

N.: Why did it have to happen in my family? Cynthia's marriage was to be the happiest day of my life, now look what I'm facing. She has betrayed me.

D.: No less than my son has betrayed me, Njeroge, and in my case I also stand to lose a very substantial amount of money. That is why I don't call this a simple act of defiance.

N.: Yes, that is an added tragedy.

D.: With extra capital in our hands we could have made a great start in the tourist trade. And we can still do that. I am determined to do it. Mohan has defied his parents but I will beat him at his own game.

N.: How?

D.: By writing frankly to my wife's cousin. It's just occurred to me that instead of hiding our dilemma from him we should really tell Sobod what's happened. He is of the older generation and will understand our position if I explain it.

N.: Will he?

D.: I'm sure he will.

N.: I'm still not satisfied, Dev, that a good straightforward talk with those two wouldn't set matters right again. I know we've already had separate talks with them but I think it's worth trying again. In fact let me tell you, just before leaving I asked Cynthia to come here with Mohan so that we could have a frank discussion together.

D.: Well, I wish I had our position straightened out with Sobod before this. I'm reasonably certain that he will appreciate our views but I would like to hear him say it; oh wait! Couldn't I phone the man? Why not actually talk to him?

N.: You mean now?

D.: Yes, if it's possible.

N.: Well, I suppose it is possible if the lines are open at this hour. Do you want to try from here? (*Nods at the phone*.)

D.: No, not from here. Anyone can come in while we are waiting for the call. I have an extension in my study. We can try from there.

N.: Do you know the number?

D.: Yes (*looking around*). It's in his letter actually and my wife's got it.

N.: All right, you get the number and I'll find out from the exchange superintendent if a radio call can be put through to California at such short notice.

D.: Excellent. If we can't get through immediately at least we can book the call. The study's open, Njeroge. I'll be there in a few minutes. Savitri might want a word with me first.

N.: I understand. (*Leaves*.)

D. (*goes to writing desk and looks inside, Savitri enters*): Oh, there you are. I was looking for that letter from Sobod.

S.: I know. I heard what you said.

D.: Well, what do you think in that case? I'm doing everything I can.

S.: I know you are, though I can't see how all this is going to end. Do you want me to talk to Cousin Sobod?

D.: No, you stay here. It's not a subject that you should discuss. And if we do get through I want Njeroge to have a word with him after me. That should convince Sobod of our sincerity. Besides, your son and the light of his life are expected here any moment. Don't tell them that we are out phoning, whatever you do.

S.: All right, though I don't know what I'll say to that girl if I am alone with her. She thinks herself so very clever. Calling me a cabbage!

D.: Calm down now. You've taken that much too seriously. She only said it in self-defence. Now where is that letter?

S.: Here it is.

D.: Well, I'd better join Njeroge. If you don't want to talk to his niece, excuse yourself and retire to the kitchen when she comes. (*Knock. Hisses while going out*) And if you want to know the truth: most men prefer cabbages! (*Hurries offstage.*)

S. (*opens door*): Come in, Mohan.

C. (*hesitating in doorway*): Isn't Uncle here?

M. (*walking in*): Yes, where are they?

S.: Your uncle's just gone out with Mohan's father. They will be back in a few minutes. Come in and sit down.

M: Come on, Cynthia, we can wait for them to return.

S.: They are expecting you; so do sit down. Shall I make some of your favourite tea, Mohan?

M.: Fine – I would like that. Don't you have any idea where they've gone to?

S.: I don't think they are very far off. Well, I'll make some tea. (*Leaves.*)

C.: Your mother's not at all comfortable at having me

around, Mohan. I wonder if I should have come.

M.: Why not, for heaven's sake! It's time they got used to seeing us together.

C.: I suppose it is all a bit sudden from their point of view.

M.: I wouldn't pay too much attention to their point of view.

C.: That's not a nice thing to say about your parents, Mohan.

M.: Maybe not, but they don't want to change their views about anything, and frankly I don't think they can at their age. Well that's not our fault.

C.: It's been a lovely day so far, Mohan. Let's not spoil it by such talk.

M.: All right. Let's talk of something else. Did you like the drive this morning?

C.: It was beautiful. When we got out of town I wished you'd just drive on and on. It reminded me of those days when you used to come down to the coast and see me on weekends.

M.: Yes, those were wonderful times. I felt that we had the world at our feet then.

C.: Do you think we can ever be so happy again, Mohan?

M.: Given the same conditions, why not?

C.: I don't know, but everything was so perfect in those days. We made so many plans. Do you think some of them will come true, Mohan?

M.: If we don't lose faith in each other, everything can come true. After all we don't want much, no more than anyone else.

C.: In those days I remember we wanted nothing but our own company.

M.: That hasn't changed, but there must be other things too.

C.: What other things?

M. (*shrugs*): Practical things. Surely you would like a house in pleasant surroundings to start with.

C.: To start with?

M.: Yes, if it's possible, why not?

C.: To start with I don't care where we live provided we are happy.

M.: Of course, that's what I mean too.

C.: No you don't – and that's what worries me, Mohan. You can't get that money out of your mind. Ever since that letter arrived you have been a different person.

M.: That's just your imagination. No amount of money could change my feelings towards you. You can't seem to believe that.

C.: I do believe it, Mohan. If I had any real doubts about you I wouldn't be here. But it doesn't alter the situation we're in. This so-called gift has become a rope round our necks. Your uncle must be an awful man.

M.: He didn't sound awful on the phone, let me tell you. He even accepted reversed charges. I told him exactly what I thought and he listened to me quietly without butting in or putting forward any of his own views. And, as you know, he's promised to send us a telegram after thinking it over.

C.: Meanwhile, we all wait on his pleasure. I hate the thought of that money now, Mohan. It's turned something natural and beautiful into a monstrous obligaion. No one has any right interfering in other people's lives in this manner. That's why I still say he must be an awful man.

M.: Look, Cynthia, let's decide once and for all between us what we want to do, or our elders will decide for us. We haven't been summoned here just to drink tea with them.

C.: I realise that and I've decided.

M.: Have you?

C.: Yes. We will wait for the message from your uncle. If it's straightforward and he withdraws all conditions from his gift, then accept it; otherwise I want no part of that money, nor will I marry you for so long as it threatens us the way it does now.

M.: You're being unreasonable again, Cynthia.

C.: I'm not. This situation can poison the rest of our lives and we've been far too happy for me to agree to any compromise.

M.: No one's asking you to compromise. I'm just asking you to be practical.

C.: I can't be practical at the expense of my self-respect. Let's not talk about it any more, Mohan. You can't see it my way and I can't bring myself to be practical. So, let's just forget the whole thing.

M.: Forget the whole thing?

C.: Yes!

M.: All right, let's forget it. (*Picks up picture.*) The bastard! (*Dashes it to floor.*) It's all his fault.

Njeroge and Dev walk in. Stop, startled, seeing picture on floor and couple standing apart, looking angry.

D. (*cautiously*): Isn't your mother here, Mohan?

M.: She is. (*Nods*) In there – cooking.

D.: Ah, then we'll wait for her. Sorry we had to get out but I had some urgent business to attend to.

M. (*sarcastic*): And did you finish it?

D. (*trying to be jovial*): No, not completely. I'm glad you came, Cynthia. We haven't seen much of you since you arrived. Is everything all right?

C. (*calm*): Yes, thank you.

N. (*who meanwhile has picked up picture and returned it to table*): Must have been a strong wind in here. (*Takes tea tray from Savitri as she enters.*) Let me take that from you, Mrs Dev.

s.: Thank you.
   Short pause.

D.: Well, now that we are all here —

M.: Yes, let's get it over with.

D.: You're very impatient today, Mohan. Do you realise we are all assembled to reach an understanding that is acceptable to everyone?

M.: I'm not here to reach any understanding, and neither is Cynthia.

D.: What do you mean?

M.: You've come here to make some sort of a bargain with us, haven't you?

N.: Bargain?

M.: Well, call it what you like. You've come here to discuss what is best for us from your viewpoint, if you like that better.

D.: We have only your good at heart, Mohan.

s.: Nothing else matters to us.

N.: And I'm thinking only of you, Cynthia. I wish you would believe me when I say that.

c. (*quiet*): I believe you, uncle.

N.: (*hearty*): Yes, of course you do. And since we are here for a frank talk, let me say it in front of everyone: I would be happier if you married a man of your own race, Cynthia.

M.: What about her happiness?

N.: She will find it among her own people. That is surely far more natural than . . . than . . . well, than marrying a foreigner.

M.: But I am not a foreigner. I was born here.

N.: All right, you were born here, but it doesn't make you an African.

M.: Why, is an African better than I am?

N.: I didn't say that.

M.: Well, what did you say then? Do you mean that like

oil and water we don't mix, or does my complexion carry a stigma in your eye?

N.: You are accusing me of race prejudice, Mohan.

M.: I'm not accusing you of anything, Mr Njeroge. But I am asking you a straight question. What's wrong with me? If it's not my race, is it some defect of character that brands me undesirable in your eyes? Or is there a suspicion that I carry some deadly secret in my origins that will rise and reveal itself only after I get married?

N.: I don't mean anything as complicated as that.

C.: This is awful. Say what you want to, all of you, and get it over with.

D.: But — (*Stops. Sudden silence. Mohan looks at them.*)

M.: It seems you don't know what to say after all. Shall I say it for you?

D.: No! I won't have you putting words into my mouth. You're very sure of your position, aren't you? You think we're being selfish, narrow-minded and petty, don't you? You aren't ready at this moment to grant us a single, decent thought, are you? Deny that if you can. (*Mohan looks embarrassed. Dev continues.*) You refuse to understand that we also have principles which are sacred to us and that we do sincerely desire what is best for you. If our standards are now considered old fashioned and rusty for modern use, then let me just tell you one thing, you only happen to be 'right' because you are young and belong to this age. But you aren't any better than us because of it. If there's any real suffering in something like this, it's on our side, not yours. The world that we knew and loved is rapidly evaporating before our eyes and don't tell me that everything new is for the better. We know it isn't. Inter-racial marriages may be things of the future, but at the moment people have hardly succeeded in breaking the simplest communal and religious barriers.

N.: Quite right, Dev. You have spoken for me as well. I have only one thing to add. I do not believe that tribe, race, traditions are bad things. They have been evolved over the centuries and we cannot now kick them over simply to suit the pleasures of the younger set. Our forefathers made certain rules through the experiences of generations and everything we possess today as a race is based on that discipline. They had foresight, and I prefer to be guided by their wisdom (*turning to Mohan*) rather than your pioneering ambitions! And (*turning to Cynthia*) Cynthia, I warn you, you will be unhappy with this man. As an immigrant of the younger generation, he is quite ready to forget his background, but there is no need for you to do the same. You are an African and must remain proud of that.

C.: I am. I can also tell you that Mohan is proud of being an Indian.

N.: Good, then that just proves what I am saying. You two can never be happy together.

C.: But we are, I mean . . . (*turns away*) we were.

D. (*after quick silence*): We all need time in this. I think that is clear to everyone by now. This is not a matter to be rushed through. If you have doubts, Cynthia, it is nothing to be ashamed of. Doubts are the mark of an educated person.

N.: There is no doubt in my mind about anything. Cynthia, you cannot give false hopes to this boy. It is not fair on him or on you. This family stands to lose a lot if you two don't reach a quick decision and I hope it has been reached at last.

C.: Mohan is free to do what he wants to as far as I am concerned.

N.: That's good enough for me.

M.: Well, it isn't good enough for me. I agree it was a mistake for me to try and rush this thing through but then anyone would have been tempted with so much money. I dare say you've given it a bit of thought yourselves.

N.: So you do admit to your mistake?

M.: Yes, I do. I've made many mistakes in my time, but being born Indian wasn't one of them. Nor is it a mistake for me to want to marry Cynthia. If she really thinks it is, let her say so. (*Silence.*)

N.: He has asked you a question, child, and we all want to know the answer.

C.: I've given my answer. He knows what I feel and think about this whole thing.

D.: There is no need for us to prolong this discussion. Your uncle's ambition for your future is a worthy and noble one.

N.: When you are both a little older you will realise that we have only acted in your own best interests.

M.: So you have been up to something?

N.: What do you mean by that?

M.: I'm just wondering what alternative plans you have in mind for us.

D.: No plans, Mohan. You're both young. Take a year to think it over. That's all.

N.: Exactly! A year is a decent, civilized period in something as grave as this. You have to think not only of yourselves but also of future generations. What will they be Africans or Indians, Christians or Hindus. Into what category will they fall and to what race will they belong?

M.: To a better race, I hope; one which knows no racial frontiers or tribal obligations.

N.: There has never been such a race in human history.

M.: Human history hasn't ended yet, though it might very

soon if we don't change our ideas of life. The human being was not created to fit into any category. If he was, then we should all be happy now. But are we? Even you are only clinging to your old prejudices now, not out of any sense of conviction but out of a blind fear of racial extinction. Our children will be free of such bogies because for them their world will be a garden glowing with colours and not the slum conglomeration of racial backyards that it is today. You condemn mixed marriages because they are breaking the old mould of society, but the sooner it's broken the better, or we will all perish in its stench. The choice before you is not whether you want to avoid having grandchildren whom you fear the world will label as half-breeds, but whether you want any grandchildren at all.

N.: I want grandchildren who look like me and your father wants grandchildren who look like you, though we hope they won't think and speak and want to act like you. What you say is clever, but it changes nothing. I trust the minimum courtesy you can show to your parents is to wait for a year before you start on the new race, which I hope never comes about.

D.: Your speech was fit only for an anarchist, Mohan. I will try and forget it. And can we have your word now that you two will let things stand as they are for a year at least?

M.: I don't make any such promise but, if Cynthia wants it that way, then I'll just have to wait.

Bell rings. Telegram arrives. Mohan, nearest door, takes it, smiles to himself, hands telegram to Savitri. She reads it, slaps forehead and slumps into chair. Dev rushes to her side; everyone is stunned. Mohan picks up telegram and reads it.

D.: What is it, Mohan?

M.: He's dead.

D.: Dead?

N.: Who's dead, for heaven's sake?

M. (*points at picture*): He is. Died of a heart attack this morning.

D. (*stunned*): I can't believe it.

S. (*grieving*): He was a very sick man. I always feared something like this might happen.

D.: If I had thought of phoning him earlier I might have talked to him. Who can say now what he really had in mind?

M.: We will never know.

S. (*rising*): Well, I know. He was a good man. If he made any mistake it was that of a generous nature. Do you think any of you are perfect? No one here has any right to judge him. (*Leaves.*)

D. (*dazed*): He must have been an extraordinary person. In death he grows even stronger than in life. (*Follows wife out.*)

C.: I'm sorry, Mohan. He was your uncle, and as your mother says we have no right to judge him now. I believe he meant well.

M.: But he had to die to prove it. For his sake then can't we just forget the past and use our own judgement from now on?

C. (*takes his hand, smiles at him*): Yes.
Njeroge, who has been watching them, shakes his head and walks out.

M. (*looking around*): They have all deserted us. We're alone . . .

C.: I think we will be for some time.

CURTAIN

The Deviant

GANESH BAGCHI

CHARACTERS

Lalit, *In his early 30's*
Shikha, *His mistress, in her 20's*
Dibu, *Their friend, in his 30's*

Time : the present
Place : Kampala

THE DEVIANT

The action takes place in Lalit's sitting room. Sunday morning. Lalit has finished having breakfast. Shikha is clearing the table. Lalit is reading a newspaper. Lalit is in his shirt and trousers, Shikha in a 'sari' and 'choli'. Lalit is seated facing the audience, except that his face is hidden behind the newspaper. Shikha hands around generally, and, when she finishes clearing the table, starts dusting the books. The scene opens without anybody saying anything for the first, say, 20 seconds.

There is a long wall behind the breakfast table — a wall with a window right behind it. The curtains are drawn apart. The furniture consists of a breakfast table and four chairs, two 'buddu' chairs, a sofa and a bookshelf. There's a table-lamp in one corner, a few paintings on the wall, a little clock on the bookshelf. There are also a couple of side tables.

Lalit is in his early thirties, Shikha in her twenties. When the curtain rises, Lalit's face is still hidden behind the newspaper. The audience can see his shoes and a part of his trousers which are bobbing up and down rhythmically.

SHIKHA: When will you marry me? (*Lalit does not answer.*) Lalit, when will you marry me?

LALIT: For God's sake, hold your tongue and let me ... read the *Sunday Nation*.

SHIKHA: What does that mean?

LALIT: That means I don't think I'll marry you at all.

SHIKHA: Why?

LALIT: Because I love you.

169

SHIKHA: Would you marry me if you didn't?

LALIT: No.

SHIKHA: So you would not marry me in any case?

LALIT: No.

SHIKHA: But people do get married.

LALIT: Yes, but not for love, not where I come from.

SHIKHA: Why do they marry then?

LALIT: For money. For children. But not for love.

SHIKHA: But that's immoral.

LALIT: I think so too.

SHIKHA: Isn't it immoral for you not to marry me!

LALIT: Are we going to begin all over again?

SHIKHA: I don't mind.

LALIT: I do.

SHIKHA: I don't.

LALIT: I do.

SHIKHA: Let me put it this way. If you don't marry me, what have I to look forward to?

LALIT: Love.

SHIKHA: That's not enough.

LALIT: What did you say?

SHIKHA: There comes a time when just love isn't enough.

LALIT: Has that time come yet?

SHIKHA: No.

LALIT: Then shut up.

SHIKHA: Lalit! (*No answer.*)

LALIT (*puts down newspaper again*): Please don't speak to me in that doleful voice, and please do not look at me with those doleful eyes.

Lalit gets up and moves on to front stage and sits on one of the 'buddu' chairs.

SHIKHA (*moving towards him*): Lalit, didn't I run away from my parents and come away with you to Kampala?

LALIT: I paid your fare.

SHIKHA: Did I ask you any questions then?

LALIT: No, you didn't. Thank you very much.

SHIKHA: If I suffer from a real sense of guilt on account of living with you without being married, what can I do about it?

LALIT: You have to do something about the way you feel?

SHIKHA: But it's killing me.

LALIT: Why didn't you think of this before?

SHIKHA: I was impulsive.

LALIT: Then go on being impulsive, can't you?

SHIKHA: But don't you suffer?

LALIT: No I don't. And I think that this question of marriage is a pathological obsession endemic among the female species of the human race. Can't you think of anything else but marriage?

SHIKHA: Yes, I can.

LALIT: Of what, for example?

SHIKHA: Of children, for example.

LALIT: Good God!

SHIKHA: Is that all you've to say?

LALIT: We can't have children.

SHIKHA: Why not? My mother had ten.

LALIT: Your mother must have suffered.

SHIKHA: She was very happy.

LALIT: Then it was very rash of your father.

SHIKHA: My father was worth ten of you, and don't say stupid things about my father.

LALIT: Then don't ask me stupid questions.

SHIKHA (*losing her temper*): It's not so stupid to ask why I can't have children? I want children — as many as my mother had and more.

LALIT (*also losing his temper*): It's an ugly world where we never stop being selfish and stupid as if the sheer pain, anguish and loneliness of existence are not enough burden for anyone of us to bear. Children, my dear Shikha, are the most beautiful things in the world, and a world that doesn't deserve them won't get them.

SHIKHA (*still excited*): But why should the sins of the world be visited upon me? I want to be whole, I want to be loved for what I am. I deserve to have children, never mind the world. I'm not the world.

LALIT (*excited*): You are the world and I am the world. And on every decision that you or I make depends the destiny of the universe.

SHIKHA: That is a lot of nonsense. You're arrogant and pompous.

LALIT (*persuasive tone*): You don't understand, Shikha. All artists, even people like you and me, shape the world with the keen edge of their perception. We can't allow this to be blunted.

SHIKHA: It still doesn't make sense to me. I can't think when you make your large, vague generalizations.

LALIT: You don't think in any case.

SHIKHA: With me feeling is thinking.

LALIT: But just feeling is not enough. What drives the engine of life is a fine mixture of thinking and feeling which we call awareness, and it moves us towards the future, towards the unknown. And this awareness is one and indivisible, every individual's burden and privilege, a fearful burden and a glorious privilege. That's why I say that on every decision we make depends the destiny of all others. We can't be irresponsible. Now you see?

SHIKHA: I see nothing. I'm most impressed with your speech, except that it's too long and it explains nothing and I see nothing. And what's all this got to do with marriage, anyway?

LALIT: How long, oh Lord, how long? You tell me why two perfectly happy people should suddenly get married after nearly two years, and be utterly miserable for the rest of their lives, coveting other people's wealth and other people's wives and husbands. Why?

SHIKHA: Lots of married people are perfectly happy.

LALIT: In all my miserable days I've seen but one married couple that's perfectly happy, and that's because they are so perfectly stupid. To be perfectly happy you've either got to be utterly lacking in feeling or utterly lacking in intelligence. Now, which would you rather be?

SHIKHA: I want to be neither. I want to be married.

LALIT: Have you heard of Lord Buddha?

SHIKHA: What has Lord Buddha got to do with marriage?

LALIT: Have you heard of Lord Buddha?

SHIKHA: Yes.

LALIT: What happened to him?

SHIKHA: What happened to him?

LALIT: He was a prince and would have been the king the day his father packed up. He was perfectly happy with a beautiful wife and children and ready access to several scores of beautiful women. Actually, my mouth waters at the very idea of the life he could have lived.

SHIKHA: You ought to be ashamed of yourself.

LALIT (*ignoring her remark*): But suddenly he became aware of life, of poverty, disease and death. Nobody could help him any more. He was utterly alone. His wife, his children and the scores of beautiful women.

SHIKHA: Your mouth waters to think of them. We know. But go on.

LALIT: Nobody could hold him back any more. And he – Prince Siddhartha – tramped all over India, following his vision. Just think of that – Prince Siddhartha walking thousands of miles – when he could afford half a dozen gold Cadillacs. That's what awareness of life does for you.

SHIKHA: You can't even afford a wife, not to speak of gold Cadillacs.

LALIT: Now, Karl Marx wouldn't approve of gold Cadillacs.

SHIKHA: Who is Karl Marx? Of the Marx Brothers? The man who wrote *The Divine Comedy*?

LALIT: No, 'divine' isn't exactly the word I'd use to describe anything Karl Marx wrote.

SHIKHA: I can never understand what you say. I ask you about marriage, and you talk about Buddha. I ask you about money and you talk about Karl Marx. One of these days I'll run away from it all.

LALIT: Run away by all means, but don't mix up Buddha with Karl Marx and Karl Marx with the romantic Italian. They are different kettles of fish altogether.

SHIKHA: I don't much care for them anyway. I don't think your books can take the place of my life. But are you telling me after all these days that you don't care if I run away?

LALIT: No, I don't. For if you make such a conscious decision you'll be saved, you'll become human.

SHIKHA: What am I now?

LALIT: You're a bit of moss, a kind of jelly-fish, a bottle top, a table-mat, a lamp-shade, even a beautiful little flamingo – but not a fully developed conscious human being.

SHIKHA: We need institutions to protect ourselves from the likes of you.

LALIT: People like you live in a world of things, conditioned by conventions, protected by institutions. And soon the coldness of things and the cruelty of institutions creep into your souls.

SHIKHA: I do not understand all this abstract nonsense, and I don't want to. I need a little protection, a little warmth, a little affection, at least a show of it to make life bearable for me. And all you're prepared to give me is a lot of words, words, words. The more I listen to you the more I feel the real, warm, human world receding from me and I feel lost.

LALIT: And I insist that your way is not the way to find our lost world. We must expose ourselves completely to wind and weather, like Lear on the heath, let winds blow and crack our cheeks, fire spit, rain spout and 'all-shaking thunder smite flat the thick rotundity of the world.'

SHIKHA: Well, I've exposed myself to you, which is worse than exposing myself to wind and weather, and I'm not protected by any institution, not even by the universally accepted institution of marriage. So, I don't see what you're complaining about.

LALIT: I'm not complaining. I'm stating my position. The moment I marry you, I accept the institution of marriage and commit the entire humanity to the unscientific and sinful practices of monogamy.

SHIKHA: Who is asking you to marry the entire humanity?

LALIT: You are.

SHIKHA: That'd make the entire humanity very miserable indeed. But do you really believe that what civilization has evolved after thousands of years of trial and error is really unscientific, a sinful practice.

LALIT: What about mass neurosis and the hydrogen bomb? Hasn't civilization evolved those as well? As a matter of fact, I should not be surprised if monogamous marriages and their consequent frustration, the docile respectability of the good citizens who watch television and mind their job, cars, wives, children and dogs, and dig in their gardens and push prams, had something to do with mass neurosis and the hydrogen bomb. The more I can't prove it, the more I feel convinced that it must be true. (*Pause.*)

SHIKHA: Lalit, can we change the subject? I feel a little exhausted.

LALIT: Why should you feel exhausted when I have been doing all the talking?

SHIKHA: Why do you talk so much?

LALIT: Because it helps me to come to terms with myself.

SHIKHA: I sometimes think that while we cling to institutions, you cling to words for protection.

LALIT: What's wrong with that? My words are my words, your institutions are everybody's.

SHIKHA: But it seems to me that you're shadow-fighting all the time. Why do you wear yourself out like this?

LALIT (*in a sudden outburst*): Because I think that the world is a house divided against itself by institutions and perverse group loyalties which lead to gang-tactics. I'm therefore against 'isms', against college crests and Eton ties, against Afro-Asian solidarity, against Public Schools and the prefect system, nationalism and NATO, public tea-parties – East African version – juke-boxes, the wide-screen cinema, nylon shirts and marriages.

SHIKHA: But, certainly the individual expresses himself through clubs and societies, doesn't he?

LALIT: Yes, in the beginning he does, but before long he develops gang feeling. There are clubs and societies in this town whose values and morals would put to shame the most corrupt bobby-soxers. They let the individual through the front-door with the most warm handshake and suave smile, but the moment he protests against the protocol, they kick him out through the back-door with the dirtiest pairs of institutional boots.

SHIKHA: Have you no loyalties?

LALIT: No group loyalties, I hope. To please a Moslem friend, I could hand over Kashmir for a birthday present. To please a British friend I could join the British Council or the Church Missionary Society, or even begin to build another empire, though that would mean a lot of hard work. That reminds me: I must go and see Babulal Patel.

SHIKHA: Can't you stay at home even on a Sunday morning?

LALIT: I can, but I'll use my divine will and go out.

SHIKHA: Is it absolutely necessary that you should go out?

LALIT: Are we animals that we should limit ourselves to the absolutely necessary?

SHIKHA: One of these days I will use my divine will and get out for good.

LALIT: Please leave the latch-key under the door-mat and shut the bedroom windows. Only last week some sharp character removed Mr Brown's lounge-suit, brand-new, with a fish-pole. Genuine Montague Burton's, nine guineas.

SHIKHA: We live together, but we have no real contact. If I want to sit down and talk to you, you run away. You live in a world of your own, and there you're protected. When you come to grips with reality, you want to get away.

LALIT: Remarkable character, David Brown. He's like a portrait done in pastels, and he's the gift of making his most stupid platitudes sound like 'Divine Comedy'. Everybody's terrified of him. He is the Manager of the Great Bank of Juggernaut. As a matter of fact, he *is* the Bank of Juggernaut.

SHIKHA: He seems to be a most interesting character. He can't be very much against the Establishment from the sound of him. Maybe I'll run away with him.

LALIT: Might be interesting to see how he reacts – he's so used to taking everything in his lumbering stride. You say, 'Mr Brown, will you run away with me?' He says, 'What securities can you offer? Land's no good.' You repeat, 'Mr Brown, will you run away with me?' What does he say to that? God, what I wouldn't give to see some of these chaps in a real, human situation! *Someone knocks on the door.*

LALIT: Come in. Oh, hello, Dibu, is it on? (*Dibu is in his thirties. He is self-possessed, aggressively critical, business-like, well-dressed, of mature personality.*)

DIBU: No, it isn't. All the chaps have cried off. I knew this would happen.

LALIT: But at least 20 people on the staff promised me they would attend the meeting.

DIBU: These things often start with a bang; but in our case it isn't even going to start. Raju has resigned from the Association. Mukund's had to go away on official business to Bangoma. The others are only lukewarm. There's a possibility that we'll do more harm than good by making a noise about it. Babulal may not get another job.

LALIT: How do you mean?

DIBU: Babulal himself is afraid that if we have an Association meeting and make representations and give it publicity in the press, they'll victimise him, and he doesn't want that.

LALIT: But we can make even more noise when he is victimised. They would not dare.

DIBU: You underestimate the strength of the Establishment. You do not understand their capacity for intrigue. There are wheels within bloody wheels. And personally I'm never sure that all the people who rant against the Establishment are not really trying to establish themselves at the expense of it.

LALIT: And personally I think you stink – the whole lot of you.

DIBU: This has gone on since the time of Antigone; how often has the individual won? And you must admit that Babulal has neither Antigone's intelligence nor her integrity.

LALIT: I don't care about that. Antigone gave Creon a damned good fight and so shall we.

DIBU: But Antigone fought alone – you're trying to use the same gang-tactics which you profess to despise.

LALIT: This isn't gang-tactics. This is the spontaneous reaction of rightly-constituted people against gang-tactics.

DIBU: Well, I'm not so sure.

SHIKHA: Will somebody please tell me what's going on?

LALIT: This has nothing to do with marriage or children, table-mats or lamp-shades.

DIBU: Don't be so superior, Lalit. You talk like the neo-fascists, those angry young men, the chip-on-the-shoulder chaps who are contemptuous of everything and everybody except themselves, chaps who hate women because they brought them into the world, who hate welfare states because they protect those subsidized louts from disease and starvation, chaps who take everything from you first and then kick you in the teeth because it's their privilege to do so.

SHIKHA: What's happened to Babulal Patel?

LALIT: Babulal's been sacked. The management doesn't like him. He's not charming enough, he doesn't say the right things, he's fluttered dovecotes which had never been fluttered before. All the one-eyed kings at this international centre of lame ducks have suddenly decided that he should be thrown out of the back. We've decided we ought to know why he's being thrown out in this high-handed manner. But after the initial show of strength everybody's settled down to his tropical apathy. I think something can be done. Dibu doesn't think so.

DIBU: I'm not so keen on fighting other people's battles for them as you are. You're always looking for a cause and magnifying it out of all proportion. People are not by nature cruel, mean or selfish as you seem to think, but insecure. Isn't it possible that the management is hitting back out of a sense of insecurity because Babulal was trying to establish himself a little more firmly than the Establishment itself, setting up a kind of competition, if you know what I mean?

SHIKHA: Will you have some coffee, Dibu?

DIBU: Yes, please. Thank you very much.

SHIKHA: What about you, Lalit?

LALIT: I must really go out.

SHIKHA: I won't be a minute.

  Exit Shikha.

DIBU: Why do you want to be mixed up in this?

LALIT: It's none of your business.

DIBU: You can be rude as hell, I don't care. I don't think you're doing the right thing. It's not right the way you treat Shikha. Before you go banner-wagging about freedom and all that, why don't you set your own house to order?

LALIT: If you don't shut up, I shall throw something at you.

DIBU: All romantic idiots are really very defenceless.

LALIT: You call me a romantic idiot because I'm concerned about justice and human happiness?

DIBU: You're a bloody fool, that's all I can say.

LALIT: It's none of your business what I am.

DIBU: What right have you to mess up this girl's life?

LALIT: Why should you mind if she wants that I should mess up her life rather than anybody else?

DIBU: I mind because she's so easily taken in by your pseudo-intellectual claptrap.

LALIT: Why don't you expose me to her?

DIBU: It might destroy her. She wants to believe you, but you make it jolly difficult for her.

LALIT: I'm not going to change myself either for Shikha's sake or for yours.

DIBU: You're a hypocritical, unmitigated bore, and you'll die of self-love.

LALIT: You're a damned snake in the grass, an effete cynic who wants to justify inaction and laziness by accusing others of being thoughtlessly, vulgarly active.

DIBU: You're just a joke, Lalit, a stale stupid joke. Nobody takes you seriously except yourself, and I don't mind telling you that I haven't much time for impostors and charlatans.

LALIT: If you provoke me any more, I shan't be responsible for what I do.

DIBU: When are you ever responsible for what you do? Soon I'll have to organize a society for the protection of Lalit Roy. And stop threatening me before you've said any more that you'll be sorry for.
Lalit advances menacingly towards Dibu.

LALIT: Look, Dibu, don't think I'm a fool. I know very well why you come here. If you don't leave Shikha alone, I'll knock your brains out.

DIBU: I thought you're against middle-class feelings and attitudes. You've told us, time and again, that you're against possessive lust, that you don't understand people who hang on to their books, cars, furniture and wives. The moment there's any challenge, you expose yourselves. You bloody intellectuals, you are so utterly mixed-up that you give me a pain in the . . .
Enter Shikha, with coffee on a tray. Dibu restrains himself.

LALIT: I'm going out. I've work to do. You two can sit

here billing and cooing to each other. I'll have this meeting and send in our protest. If nobody comes to the meeting, I'll hand this over personally to David Brown. (*Showing Dibu and Shikha an envelope.*)

DIBU: David Brown is usually at the Summit Club on Sunday mornings, drinking John Collinses and working up an appetite.

LALIT: All right, I'll go to the Summit Club then.

DIBU: Are you kidding? You'll be thrown out. Freedom of Association means, in this country, freedom of *not* associating with bank clerks like you.

LALIT: Allow me to sort that out.

DIBU: Will you let me have a look at what you've written?

LALIT: No, my guardian angel, I don't think I want to do that.

DIBU: Lalit, it's easy to lose your job, but not so easy to get one.

LALIT: The day I begin to worry about jobs and money, I'll 'cease upon the midnight' with a bullet in my brains.

SHIKHA: Why should he worry? He has no wife or children to worry about.

LALIT: I'd do exactly the same even if I had twenty wives and fifty children to worry about. I must go now. What about you Dibu?

DIBU: I should be content with three or four wives. I think, on the whole, twenty is too many.

LALIT: Dibu, what I really wanted to know, finally, was whether you were coming to the meeting or not.

DIBU: Finally, I'm not. I'm going to stay right here and talk to Shikha.

LALIT: You'd make an ideal couple, the two of you.

DIBU: As a matter of fact that's an idea which has crossed my mind from time to time.

SHIKHA: Some coffee, Dibu?

LALIT: Why don't you give him the nectar of the Gods?
   I'm soon going out!

SHIKHA: I'm a free agent, am I not? I'm not even married.
   Do you mind very much what we do? (*Shikha sits down
   with her knitting.*)

LALIT (*vehemently*): No, I don't. (*Proceeding towards the door.*)
   Goodbye.

DIBU: Lalit, before you go and do something rash, just
   answer one question for me, will you?

LALIT: Go ahead.

DIBU: What's the date today?

LALIT: Don't play the fool with me, Dibu.

DIBU: Would I dare play the fool with you? I'm serious.
   Tell me the date today.

LALIT: I don't know and I don't care.

DIBU: Yes, you, the world's great giver, have forgotten –
   I haven't. You are always oozing with sympathy,
   aren't you? Angola, Bizerta, Sharpeville, Congo,
   Algiers, Little Rock – all the poor downtrodden people
   of the world – your heart bleeds for them. Mine
   doesn't. I'm not prepared to give even a little more
   to anybody. People get what they deserve. And people
   who always fall over backwards – giving, giving, giving
   all the way – will get nothing but contempt. What does
   Bizerta mean to me? Nothing. Why should I care what
   happens to the Algerians? An African friend of mine
   said to me the other day, 'Oh, how I hate people who
   love Africa': I know exactly how he feels. You wear yourselves out, and you wear others out – with your love.

SHIKHA: What is the date today? I wish somebody would
   answer that question first.

DIBU: I know the date today and I think . . .

SHIKHA: Never mind what you think. If somebody doesn't
   tell me soon I'll have hysterics.
   (LALIT *has looked up his diary*).

LALIT: Ladies and gentlemen, for the satisfaction of all concerned, I'll answer this pregnant question – it's 6th August, 1961. May I go now?

DIBU: No, you may not. Listen to me first. Exactly sixteen years ago – in 1945 on 6th August at fifteen minutes past eight in the morning – Japanese time – a bomb was dropped at Hiroshima; sixty thousand people were killed and a hundred thousand injured or mutilated. And today there's no mention of it in the newspapers which are full of compensation schemes for expatriate officers and wedding photographs.

SHIKHA: We have to readjust ourselves and go on living. Why blame the poor people for forgetting? If there's anything I want to forget, if there's anything I want to pretend never happened, it's Hiroshima and Nagasaki.

DIBU: I'm not blaming the people. I'm talking about the rebels and reformers who said they would not let this happen again.

LALIT: We've forgotten, but not altogether. Babulal Patel and Hiroshima are the same thing. When we're drawn into this business of living and partly living, we forget, but our sorrows do not leave us, Dibu, and one day we'll build a niche in every house and call it Hiroshima and burn incense before it, and we shall all say 'Oh, Hiroshima, if we forget thee ever again, let our tongues cleave to the roofs of our mouths'.

DIBU: I'm not so sure.

LALIT: You're welcome to your cynicism, but you're not going to corrupt me. I'll wear myself out – I'll wear myself out over Hiroshima and wear myself out over Babulal Patel. And when the insane fever is gone, we'll sit and remember, and we shall hang harps upon the willows and weep, and you, Dibu, will be with us. Goodbye.

Lalit goes out.

DIBU: I can't make him out.

SHIKHA: I've been trying hard, too, for these two years.

DIBU: Have you found out anything?

SHIKHA: He's not what he seems. I think he feels very lonely and insecure.

DIBU: If he feels lonely and insecure, why is he so pompous?

SHIKHA: I want to believe in him. Don't make it difficult for me.

DIBU: Did you ask him when he was going to marry you?

SHIKHA: Yes.

DIBU: What did he say?

SHIKHA: He said he wasn't going to marry me ever.

DIBU: Why don't you marry me, then? How long am I going to hang round?

SHIKHA: I really don't believe in marriage. You see — marriage is an institution and institutions are generally corrupt.

DIBU: I've never heard you say this before.

SHIKHA: I don't see why you and I, two perfectly happy, perfectly normal people should suddenly decide to get married and be perfectly neurotic and unhappy for the rest of our lives.

DIBU: Plenty of married couples are perfectly happy.

SHIKHA: In all my miserable days I've seen but one married couple that's perfectly happy and that's because they're so perfectly stupid. To be really happy, you've to be either perfectly lacking in intelligence or completely lacking in feeling. You see?

DIBU: You confuse me. You sound almost like Lalit.

SHIKHA: You see it's not enough to feel. We must think. And of late I've been thinking.

DIBU: I see.

SHIKHA: You see nothing. I'm telling you, Dibu, we all live in a world of things, conditioned by conventions,

G

protected by institutions, and before very long the
coldness of things and the callousness of institutions
corrupt our very souls.

DIBU: So you're perfectly happy as you are?

SHIKHA: No, not perfectly happy, for to be perfectly happy
one's got to be either an idiot . . .

DIBU (*cutting her short*): Stop playing this game with me.

SHIKHA: This is not a game. I'm trying to believe everything Lalit says.

DIBU: Are you getting anywhere?

SHIKHA: No. The knowledge of good and evil followed
when the first man and first woman fell from grace. I
fell the day I loved Lalit. I've given everything away,
Dibu, and I've nothing more to give. I can't take back
what I've given away, Dibu, can I?

DIBU: How much do you care for me?

SHIKHA: So much that I wish you were Lalit or Lalit were
you or something . . . I don't quite know what!

DIBU: The only way to get him is to demolish him. Give
him up and you might get him. How can you go on
like this?

SHIKHA: I can't. But if I call his bluff, he might crumble.
So, I let him talk. I try to believe in him. When he's
around I feel I must protect him, and when you're
around I feel protected. I need you and he needs me.

DIBU: Who's going to work this out?

SHIKHA: I don't know.

DIBU: You know, but you don't want to say it, not even
to yourself. You don't realise that you can do a lot of
harm by giving without expecting anything in return.
He is destroying you – piecemeal – every day. I *will*
not let him destroy you.

SHIKHA: What do you want me to do?

DIBU: Come away with me.

SHIKHA: It's so difficult.

DIBU: Please, Shikha, don't let loving and giving become a habit. You've a right to protect your ego from being hurt. It's a precious thing – one's ego – and if you ignore it or destroy it – you're finished. Why should you let his ego become bigger every day at the cost of yours?

SHIKHA: Will you take me away, Dibu, far away from here?

DIBU: Yes, I will.

SHIKHA: Will you protect me from more hurt?

DIBU: Yes, I will.

SHIKHA: Then I'll come with you and let Lalit sort it all out with himself.

DIBU: You won't change your mind?

SHIKHA: Never.

DIBU: Do you want *me* to tell Lalit about our decision?

SHIKHA: I would like to tell him myself. When can we go?

DIBU: Today, if you like. There's no difficulty at all. In matters of love, 'More haste, less waste' is the golden principle.

Dibu holds Shikha's hands when Lalit enters. Lalit looks crushed by some unforeseen calamity. He comes in quietly and slumps down on a chair without taking any notice of either Shikha or Dibu.

SHIKHA (*looking concerned*): What's the matter, Lalit? Didn't you have a meeting?

LALIT: No.

DIBU: Why not?

LALIT: Nobody was interested. They're all too busy looking after themselves.

DIBU: I think this is the best thing that could have happened.

LALIT: I don't feel like getting into another argument with you.

DIBU: There's something comforting in other people's misfortunes, you must admit.

LALIT: Leave me alone, Dibu.

SHIKHA: There's something very important I want to tell you, Lalit. You must listen to me carefully.

LALIT: I've got to sort out a lot of things before you or anybody else tells me anything important.

SHIKHA: What is the matter, Lalit? You sound most distressed.

LALIT: I went to the Bridge Club first and tried to persuade the people there to come to the meeting. They would not leave their bridge table.

SHIKHA: I understand you're upset, but, please, listen to me. I've got to explain everything before I leave.

LALIT: Funny! I never understood people who grew up with the fear of the Establishment in their guts. I was so sure I could defy people like David Brown and everything they represented.

SHIKHA: It's always you, you, you. You reduce everything to size and your own ego becomes bigger and bigger every day. You haven't even the time to listen to other people. If there is ever a real challenge . . .

LALIT: I'm through with myself, Shikha.

DIBU: What are you talking about?

SHIKHA: Every time I've decided to do something, you've upset my plans completely. This time I don't want to hear anything you've to say. I shan't change my mind.

LALIT: You know, Shikha, we didn't have the meeting. So I strode off to the Summit Club to see David Brown, and there he was, outside the entrance of the club, talking to half a dozen of his club chums. I thought I'd take him down a peg or two, tell him exactly what I thought of him and the bank before I handed over the letter to him.

DIBU: I really admire your courage, old boy.

SHIKHA: And of course, you didn't think what would happen to me when you lost your job and the other banks refused to give you one, did you!

LALIT: Don't worry, Shikha, I haven't lost my job, but I've lost something more precious – my confidence, my self-respect.

DIBU: Maybe you had too much of it.

SHIKHA: You needn't be quite so brutal now. What happened, Lalit?

LALIT: As I was saying, I found David Brown, talking to his club-mates, standing near the club entrance, perfectly harmless, almost ridiculous in his English shorts. He looked so comical that I felt definitely superior to him, but as I approached him my courage gave way. And I stood in the middle of the car-park feeling completely lonely and defenceless. My mouth was dry with apprehension. I could not take another step towards him. The club was suddenly transformed into an amphitheatre with the serried ranks of high-powered administrators and executives seated on the endless, semi-circular tiers of seats, looking down at me, half in contempt, half in amusement. To defy them, I tried to feel in my pocket for my letter of protest, but a horrible laughter of derision filled the air, and I felt paralysed. Suddenly half a dozen mad bulls charged at me, while men and women cried out for my blood, and I fled; I fled without once looking back, fled in sheer panic.

SHIKHA (*moving towards him*): Sit down, Lalit and don't think of that just now.

LALIT: I don't think I'll recover from this, Shikha.

DIBU (*trying to comfort Lalit*): Oh, don't worry, old boy. The individual often loses battles, but wins the war.

LALIT: What's happened to our cynic? I didn't know you

were so hopeful of the ultimate victory of the individual.

DIBU: We all are. The most unctuous, oily and servile
representatives of the Establishment are little kings
unto themselves in their fantasy world. Otherwise we
just couldn't go on. Nobody can escape his ultimate
loyalty to freedom. That's our fate. But good Lord!
I sound so pompous when I talk to you, Lalit. You
always do this to me.

LALIT: I'm almost beginning to listen to what other people
have to say. And, strangely enough, even what you
have to say seems to make sense. And, Shikha, what
was it you were going to tell me? I've a vague recol-
lection it was terribly urgent.

Dibu and Shikha exchange glances

SHIKHA: Well, believe it or not, I was thinking of marriage
again. You see, there's something so soothing, so
comforting about the idea of marriage that in moments
of stress and strain I inevitably think of marriage; I
hope you understand.

LALIT (*aggressively*): You're altogether impossible.

DIBU: You don't quite understand the situation, Lalit.
You've just lost a crucial battle. Your defeat was as
a matter of fact, a masterpiece of strategy, because
by losing this battle, you've finally had your victory
over me. Goodbye, Lalit. Goodbye, Shikha.

CURTAIN

Fusane's Trial

ALFRED HUTCHINSON

CHARACTERS

Fusane	La-Ngwenya	Judge
Mfundisi	La-Shabalala	Lawyer
Ma-Magwaza	La-Mkize	Orderly
Ma-Mtetwa	Nduna	
Shabangu	Wardress	
Magagula	Clerk	
Mtetwa	Prosecutor	

FUSANE'S TRIAL

SCENE ONE

Fusane's Trial *is set in Mashobeni, a district in Swaziland, a stone's throw from the South African border.*

A room in Mfundisi's house.

FUSANE: Mfundisi, I'll kill myself!

MFUNDISI: Now, now, now. There's no need to talk like that, Fusane.

FUSANE: *I mean it, Mfundisi.*

MA-MAGWAZA: I don't blame the girl. I'd kill myself too.

MFUNDISI: Patience, you're not helping things – talking like that.

MA-MAGWAZA: That's how I feel. It's a shame.

MFUNDISI: I agree. But . . .

FUSANE: I'll kill myself before I become Shabangu's wife.

MFUNDISI: It won't come to that. It will be all right.

MA-MAGWAZA: All right! Would it be all right if our Nozipho was being forced to marry a man she did not want?

MFUNDISI: Be reasonable, Patience.

MA-MAGWAZA: Reasonable! That wicked old man! Why Shabangu's old enough to be her grandfather. Reasonable, indeed! And he has five wives already!

MFUNDISI: You won't have to marry him, Fusane. Nobody can force you.

FUSANE: My father's forcing me. He says I am Shabangu's wife because Shabangu paid him lobola of five cattle when I was a child . . .

MFUNDISI: Still, he can't force you.

FUSANE: I won't go, Mfundisi. I'd rather die.

MFUNDISI: No need for that kind of talk. This thing must be stopped. I don't know why the District Commissioner hasn't answered my letter. When did I write, Patience?

MA-MAGWAZA: Last week – Thursday.

FUSANE (*crying*): I won't. I won't. I won't.

MFUNDISI: You won't. All right, you won't.

MA-MAGWAZA: Poor child. There, there. No need to cry. No old goat will get you.

MFUNDISI: There's still time. The wedding's not till next month.

FUSANE: Shabangu says he wants me next week.

MFUNDISI: Next week! Where's your father, Fusane? At the lands?

FUSANE: No. I left him at home, Mfundisi. He will be going to a beer-drinking party at Shabangu's in his honour.

MFUNDISI: I'll see him today. Before this evening's service. I'll talk to him.

FUSANE: Try, Mfundisi. But he won't listen.

MA-MAGWAZA: What does your mother say?

FUSANE: What can she say, Ma-Magwaza?

MFUNDISI: I'll talk to him. And to Shabangu. And first thing tomorrow morning, I'll send a telegram to the District Commissioner.

MA-MAGWAZA: Fancy selling one's own child! It's barbarous . . . criminal!

MFUNDISI: He doesn't see it that way. He thinks he's within his rights.

MA-MAGWAZA: Rights!

MFUNDISI: Yes, rights. It's the tribal custom.

MA-MAGWAZA: But this is the twentieth century.

MFUNDISI: And so it is. Times have changed but some old customs survive – misfits in these times.

MA-MAGWAZA: Huh! How's Nduna, Fusane?

FUSANE: He's all right, Ma-Magwaza. He wants us to run away.

MFUNDISI: Run away together? No. No. That won't do. We'll fight this matter. It can't be allowed to happen. Tell Nduna to come and see me.

FUSANE: Yes, Mfundisi.

MFUNDISI: Don't worry my girl. I'll marry you to Nduna yet! You'll see.

FUSANE: Mfundisi and Ma-Magwaza, I can't tell you how grateful I am to you. I feel so much better after seeing you!

MA-MAGWAZA: Come whenever you want. Come any time. This is your home, my girl.

FUSANE: Thank you, Ma-Magwaza.

MA-MAGWAZA: How's the dressmaking, Fusane?

FUSANE: All right, Ma-Magwaza.

MA-MAGWAZA: I've always said that you were the best dressmaking pupil I ever had.

FUSANE: You are too kind. Well, good-bye, Mfundisi. Goodbye Ma-Magwaza.

MA-MAGWAZA: Goodbye, my child.

MFUNDISI: Goodbye. And don't forget what I told you. I'll marry you and Nduna yet.

Exit Fusane.

SCENE TWO

Interior — a hut at Mtetwa's.

MA-MTETWA: Fusane, if you don't listen to your father the ancestors will turn their backs on you.

FUSANE: Mother, I've told you – I'm not going to Shabangu.

MA-MTETWA: And what do you expect your father to do? Think of that.

FUSANE (*emphatically*): I'm not going to Shabangu, mother.

MA-MTETWA (*sighs*): What do you think I am going to do? (*Change of tone*) Tut, tut, Fusane. What's wrong with Shabangu? He's not a cripple or anything. He's old. You can't blame him for that. He'll look after you. It's said that old men make good husbands. Moreover, being old, he won't trouble you much. He hasn't even tried . . .

FUSANE (*desperately*): I'd kill him if he tried!

MA-MTETWA: That's what I thought about your father. Look at me, Fusane. Look at me properly. Do you see anything wrong with me? Is there a mark, a brand on me? You see, nothing's wrong with me, is there? Well, I was just like you. My father gave me to your father. Here I am. I've given birth to you and your brothers. I'll tell you something else, Fusane – I also had someone I loved. Just like you. It's hard at first but one gets used to things . . . gets used to things . . .

FUSANE: Did you love him very much, mother – your sweetheart?

MA-MTETWA: Love! Love? Those are beetles buzzing in a girl's head . . . I'm sorry, my child. My heart bleeds for you. But there's nothing you can do. Nothing that I can do. It's the law. Ma-Ngubane was here to see if you'd finished her dress. She's coming tomorrow morning.

FUSANE: It's nearly ready. I'll finish it now.

MA-MTETWA: Think about what I've said to you, Fusane. It will be all right.

FUSANE: It's no use, mother. I won't go to him.

SCENE THREE

A hut in Shabangu's kraal.

SHABANGU: Drink, Mtetwa. Drink, father-in-law. Eat meat. This is your party. He bore me a beautiful wife – eh, Magagula?

MAGAGULA: Hau! A real gun of a girl. She puts out the sun.

MTETWA: I played with you, Shabangu, I should have asked for ten head of cattle. Ten? No, fifteen.

SHABANGU: Hey, do you hear that, Magagula? Fifteen head of cattle for an infant. Something I wasn't even sure would live and grow up. (*Laughs.*)

MTETWA: I played with you. A real missis – that's what she is. And she works like an anteater.

MAGAGULA: Au, a gun of a girl! A real rifle.

MTETWA: It was hard work making her. I sweated, I tell you. Bruised my knees and elbows. And what do I get, eh? A miserable five.

SHABANGU: We all know the work you're talking about (*laughter*). But don't forget that once she's here I'll have to feed and clothe her, like those others there . . .

MTETWA: She looks after herself with that sewing machine of hers. She'll be no trouble.

SHABANGU: Look at my wives! See how they glisten in the sun. The earth quakes where they walk. They finish my grain.

MAGAGULA: There's no starvation in your kraal, Shabangu. Everybody sleeps with a full stomach.

MTETWA: We also eat at my kraal. Any trouble, any ill-treatment, and my daughter comes back home. She's not coming here to beg for food! We Mtetwas never begged for anything . . . Straight back home. There'll always be a place for her.

MAGAGULA: The women of this kraal live like queens.

SHABANGU (*shouting*): Hey you, La-Ngwenya, bring us another pot of beer. Eh! Where's La-Nkosi?

LA-NGWENYA: I don't know, Shabangu. She was here just now.

SHABANGU: Yes, it's just like La-Nkosi. Once there are men around she can't sit still – I know her. One of these days I'll tell her to pack up and go back to her people.

(*The women occupy another part of the stage, possibly separated from the men by a low partition.*)

LA-NGWENYA: He's started – the old fool!

LA-SHABALALA: Call this a kraal? More like a prison!

LA-MKIZE: Aw, look at his eyes. Everywhere. He must be sorry he can't see round corners. Jealous old fool!

LA-NGWENYA: That fool Mtetwa sending his daughter to this kraal!

LA-MKIZE: Eh, Fusane. She's the one who'll suffer. No wonder she's digging up red earth. Call this being married – to a thing that's old and finished. What does he want with another wife?

LA-SHABALALA: I curse my father who drove me here with a stick. If I'd known it would be like this, I'd rather have died.

SHABANGU (*calling*): Hey, you women! What's the muttering about? Hatching a plot to bewitch me, eh? Let me tell you, others have tried and failed. This is Shabangu, this! I sent a witch flying to her mother! La-Ngwenya, hurry up with that beer. What have you been doing all this time? Putting in poison? Come on, drink. Enough. I didn't say drink all the beer. (*Lowering voice*) Women, Mtetwa! I don't know why God made the useless things. Lazy! You should see my lands – overgrown with weeds! Now look at that! You see! Hey you, son of Sithole, what do you want there among the women? Get back to the other men!

LA-MKIZE: I called him for a drink.

SHABANGU: Because you're too full of my beer, eh, La-Mkize! I've a good mind to spill the beer. (*Lowers voice*) That's how it starts, Mtetwa. These boys haven't come to eat and drink. Before you know it they're on top. I know them. (*Aloud*) It's late – all of you! Drink up and go to your kraals. Drink and go. The party's over. I have given you meat and beer . . .

VOICES: Shabangu!

SHABANGU (*bitterly*): Yes. Shabangu! Shabangu! And all the time you're planning to bite my ankles.

VOICE: No, Shabangu.

SHABANGU: Oh, yes, I know you! I wasn't born yesterday. Drink and go.

MAGAGULA: You have feasted us, Shabangu.

SHABANGU: Waste of my beer on hyenas. Eh, Mtetwa, it's a pity Fusane and her mother couldn't come. My beer's been wasted on these dogs and hyenas. What does she say, Mtetwa, what does Fusane say about coming here?

MTETWA: What can she say, Shabangu?

SHABANGU: Eh, I think your Mfundisi wants her for him-self. He was here today . . .

MTETWA: Oh, he's mad, Shabangu, mad! Forget him.

SHABANGU: But, Fusane, is she happy? What does she say?

MTETWA: Err . . . Well . . . What can she say?

SHABANGU: Well, next week, eh? Next week. Mtetwa, you dog, you made me wait a long time. She was ripe long ago.

MTETWA: Oh, no, Shabangu, she was still growing. Treat her well, eh? But I played with you, Shabangu. I should have made a big gap in your herd.

MAGAGULA: Aw, not in Shabangu's. No, not in his herd. There would have been no sign that any cattle had left. This is Shabangu-who-doesn't-get-finished. Why, he can lobola all the girls in this district . . .

SHABANGU (*softly*): Fusane, Fusane. My wife. Eh, you bore me a beautiful wife, Mtetwa.

MAGAGULA: A gun of a girl.

SHABANGU (*with resolution*): Mtetwa, tie up your dogs tonight.

MTETWA (*alarmed*): Eh?

SHABANGU: You heard me, Mtetwa. I'm visiting her tonight. I'm seeing the missis.

MTETWA: No, no, Shabangu! Not tonight, wait until next week . . .

SHABANGU: What, no? I'm coming. Tie up your dogs. (*Chuckles*) Fusane. I'm visiting the missis. (*Shouts*) La-Mkize, shake your fat buttocks and bring some beer for my father-in-law. (*Softly*) Tonight is tonight . . .

SCENE FOUR

At Mtetwa's: the hut of Fusane.

FUSANE: Get out! Get out of my hut!

SHABANGU (*speech is slurred*): But my wife. My darling *dudu s'thandwa sami*. My little missis. Come . . . Eh, she has spirit. (*Chuckles*) I like that.

FUSANE: Father Shabangu, you're drunk. Go away!

SHABANGU: Now, now. None of that! Father! Eh, look at this! A bed. A nice bed with nice soft springs. He! He! *Ntsefestefestefe*! I'll sleep nicely tonight ... Ah, my little wife ... come. Give your old man a kiss.

FUSANE: Keep away from me!

SHABANGU: A spirited young heifer this. But I'll tame you. I'll tame you – or this wouldn't be Shabangu! Got you! Come on now. This won't do ...

FUSANE (*panting*): Leave me! Let go of me!

SHABANGU: Ah, they all say that ... but after ... Ha, ha! Then they sing my praises. (*Struggling and panting*) There ... on the bed ... that's where you belong ...

FUSANE: Leave me! Leave me ... or I'll ...

SHABANGU: I've left you ... too long ... as it is. I want to find out what my cattle bought. So you'd bite me, eh? There ... eh, but she's a strong young heifer, this one ... Ha, but you've met an old bull ...

(*Fusane hits Shabangu with her wooden pillow several times. Shabangu groans and Fusane screams repeatedly. Mtetwa and Ma-Mtetwa come running into the hut.*)

MA-MTETWA: Fusane! Fusane!

MTETWA: What is it? Oh God!

MA-MTETWA (*seeing Shabangu*): Oh! Shabangu! Shabangu! (*Fusane sobs hysterically. The sound of running footsteps is heard.*)

NDUNA: What is it? What's happening?

MA-MTETWA: Oh, Nduna! It's Fusane. She's hit Shabangu with her wooden pillow. Look.

MTETWA (*alarmed*): I can't hear him breathing.

NDUNA: Let me listen. (*Pause*) He's *not* breathing. He's dead.

MA-MTETWA: Dead?

MTETWA: Dead!

NDUNA: Dead.

MA-MTETWA: Fusane, what have you done?

MTETWA: Shabangu dead? Dead?

NDUNA: Oh, Fusane, my dear. My darling.

FUSANE: Oh, Nduna, Nduna. He tried to rape me.

MTETWA: What are we going to do now.

(*Ma-Mtetwa gives death ululation.*)

SCENE FIVE

Visitor's room in prison. There is a fierce din of voices.

WARDRESS: Fusane Mtetwa! Fusane Mtetwa! Are you sitting on your ears! Wake up! This isn't your mother's house. This is prison. You're used to killing people. Take. Things for you. That old man there!

MTETWA: Here. This way, Fusane. It's your father. I'm here. Oh, this noise. How are you Fusane? Can you hear me?

FUSANE: Yes, I hear you. I'm all right.

MTETWA: Your mother greets ... Oh, this noise. Mother greets you. And Mfundisi. They greet you. Do you hear me?

FUSANE: Yes, thank them, father.

MTETWA: What, Fusane? What did you say? I don't hear you.

FUSANE: Thank Mother and Mfundisi.

MTETWA: Yes. Yes, I'll do that. Is there anything you want?

FUSANE: No. Nothing. I'm all right.

MTETWA: We're buying you a lawyer. Do you hear? We're buying you ...

WARDRESS: Time up! I said time up! Next.

FUSANE: Goodbye, father.

WARDRESS: Are you deaf, you murdering bitch! Old man,

go away. Don't cry. They haven't hanged her yet. Next. Look sharp.

SCENE SIX

In the court.

CLERK: In the Supreme Court of Swaziland at Mbabane, Regina v Fusane Mtetwa. That the accused, Fusane Mtetwa, is guilty of the crime of Culpable Homicide. In that on the 19th day of September 1964 (*begin slow fade*) and at Mashobeni, within the jurisdiction of the above court, the accused did . . .

PROSECUTOR: . . . and that by repeatedly striking the deceased – an old man – on the head used force in excess of that warranted by the situation. In short, your Lordship, the Crown will prove that the accused is guilty of the alleged crime of Culpable Homicide. The Crown will call two witnesses. (*Pause.*) Your Lordship, I now call Police Sergeant Amos Nkomo. (*Pause.*)

CLERK: Place your right hand on the Bible and repeat after me: I swear that the evidence which I shall give . . .

PROSECUTOR: Thank you.

JUDGE: Does the defence have any questions?

LAWYER: No questions, your Lordship.

PROSECUTOR: I now call witness for the prosecution, Nduna Nkosi.

ORDERLY: Nduna Nkosi.

JUDGE (*pause*): Swear in the witness.

CLERK: Place your right hand on the Bible and repeat

after me: I swear that the evidence which I shall give . . .

(*The previous expressionistic scene is blocked out momentarily. The lights now go up on a relatively realistic depiction of Nduna in the witness box.*)

NDUNA: Yes, sir. He was dead.

PROSECUTOR: Thank you. The Crown rests, your Lordship.

LAWYER: Are you well acquainted with the accused?

NDUNA: Yes, sir. I wish to marry her.

LAWYER: Does that mean that you are betrothed to her?

NDUNA: No, sir. That was not possible.

LAWYER: Would you please explain why.

NDUNA: Her father pledged her to old man Shabangu. (*Hotly*) She hated him. He was forcing her. But she loves me. We were going to run away.

(*Murmur in court.*)

ORDERLY: Silence in court.

LAWYER (*considerately*): Just one more question. On the night in question, did the accused ask you to do anything?

NDUNA: Yes. She asked me to report to the police.

LAWYER: And did you do that?

NDUNA: Yes, sir.

LAWYER (*gently*): Thank you. No further questions, your Lordship. With your Lordship's permission, I will call my first witness, the Reverend Alfred Magwaza.

(*Murmuring of crowd.*)

CLERK: Place your right hand on the Bible and repeat after me: I swear that the evidence which I shall give . . .

MFUNDISI: Yes. I went to see her father that evening. And I also talked to Shabangu.

LAWYER: And what did they say?

MFUNDISI: They were determined to go through with it.

LAWYER: In your opinion, is the accused a violent or reckless person?

MFUNDISI: Oh, no, indeed not. She is a very gentle and conscientious young woman. And hardworking too. She helps to support her family with her dressmaking.

LAWYER: Thank you, Reverend Magwaza.

PROSECUTOR: Reverend Magwaza, this assessment of the accused's character is, of course, just your own opinion.

MFUNDISI: Well, yes.

PROSECUTOR: Would it be true to say that generally speaking people are on their best behaviour with ministers of the church?

MFUNDISI: Perhaps, I don't know.

PROSECUTOR: Isn't it possible that you saw only the best side of the accused's nature?

MFUNDISI: Well . . . I have known her many years.

PROSECUTOR: Thank you.

LAWYER: I now call the accused's father, Kufa Mtetwa.

JUDGE: I think this is a convenient time to adjourn. We will hear the next witness' evidence when the court reassembles.

ORDERLY: Rise in court.

(*Murmur of voices.*)

SCENE SEVEN

In court.

LAWYER: Do you love your daughter, Mr Mtetwa?

MTETWA: Yes, she's my child.

LAWYER: How old is she?

MTETWA: Eighteen.

LAWYER: How old was she when you betrothed her to Shabangu?

MTETWA: She was six.

LAWYER: She is a mature girl. Why hadn't she gone to Shabangu before this?

MTETWA: Shabangu kept asking for her. He said she was old enough, but I kept putting him off until I could do so no longer. He wanted her with red eyes.

LAWYER: And why have you kept her at home all this time?

MTETWA: I wanted her to grow up.

LAWYER: Isn't it true that you wanted her at home because she supported the family with money from her dress-making?

MTETWA: Well, yes. The harvests have been bad.

LAWYER: What were your daughter's feelings towards Shabangu – the man you betrothed her to?

MTETWA: She didn't want him.

LAWYER: And knowing this you were forcing her to go to him?

MTETWA: She was already betrothed. Shabangu paid five head of cattle.

LAWYER: But she did not want him.

MTETWA: She is my child. She has to do what I want.

LAWYER: Including marrying a man she did not want? Leaving the man she had chosen herself?

MTETWA: I am her father. Shabangu was wealthy. He would have looked nicely after her.

LAWYER: You were forcing her – weren't you?

MTETWA: Female children have no choice . . .

LAWYER: What about male children?

MTETWA: They're different. They are men.

LAWYER: On the night in question did you know that Shabangu was going to visit your daughter at your kraal?

MTETWA: I did.

LAWYER: You did not stop him?

MTETWA: No. It was his right to do so.

LAWYER: And don't you think it's wrong to force your daughter?

MTETWA: No. It's the custom. Her mother was given to me. It's the custom of my people. It may be hard but I was doing nothing wrong. I was doing nothing wrong (*sobs*).

LAWYER: Are you sorry that your daughter is in this trouble?

MTETWA: I could die. But what could I do? Tell me? I had eaten Shabangu's cattle . . .

LAWYER: You could have let her marry the man she loves – Nduna Nkosi.

MTETWA: Yes, I could. I should have listened to Mfundisi Magwaza. But I am an old man, I follow the old ways. Times have changed. But it's the custom. The custom. (*Breaks down in sobs.*) My poor child. My poor child.

LAWYER: That is all, your Lordship.

PROSECUTOR: I have no questions, your Lordship.

JUDGE: Orderly, help the old man down. (*Pause.*) Does Counsel for the Defence wish to address the court?

LAWYER: If it please your Lordship. Your Lordship, this is an obvious case of self-defence. I submit, your Lordship, that the Crown has failed to prove that the accused acted recklessly or in any way used more force than was necessary to defend herself. I submit that she struck the deceased . . . She is a victim of a custom that belongs to the past. Are we to allow ourselves to be encumbered by dead, sterile and barbarous customs as we march into the future? Your Lordship, I hope not. I respectfully ask this court to return a verdict of not guilty.

(*Murmur in court.*)

SCENE EIGHT

In court.

JUDGE: ... and after consultation with the Assessors, I find the prisoner not guilty of the charge. I therefore direct that she be released from custody forthwith.

(*Loud murmur in court. Traffic noises. The rest of the action takes place approaching, or near, the door leading from the court – or perhaps nearest the auditorium.*)

MA-MTETWA: Fusane, my child! Oh, Fusane!

FUSANE: Mother! Mother! (*Sobs.*)

MFUNDISI: Let them weep.

FUSANE: Oh, father.

MTETWA: Fusane! My daughter. My own little daughter. You forgive your father. You forgive your old father.

MFUNDISI: It's over. It's all over.

FUSANE: Mfundisi and Ma-Magwaza?

MA-MAGWAZA: How are you my girl?

FUSANE: I'm all right, Ma-Magwaza. I'm all right. Thank you for all you've done for me. Oh, the sky and the sun and birds circling high!

MFUNDISI: Have you forgotten Nduna?

FUSANE: Mfundisi!

MFUNDISI: Yes, I know. We were young too ... once, eh, Patience?

MTETWA: Take her, Nduna, son of Nkosi. Take her my son. Look after her nicely. She's yours.

MFUNDISI: Didn't I tell you, Fusane, didn't I tell you I'd marry you and Nduna? I did. Yes, I did.

CURTAIN

The Opportunity

ARTHUR MAIMANE

CHARACTERS

Minister of Foreign Affairs
Solomon, *An old political associate*
Emma, *Solomon's wife*
Monica, *Their daughter*
Joseph, *Monica's fiancé*

THE OPPORTUNITY

SCENE ONE

Office of the Minister of Foreign Affairs. There is a knock at the door.

MINISTER (*sharply*): Come in. Hello, Solomon! Right on the dot, and you're here!

SOLOMON (*respectfully*): Good afternoon, Minister.

MINISTER: Now, Solomon! Minister, indeed! You? Calling me that? After we've known each other all these years? Years of struggle for our country's independence? Now, Solomon! Sit down.

SOLOMON (*laughing hesitantly*): Thank you. But you *are* a Minister, now, aren't you, Frederick? I must show proper respect.

MINISTER (*playfully*): Ah, then I must call you Mister Organizing Secretary!

SOLOMON: But that's only a post in the party, Minister. It is not as important as yours.

MINISTER (*expansively*): You know what the Prime Minister thinks of the party, Solomon!

SOLOMON (*quietly*): But the party has done its job, hasn't it? We shall be independent in a month.

MINISTER: But that does not mean the Prime Minister has forgotten you, you know.

SOLOMON: Well, of course I know the importance of the party, Frederick. But now that the cabinet has been appointed, what's left for people like me?

MINISTER: There's still plenty of jobs, Solomon! You could be chairman of the National Bank –

SOLOMON (*a little sharp*): I know nothing about banks.

MINISTER: You want to remain in politics! Is that it?

SOLOMON: Mr Minister, I am prepared to serve my country in any capacity. But I have been in politics a long time now – many years.

MINISTER: I know that, Solomon! We all know that – even the Prime Minister! That is why you're here today. That is why I asked you to come to my office. (*Pause.*) Don't you understand, Solomon . . . ?

SOLOMON (*slowly*): Well, you're in charge of foreign affairs, so . . .

MINISTER: So I want you to be an ambassador! Mr Senior Ambassador!

SOLOMON: What?

MINISTER (*laughing*): After being your junior in the party, now I'll be your boss! What d'you think of that?

SOLOMON: Don't think that I feel – you don't deserve your post, Mr Minister. After all, you're better educated than I am—

MINISTER (*a little exasperated*): But don't you realise what I'm offering you?

SOLOMON (*flustered*): Oh, I do appreciate it! I'm very grateful, but I just wanted to make it clear that—

MINISTER: Oh, I understand, Solomon! You don't have to explain. (*Pause.*) D'you think education is important, Solomon?

SOLOMON: Of course I do – you know that. That's why I don't complain because – that's why I sent my daughter Monica on scholarship to the U.K. I was only a primary school teacher myself, but I know the value of a good education.

MINISTER: I'm glad you agree with me! It is important, education. And yours – yours has been increased by experience, has it not? That is why we are sure you will make a good ambassador. And you are a good speaker, too. (*Laughing*) Those speeches you used to make! '*We want our Freedom*'!

SOLOMON: Speaker? But ambassadors don't have to be good public speakers!

MINISTER: The United Nations, Solomon! The world's greatest platform!

SOLOMON: What? Me?

MINISTER (*laughing*): Yes, you Solomon! You talked us into independence, now you must talk us into history!

SOLOMON: The United Nations ... ! That would be wonderful!

MINISTER: Do you want the post?

SOLOMON: Yes!

MINISTER: I would like you to have it too, Solomon. (*Pause.*) But there are many problems.

SOLOMON (*humble*): Problems? What problems?

MINISTER: We were talking about education just now.

SOLOMON: Yes.

MINISTER: Your wife, Solly. She does not have it.

SOLOMON: I see.

MINISTER: You realise, don't you, that an ambassador's wife is almost as important as he is? She has to do a lot of entertaining for him. For that, a wife must have education, Solly – you understand?

SOLOMON: I think so. I just never thought of it ...

MINISTER: I have seen it with my own eyes, I tell you! In some of these independent African countries, the ministers got married donkey's years ago, and their wives are not educated. They take them to these cocktail parties – and these women can't speak to anybody! They all sit together in a corner, ignored by everybody. We don't want that to happen with —

SOLOMON (*quietly*): Is that why I did not get a ministry?

MINISTER (*gently*): No, Solomon. At least, I don't think
so. The Prime Minister decides those things. (*Heartily*)
Anyway, educated wives are not so important at home
as overseas. An ambassador must embody the
progress of his country within his person. And so
must his wife. If he's uneducated – or his wife is –
those white people will think we're *all* savages!

SOLOMON (*a short silence*): So I can't get the job?

MINISTER: That's up to you, Solomon.

SOLOMON: How?

MINISTER: You can't take your wife to New York.

SOLOMON: That will be difficult, Frederick. We have
been married almost thirty years now. If I go, and
can only see her once a year, our marriage will be
meaningless.

MINISTER (*emotionless*): But you can't go without a wife.

SOLOMON: What? How can I leave my wife behind and
still —

MINISTER: You'll have to marry again. An educated woman
this time.

SOLOMON: You mean I must divorce my wife?

MINISTER: You can't really call it divorce, Solomon. You
were married by native custom.

SOLOMON: I see . . .

MINISTER: So? Will you do it? It's for the good of your
country, you know. You said yourself that you're
prepared to serve the country in any way. This is how
you must serve our country.

SOLOMON: But . . . how do I find a wife, an educated one –
which means a young woman – in such a short time?

MINISTER: Oh, you haven't been doing too badly, Solly?

SOLOMON: What d'you mean?

MINISTER: What about that secretary at party headquarters?

SOLOMON (*defensively*): Which one?

MINISTER: The one you've been – well, you don't want me to go into details, do you? We know these things, Solomon ...

SOLOMON (*dully*): You mean Veronica. I have been trying to keep it quiet.

MINISTER: If that's her name.

SOLOMON: But how can I divorce my wife after all these years? What about my children?

MINISTER: You are a politician, Solomon – or you want to be one. You know that to do well in politics, you have to grab opportunities. This is yours! And we must make sacrifices for our country. All of us!

SOLOMON: But such a big sacrifice! Does the Prime Minister insist?

MINISTER: *I* insist, Solomon. *I* am the Minister of Foreign Affairs. The Prime Minister acts on *my* advice in matters concerning my ministry.

SOLOMON: So it would be useless to talk to him ...

MINISTER (*coldly*): You would be useless to me if you did. (*Heartily*) Now come on, Solly! I don't want to push my authority in your face, you know ... (*Pause.*) So?

SOLOMON: I must think about it.

MINISTER: Of course you must, Solomon ... Though you understand that a man who will have to make quick decisions for his country at the United Nations – with my guidance, of course! Well, – he must be somebody who does not waste time reaching decisions.

SOLOMON (*dully*): Yes. Yes, I understand.

MINISTER (*briskly*): Good. I'll expect to hear from you later this week. Goodbye, Solomon.

SOLOMON: Goodbye, Minister.

SCENE TWO

A room in Solomon's house — the Lounge/Sitting-room.

EMMA: Solomon, why are you still sitting here so late at night? You must come to sleep, my husband.

SOLOMON (*dully*): Just now, Emma.

EMMA: It is three nights now that you do this. What is the trouble?

SOLOMON (*tired exasperation*): No trouble at all, Emma. I'm just thinking.

EMMA: I know you too well, Solomon.

SOLOMON (*sighing*): Ah, sometimes one has to make difficult decisions.

EMMA: If you know what is right and what is wrong, then they are not so difficult to make. You know that, Solly.

SOLOMON: Even if they hurt you?

EMMA: Do you mean hurt me? Or just the person who makes them?

SOLOMON: You, them, me, – anybody!

EMMA: If you know what is right, you make them.

SOLOMON: Like when the district commissioner dismissed me from teaching because of politics?

EMMA: You helped to free our country, did you not? Next month we shall be independent.

SOLOMON: You mean you were never angry with me even though for months I was unemployed?

EMMA: You were right, and I agreed with you.

SOLOMON: Because I was helping us to get independence? What would you say if I now told you that I must leave you because of this independence?

EMMA: Leave me? How leave me?

SOLOMON (*bitterly*): I mean divorce you!

EMMA: Solomon! How can you say such things? I am glad the children are sleeping and cannot hear you!

SOLOMON: I am serious, Emma. They want me to become

an ambassador. To speak at the United Nations.

EMMA: That is a very important job, is it not?

SOLOMON (*extremely bitterly*): Oh, it is, Emma. Very! That is why they say I must divorce you. Because you are not educated.

EMMA: They think I will shame you?

SOLOMON: Yes.

EMMA: I would be lost in a place like that. It is somewhere in America, is it not?

SOLOMON: In New York.

EMMA (*thoughtfully*): Yes, in New York. Do you want to go?

SOLOMON: It is my big chance. If I refuse it – well, I don't know.

EMMA: You have done big things for our country.

SOLOMON: I have suffered for my country. Unemployment and even jail.

EMMA: Now it is my time to suffer.

SOLOMON (*with relieved surprise*): You agree then, Emma?

EMMA: No. I do not agree, Solomon. But you want to go. And I cannot go. My father and mother gave me to you as a wife, so you must do for me what you think is right.

SOLOMON: But I don't think this is right!

EMMA: But you want to go. I know you too well, Solly. If you do not get what you want, there will be no peace for you or for me. You will make life unhappy for both of us.

SOLOMON: Oh, Emma, Emma! Am I that bad? Why can't I pretend to you? Why couldn't I pretend to be strong and decisive to you – I'm sorry, Emma.

EMMA: Sorry? You forget that I was not born in the town, Solly. I am a country woman, where men are expected to make all the decisions.

SOLOMON: But what will the children say about a divorce? Especially Monica?

EMMA: That one is worse than the white people, I know.

H

Too much education. Monica! My own daughter, and most of the time I have no idea how she thinks, or why?

SOLOMON: Yes, Monica. What is she going to say when you – when we tell her?

EMMA (*ironically*): *You* must tell her. It is you two who are educated, and *you* know how she thinks. So you can tell her in a way that she will understand.

SOLOMON: You are laughing at me now, Emma. Don't you think—

EMMA: No, Solly. You must tell her. It is with her that you must show what a strong man you are in your mind. With me you can be easy and tell me whatever you think. But with her you must be strong. That way she will always respect you.

SOLOMON: Have I not been strong with her?

EMMA: Oh, you have been, my dear. But in the way of the white man.

SOLOMON: D'you want me to put her over my knee and—

EMMA (*laughing*): That is not our only way, Solomon. You know that.

SOLOMON: Well, I'll talk to her. But I may need your help. So you must be there.

EMMA: Very well, Solomon. We'll do it tomorrow. But please come to bed now – it's so late.

SCENE THREE

The dining-room or the kitchen of Solomon's home. Next morning at breakfast. Wakey-wakey music on radio. Door opens and is banged shut.

MONICA (*cheerily*): Good morning, Papa. Good morning, Mama.

SOLOMON: Good morning, Monica.

EMMA (*scolding softly*): You must not always be late for breakfast, my child. Eating in a hurry is not good—

MONICA (*laughing easily*): I know, Mama. It's not good for your digestion! But then a good digestion means you put on weight – and that's the last thing I want to do.

EMMA: Ah, you modern girls. Figure, figure – that's all you think about. When I was a girl—

SOLOMON (*uneasily*): Is the modern girl going to be home early tonight?

MONICA: We-l-l, I don't know yet, Papa. Perhaps. It depends on what Joseph and I decide to do tonight. But I'll probably be home about—

EMMA (*motherly*): And how is Joseph, Monica? I have not seen him for a long time!

MONICA (*laughing with Solomon at an old family joke*): Oh, yes, we know, Mama! Three days can be a long time, when a loving mother like you is worrying if her daughter is ever going to get married. Oh, don't worry, Mama. Joseph will marry me any time I say so.

SOLOMON (*jokingly*): Isn't it for the poor boy to decide?

MONICA (*mock surprise*): Has any man ever done so, Papa? Eh, Mama? Doesn't he know yet that it is the women –

EMMA: Hush now, my child! That is not the way for children to talk.

MONICA (*some annoyance*): Oh, of course! Always a baby! Even if I'm grown up.

SOLOMON (*hurriedly*): I was asking if you're coming straight home because I – we want to talk to you, Monica. Something important.

MONICA (*after a brief, offended silence; grudgingly*): A family conference?

SOLOMON: Well, yes. I suppose you can call it that.

MONICA: What's it about?

SOLOMON: We'll tell you tonight, my girl.

MONICA (*a bit sharp*): The little girl treatment again!

SOLOMON (*resignedly*): Well, it's about my new post in the government. After independence.

MONICA (*more friendly, with curiosity*): Are they going to give you a big job at last, Papa? What is it? They've already appointed all the ministers, and—

EMMA: Tonight, school teacher. You are getting late.

MONICA (*ironically*): That's right, Mama. Well, I'm off, people! See you tonight.

SCENE FOUR

As for Scene Two. Same evening. Scene opens with closing of the BPC News.

SOLOMON: Hm, hm, that makes it ten past seven, and she isn't here yet.

MONICA (*cheerily*): Good evening, Mama, Papa! Here I am – almost on the dot!

EMMA: Hm. Did you see Joseph today?

MONICA (*laughing lightly*): Yes, Mama. And your-son-in-law-to-be will be coming to see *you* later. When he comes to pick me up. Well, Papa? Here I am, ready to hear all the good news!

SOLOMON: It's good news and it's bad news too, my girl.

MONICA: How d'you mean, Papa?

SOLOMON (*clearing his throat*): Well, as you know, we're going to be independent very soon. Something we have fought for for a very long time. And independence means that we must have ambassadors who will represent their country—

MONICA (*excitedly*): Oh, Papa! Is that what you're going to be? I'm—

SOLOMON: Just wait a minute, my girl. Just listen quietly and understand everything I'm going to tell you. Remember I said it was good news and bad news too. (*Pause.*) Now, Monica, you're an educated girl – one of the best educated we have. *I* saw to that. So you will understand when I say that an ambassador – especially a senior one like I'm going to be – needs to have the kind of wife who can mix properly with the officials of foreign governments. Especially these imperialist governments, who don't really believe that we can rule ourselves. Is that not so?

MONICA (*slowly, after a pause*): Go on, Papa.

SOLOMON (*clearing his throat*): Your mother is not that kind of woman. She is not educated.

MONICA: So?

SOLOMON: So I will not get this posting if . . . if . . .

MONICA (*fiercely*): Go on!

EMMA (*speaking into the silence that follows*): What he means, my child, is that he wants to divorce me. And marry an educated girl.

MONICA: What! Is that true, Papa? You want to – I can't believe it! I always thought you loved Mama —

SOLOMON: What has love got to do with it?

MONICA: Everything! Love is the most important thing in the world!

SOLOMON: That's your white man's education talking, my girl. Respect! That is the important thing! When your mother and I got married, respect was the thing that mattered.

MONICA: And now you don't respect her any more? She can't read and write well enough for an ambassador's wife?

SOLOMON: History is moving fast, and your mother has been left behind.

MONICA: Do you agree to this, Mama?

EMMA: What is agree? What can I do? What can any of us do? I must not stand in your father's way, my child.

SOLOMON: I am glad to hear you speak like that, Emma.

MONICA: Well, I'm not! I don't want to have divorced parents!

SOLOMON: I am doing it for our country.

MONICA: Our country! Is this 'country' thing more important than the people who live in it? I say to hell—

EMMA: Monica! Remember who you are talking to!

MONICA: All right, I'm sorry I swore in front of you. But tell me, what is this country if not us? Tell me that!

SOLOMON (*quietly explanatory*): We are the country – each single one of us. But the individual is of no importance. It is only as a people – as a nation – that we matter. Each *one* of us is nothing without the others.

MONICA: I don't see these ministers we have behaving like that. As far as they're concerned, they're the only things that matter! Driving around in their big, shiny cars as if—

EMMA: They are big and important men, my child.

MONICA: And your husband is also going to become big and important? So he starts by driving his big and shiny ambitions over you – over the faithfulness, respect and everything you have given him for more than a quarter of a century? If that's the meaning of importance, I'm glad I'm not important!

EMMA: Let your father speak, my child. I want to understand him again.

MONICA: But what more can he say? He's said it all! And you sit there quietly, saying there's nothing you can do. Well, you can if you want to! You can—

SOLOMON: Monica! You'd better stop right there!

MONICA: All right, Father. Tell us. Who *are* you going to marry? Who is fit to be an ambassador's wife?

SOLOMON: We don't have to talk about that now.

EMMA: But you must tell her, Solomon. As our eldest child she must know everything.

SOLOMON: Very well, you know her. Veronica. The niece of the Minister of Education.

MONICA: What! That – that –

SOLOMON: Be very careful what you say about her, Monica. She is going to be your *mother* too, so you better start showing her some respect.

MONICA: She was my junior at secondary school – and not a bright girl at all, from what I heard and saw of her. Veronica!

SOLOMON: It's probably just as well she's not as clever as you! Because you're so full of cheekiness and arguments!

MONICA: And she has accepted your proposal, Papa? Or wasn't that necessary? Is this to be *her* sacrifice to the nation? Her uncle, the minister, just tells you to marry her for the good of the nation and – snap – it's all arranged?

SOLOMON: She has accepted my proposal.

MONICA: You mean you just made an appointment for her to come to your office at party headquarters, popped the question and she said yes?

SOLOMON: Of course not!

MONICA: D'you realise what you're saying, Papa? You're implying that you have been having a love affair with this – this Veronica?

SOLOMON (*furious*): What business is that of yours? Eh?

MONICA: So it is true. Did you know about this, Mama?

EMMA: We always know these things, my child.

MONICA: And you accept it?

SOLOMON: What kind of a child did I bring to life? What has this education—(*Knock at the door.*) Who's that?

MONICA: I'll answer. I think it's Joe. I told you he was coming tonight. (*At door*) Hello, Joe. Come in.

JOSEPH: Hello, dear. (*Entering.*) Good evening, sir. Good evening, Mother. I hope you are both well tonight.

SOLOMON: Good evening, Joseph.

EMMA: Good evening, my son.

MONICA: None of us are *really* well tonight, Joe – at least not in spirit.

SOLOMON: Be quiet, Monica!

MONICA: Quiet? But Joe is as good as one of the family – what *was* a family, anyway. Don't you think he has a right to know what's happening to the family he's marrying into?

JOSEPH: I'm afraid I don't quite understand what's going on . . .

EMMA: Would you like to have some tea, Joseph?

JOSEPH: Yes, Mother, please.

MONICA: Well, go on, Father. Tell Joseph what's happened.

SOLOMON: I suppose you have heard, Joseph. That I have been offered an ambassadorship?

JOSEPH: Yes, sir. And I was very pleased. But I was not sure if it was time to congratulate you.

MONICA: It's not. It is a time for crying and the gnashing of teeth. How can anybody ever make such a demand of another man?

SOLOMON: It's not a demand, Monica.

MONICA: Tell me, Joe, d'you think it's right?

JOSEPH: What demand? I – I'm not sure I understand.

MONICA: Yes, you do! You're in the Prime Minister's office. Answer a simple question! Is it right for your government to demand that my father divorce my mother – just to become an ambassador.

JOSEPH: Divorce! . . . Well, they want to send him on a very important mission—

MONICA: The importance has nothing to do with it! It's the principle that matters! I say it's immoral!

SOLOMON: But you're missing the whole point, Monica.

EMMA: Here is the tea. I don't know what time we shall eat supper tonight with all this talk.

MONICA: You've come back just in time, Mama. Papa has finally come to the whole point. Go on, Papa.

SOLOMON: It's simple. I have explained the duties of an ambassador's wife, and it is quite obvious that she must be an educated woman.

MONICA: I see ... d'you mean that even if they hadn't made the condition you'd still've divorced Mama to marry that girl?

SOLOMON (*sharp*): I didn't say that.

MONICA: But you mean that.

SOLOMON: Joseph, please explain the facts of life to this hot-headed idealist of yours!

JOSEPH: Well – I don't know how to say it, sir. All I think I can say is that your father's right, Monica. A senior ambassador, like he's going to be, needs an educated wife.

MONICA: And what about the Private Secretary to the Prime Minister? Am I educated enough for you, Joe? All I have is a B.A. you know.

JOSEPH (*laughing nervously*): You'll do. You're educated enough.

MONICA: Enough! Just as my mother was educated enough for my father twenty-seven years ago? But what's going to happen when they offer you a bigger job?

JOSEPH: I'm quite happy with my job.

MONICA: So was my father, twenty-seven years ago!

JOSEPH: You don't have to start quarrelling with me now, Monica.

MONICA: I'm not quarrelling ...

EMMA (*interrupting*): Why don't we talk about something else? It is not good to have hot talk with your food. (*Turns to Joseph*) And how have you been?

Conversation and business ad lib during tea-drinking. Emma clears table and begins to exit with remains of cake etc.

SOLOMON: Ah, that was very good tea, my dear. And now I shall go and help you wash up! Will you young people stay for supper, or are you going out?

JOSEPH: Well, sir, we were planning to go—

MONICA: I don't think I want to go anywhere. I couldn't face people tonight.

JOSEPH: All right.

SOLOMON (*going off – with tray of crockery; at a distance*): Hold the door for me, Emma, please.

JOSEPH: Whew! I didn't know I was going to walk into anything like this, sweetheart.

MONICA: Would you've preferred not to be involved?

JOSEPH: Well, to tell you the truth, yes. I mean, your father's an important person, and I couldn't disagree with him and—

MONICA (*eagerly*): Then you think he's wrong?

JOSEPH: Well – don't let's jump to conclusions, sweetheart. He was right on some things, but not on others.

MONICA: I see ... Even though you don't make sense, I see.

JOSEPH: Oh, you're a bright girl, sweetheart. The most intelligent girl in this country.

MONICA: Is that why you want to marry me?

JOSEPH: Well, that's got something to do with it.

MONICA: Would you still want to marry me if I was just an ordinary girl? Without a London University degree?

JOSEPH: How can I answer that? I've only known you as such a girl.

MONICA: But let's say you'd met me here, before I went to London?

JOSEPH: That's an unfair question, sweetheart.

MONICA: Oh, no, it's not! What do you love? Me or my education?

JOSEPH (*exasperated*): Monica, people are what they are because of their background. You have the personality I love, partly because of your education. I know I wouldn't love you if you were uneducated.

MONICA: So it is my education! Just like Papa married Mama because she could read and write! Today you love me because my education is good enough for you. But in ten years' time? He said Mama didn't keep up with him. What happens if I don't keep up with you? Will you also—

JOSEPH: None of us can look into the future, Monica.

MONICA: So! When we get married, you'll promise to love and protect me – till death do us part. But you won't mean any of it, will you? Because you can't foretell the future! You're a bright young man, Joseph – one of our very best. And though you say you can't foretell the future, you know it's going to be bright enough to fulfil your ambitions! And what about poor little me then? Eh? Tell me that!

JOSEPH (*light sarcasm*): If there's going to be any bright future in this country, you'll be there, Monica. I know you that well.

MONICA: Then you know me better than I know myself! I'm just a school teacher now, and I'm happy with it. I'm satisfied. I don't want to become a politician who places his country before his own family. All I want to be is a good wife to you and a good mother to our children. Like my mother! Oh yes! *I* am *proud* of my mother, if nobody else is! I want to be like her. So are you going to abandon me too when you have the chance to be a big shot who needs the other kind of a wife?

JOSEPH: I don't know what to say when you speak like that, Monica. All I can say is that I love you, and I want you to be my wife.

MONICA: And all I can say is that I'm not so sure if I still want to marry you. Perhaps I should look for a junior civil servant without your ambitions. You men of ambition! Who can trust you?

Door opens.

SOLOMON (*approaching*): Well, supper will be ready soon, my children! I'm sorry that you had to find us in the middle of such an embarrassing argument, Joseph, my son. But now everything is all right. The old woman and I finalised things in the kitchen.

JOSEPH: I'm glad to hear that, sir.

MONICA: And I'm glad for you too, Papa – though I'm sorry for you as well. And while you have been finalising things, we have been doing the opposite in here. We have broken things up.

JOSEPH (*pleading*): Oh Monica!

SOLOMON: What d'you mean by that?

MONICA: Oh, yes, Papa. There's going to be more than one divorce in this family. At least I think so. I haven't quite made up my mind yet. But I'm thinking that I shouldn't make the same mistake my mother made. Because Joe is ambitious like you, Papa. And you ambitious men cannot be trusted. (*Solomon protests.*) At least by unambitious women like me and my mother. Veronica probably said she'd marry you because you were a big shot. Unlike the men of her own age, who are still working their way up. She's just the kind of wife you need to push you and push you to the top.

SOLOMON (*interrupts*): But, Monica, you don't . . . !

MONICA: But don't think you'll get there! Because the brilliant young men like Joe will already be waiting near the top – pushed up there by their ambitious wives. And they'll kick you in the teeth when you try and go past them to the very top.

JOE (*interrupts*): How can you . . . ?

MONICA: I don't think I want to be involved when that happens. So maybe I should disengage myself now, and leave the opportunities to you great men of ambition!

SOLOMON: Monica!

JOSEPH: Monica, please!

MONICA: I don't think I want to see you again, Joseph. Here's your ring . . . If you want me, Papa, I shall be in the kitchen – with mother.

Sharp exit. Momentary hush. Sobbing audible off; soft consolatory noises . . .

QUICK CURTAIN

Maama

Go and catch a falling star,
Get with child a mandrake root,
Tell me where all past years are,
Or who cleft the Devil's foot;
Teach me to hear mermaids singing,
Or to keep off envy's stinging,
    And find
    What wind
Serves to advance an honest mind.

John Donne

CHARACTERS

Akwaamu, *The Chief*
Ataapem, *The Chief's advisor*
Maami Efua, *The Chief's youngest wife*
Maama, *The daughter of Maami Efua*
Maami Araba, *The Chief's eldest wife*
Joseph Baden, *A medical practitioner*
Kodwo ⎫
Kweku ⎭ *Peasants*

Scene: A village in ancient Gold Coast

MAAMA

SCENE ONE

A desert heath

ATA: I don't think you're right, Nana. You mustn't send Maami Efua away just because she hasn't given you a child.

CHIEF: I have many reasons for sending Maami Efua away, Ataapem. You know that in our village a chief's wealth is measured by the number of his children and wives. The witch doctor says Maami Efua will never have a child. It could be that she has angered some god who has brought this punishment on her. Don't you think that if I keep her in my house we may all suffer the wrath of the god?

ATA: As I see it, the gods may have done this to test your love for your wife. She may have a child hidden somewhere, you know.

CHIEF: You carry your frivolities everywhere, Ataapem. Why should she pretend to be childless? Do you think she is mad? A woman without a child is a curse to her people. No, I shouldn't listen to you.

ATA: What does it profit a man to seek treasures in children?

CHIEF: Don't speak to me in parables. Your wisdom is a very shallow one. It does profit a man a great deal, greater than you can imagine. Maami Efua will go whether you think I am right or not.

ATA: The final decision rests with you, of course, but

remember, Nana, that the course of life is obscure and uncertain.

CHIEF: Life is what you make it, my child. If you want to be rich and you have faith you will be rich.

ATA: In the same way, if you want to have children you will have them if your faith is strong enough.

CHIEF: That's right.

ATA: Well, then, are you blaming Maami Efua because her faith is not strong enough?

CHIEF: Children, though, are given by the gods.

ATA: If children are given by the gods, why don't you pour down libation to the gods to grant you your wish?

CHIEF: Do you think we can harass the peace of the gods for our own selfish ends?

ATA: But Nana . . .

CHIEF: Stop talking nonsense. I can't bear such a situation.

ATA: Of course you can. Man must be able to face what comes his way. He must accept it as his lot and be satisfied with what he has, looking up to Jesus, the man who laid down his life for all mankind. In the hour of his distress he must cherish the hope that the future holds something good for him, because sorrows cannot last forever.

CHIEF: I know! I know! That's what you've learnt from that erudite priest. But I am the chief and in this matter my word is most important. Maami Efua ought to go back.

ATA: You did send her away once, for two years.

CHIEF: Quite true! I called her back because I wasn't strong enough. Mind you, I wouldn't have done that for any of my other wives.

ATA: She did write to say she was expecting a child, did she not?

CHIEF: That's right! But where is the child?

ATA: That's what I said. The child may be with the parents of Maami Efua. (*Pause.*) The doctor said that Maami Efua is not barren.

CHIEF: The witch doctor?

ATA: No, no, the educated one. He knows better than the witch doctor.

CHIEF: Why do you say that? That doctor is in love with Maami Efua, I can tell you that. Maami Efua is beautiful, educated and she gets on better with the doctor than with me. I don't believe in educated doctors.

ATA: From where else will you seek help for Maami Efua?

CHIEF: I have asked myself that question many times. I always got the same answer: the rustling of the trees, the ominous hoots of an owl, the dryness of a sultry wind and the burning heat of the sun, all tell me that Maami Efua must return to her parents.

ATA: There's the doctor.

CHIEF: Where?

ATA: There, taking pictures.

CHIEF: He probes into everyone's private affairs with that ugly camera. He's an idiot. Come along.

Exit the chief. Enter the doctor.

DOCTOR: It's a very hot afternoon.

ATA: Yes, doctor.

DOCTOR: How's the chief and his wife?

ATA: The chief is rather desperate, doctor.

DOCTOR: Desperate? Why should he be?

ATA: About his wife, Maami Efua.

DOCTOR: What about her?

ATA: You know she can't have a child.

DOCTOR: Yes, I know. Why should that make him desperate? Why should a man despair, at all? Simply because there has been a failure caused by a knotty snag somewhere? Look! If life were all a rose without a thorn, man would lose the power to reason. Don't you think so?

ATA (*mystified*): Yes.

DOCTOR: Tell the chief that.

ATA: I can't.

DOCTOR: Why?

ATA: He has already made up his mind to send Maami Efua away.

DOCTOR: Is your chief such a bastard?

ATA: No, his father is still alive.

DOCTOR: How many children has he?

ATA: Twenty-eight! Already three of his wives are pregnant.

DOCTOR: I see.

ATA: Would you like to talk to him? He might change his mind.

DOCTOR: No, I don't meddle in the affairs of other people, especially where a chief like that is involved. Goodbye.

ATA: Goodbye, doctor.

Exeunt in different directions. Enter two peasants returning from the farm.

KODWO (*wiping his brow*): It's been a terrible day.

KWEKU: Yeah, one of them bastard days.

KODWO: The sun's going down.

KWEKU: Yeah, we need cool our hearts a bit.

KODWO: You want some water?

KWEKU: No, no! I've got me beer with me all the time.

KODWO: D'you like beer very much?

KWEKU: Just palm-wine. That's my beer. You know, matter of taste, like. Just like I told you. Some blokes like children, some don't.

KODWO: I suppose it depend.

KWEKU: Yeah, it depend on your performing power.

KODWO: You don't expect a man to sweat in the hot sun the whole day and come home ready for it.

KWEKU: Ready for what?

KODWO: Ah, Kweku, you know what I'm talking about. Ready for the kill.

KWEKU: Yeah, a man can kill by loving too much.

KODWO: It's been a nasty hot day.

KWEKU: Yeah, the night will be one of them nights. The witches come down tonight.

KODWO: What witches?

KWEKU: Them witches who hate men.

KODWO: Ah, I heard about them.

KWEKU: I fear them witches even when they give gifts.

KODWO: Could be the chief would do with one of them gifts.

KWEKU: Once in a while, a tree or a stone or even a snake may turn into a man. But the gift of a witch . . . not me. I'd rather die first.

KODWO: Yeah.

KWEKU: You know, Kodwo, Nature owes us nothing. We owe Nature everything.

KODWO: That's what them gentlemen call wisdom of the ages.

KWEKU: I ain't no 'gentleman', friend. I dig the soil and turn it over, that's all. I know a good soil from a bad one . . . that's all.

KODWO: Hey, Kweku, do you know the doctor?

KWEKU: The witch doctor?

KODWO: No, the educated one.

KWEKU: What's the matter?

KODWO: He's chasing the chief's wife.

KWEKU: The chief has fifteen wives; which one?

KODWO: The new one.

KWEKU: That's not true, Kodwo. That woman is sick.

KODWO: Sick?

KWEKU: Yeah, she is under a curse.

KODWO: A curse?

KWEKU: The doctor tried to help her, but no use. The chief's too jealous.

KODWO: So what's happened?

KWEKU: I don't know. That don't bother me. My wife is waiting for me. One is enough for me.

KODWO: It's bad enough, I mean having a nagging wife around.

KWEKU: You've got a nagging wife?

KODWO: Terrible!

KWEKU: Probably you snore in bed. Well, do you?

KODWO: How the hell can I know?

KWEKU: My wife is waiting. She don't snore in bed. She don't nag. When I say to her: sit down, she sits down, get up, she gets up, turn round, she . . . you know what I mean.

Exeunt. Steadily the sky darkens and night falls. A strong wind gathers force, turns into a hurricane. Thunder and lightning. Weird voices rise on the heath. It begins to rain. For a time there is no light around except the flashes of lightning, no earthly sound but the pattering of the rain and the hoots of an owl mixed with the weird cries. Then gradually all dies away. A distant starlight and a quarter moon. A dog is baying. The moon enters the clouds, the starlight disappears and the baying fades away. It dawns. The chirping of birds, the sound of automobiles, the tip-tap of dew on the wet ground. Dawn breaks. Morning. The sun begins to shine. A light wind blows. It is afternoon.

SCENE TWO

The Chief's Garden

CHIEF: Twelve years! Twelve years and I still remember

her. Isn't it strange, Ataapem, that after twelve years
I still love Maami Efua?

ATA: She is a very faithful woman, Nana. No woman
would wait for divorce all that long.

CHIEF: Of course, I haven't divorced her yet. I can always
call her back, can't I?

ATA: Well, you are the chief and she is your subject.

CHIEF: Do you think I should ask her back?

ATA: Do you want to call her back?

CHIEF: One part of me says yes, the other part says no.
I think I am behaving like a fool. Only fools can't
make up their mind. Yes, yes, I will call her back.
Why should I fool myself? Some have got, they can't
use; others haven't got but they want to use; I have
got and I am going to use. But some idiots will think
I am a fool. No, I won't call her back. After all, I have
fourteen wives, two for each day. I must admit I get
very exhausted. (*Pause.*) Why don't you say something?
(*Pause.*) I have already sent for her.

ATA: It is not very often that a chief behaves wisely in these
parts.

CHIEF: Do you approve of my action, or not?

ATA: I don't know, Nana. You always have the last
word.

CHIEF: Do you resent that?

ATA: No, how can I? But twelve years . . . many things
have changed. After twelve years do you still believe
in polygamy?

CHIEF: So long as I have the power to perform, why not?

ATA: You just said that you are exhausted.

CHIEF: I never said I am exhausted. After a little sleep
I feel refreshed and ready. You probably think that
I will appear ridiculous in the eyes of my subjects,
but here, the chief sets the fashion, you know. Very
soon you will see how many people will be running
round looking for their deserted wives and husbands,

impotent husbands who had run away to avoid disgrace before their wives, cultured wives who longed after variety to avoid boredom. Anyway, I have sent for her. She may come or she may not come. In any case I will make ready to welcome her. Maybe she will come back; after all, she is still my wife and I love her. (*Pause.*) Tomorrow we shall start cutting down the oak tree in the garden.

ATA: The oak tree! That reminds me: great things have small beginnings.

CHIEF: You are too commonplace, Ataapem.

MAAMA (*enters*): My mother says I must come to the chief and pay my respects. If the chief likes me for a daughter, he will ask my mother to come to his presence.

CHIEF: And who is your mother?

MAAMA: My mother is Maami Efua.

CHIEF: And who is Maami Efua's husband?

MAAMA: I do not know. I am told that my father is a chief.

CHIEF: Ha, nonsense. You don't look like a chief's daughter.

ATA: Doubt is a helpless feeling, Nana.

CHIEF: Where is your mother?

MAAMA: She is waiting.

CHIEF: Go and bring your mother.

MAAMA: Yes, stranger. (*Exit.*)

CHIEF: She called me stranger.

ATA: And so you are to her. You should have embraced her, Nana. You ... we don't belong to her world, the world she alone knows, poor child! She bears a part of her mother's griefs.

CHIEF: Now you see! Do you now realize the amount of strength I have in me! I didn't send her away empty that day, you know.

ATA: How do you know that girl is truly your daughter?

CHIEF: You always believed Maami Efua is a faithful wife.

ATA: And so she is. Yet somehow, that child seems to carry the fate of men in her.

CHIEF: You have too much imagination. She is my daughter. Stop babbling nonsense. I must think of how best to welcome my dearest wife. Ask my eldest wife to come here at once.

ATA: Yes Nana. (*Exit.*)

Enter Maami Efua and Maama.

CHIEF: You are already here, Maami Efua. I have had no time to plan a true royal welcome. Though twelve years may have passed since you went away, you look younger than when you left.

EFUA: Nothing is impossible, Nana.

CHIEF: True! So you have a daughter, I see.

EFUA: Yes, we have a daughter.

CHIEF: How old is she.

MAAMA: Twelve years.

CHIEF: And what is your name?

MAAMA: Maama.

CHIEF: A powerful name, but I should have given you a name.

MAAMA: It makes no difference.

CHIEF: It's all right having such a beautiful daughter, but I wonder if she can comport herself as a royal daughter should, since she has not been brought up in this royal palace.

Enter Araba and Ataapem.

CHIEF: Maami Efua is back, Maami Araba. And this is my daughter. You must welcome them both into this house as custom demands. Come, daughter, I will show you to your many, many brothers and sisters, and to your step-mothers. (*Exit with Maama.*)

ARABA: So you came back.

EFUA: Yes, I came back.

ARABA: Did you come back to die?

EFUA: I have come back to stay.

ARABA: Humph! And is that all you could bring? A doll? Your daughter is a doll.

EFUA: She is much more beautiful, much more intelligent than all your children put together, you ugly bitch.

ARABA: Dare you call me a bitch?

EFUA: The time's past when I could endure your arrogance in silence, when you could taunt me and make me cry. Now I am a woman.

ARABA: Are you? You look more a girl than when you left. How can we believe that you did not steal the girl?

EFUA: You don't have to believe that, you wizened witch. Was it not you who always used your spell to prevent me from having a child? The spell is now broken. Say it isn't so, you witch. Deny it.

ARABA: Shut up! Shut up before I lose my head.

ATA: That's enough! Enough from both of you. What are you quarrelling about now? You have no cause to quarrel. Go into the house, Maami Efua. Perhaps the chief is already waiting for you in his bedroom. He is always refreshed and ready. You Maami Araba, you are far older than Maami Efua. You ought to be more sensible than that. Have you no human feelings? You must be more sensible than that.

Solitary drumming.

SCENE THREE

A desert heath

CHIEF: She is wonderful, Ataapem. A wonderful daughter.

ATA: You are the luckiest of men, Nana.

CHIEF: She is quite different from any of my other children and rather wise for her age.

ATA: She must have been kept specially for you by Nature, Nana.

CHIEF: She must have been. All-knowing Nature, aware of a mother's suffering, has given to the world one of her own mysterious children.

ATA: Would it be wise if we made a sacrifice to Nature to thank her?

CHIEF: That I have already done, but I will do more.

ATA: The gift of Nature must not be lightly esteemed for it could bring sure happiness or uncertain disaster.

CHIEF: You must get married, Ataapem. You must get married and start sowing seeds.

ATA: I will bide my time, Nana. I can see no cause to rush into anything. If it were possible to have everything for nothing, I would not choose to sit at home and twiddle my thumbs. I'd rather work for my living.

CHIEF: Look at her coming. Isn't she a daughter among daughters?

ATA: Her presence in your house has already worsened the feud between Maami Efua and your other wives. Would it not be wise to show less affection towards her?

CHIEF: At last your too-much wisdom is breeding in you womanish fears.   (*Enter Maama.*)

CHIEF: You've come in good time, my daughter. Your presence always seems to weave a spell over my senses.

MAAMA: Is it possible for a child to advise a king?

CHIEF: Yes, it is possible, if that child contains in herself the wisdom of the ages.

MAAMA: Wisdom?

CHIEF: She must be all-knowing, like Nature herself.

MAAMA: And if that child is a man?

CHIEF: He must not only know how to hold a gun. He

must also be brave enough to drink hemlock without any sign of pain. He must be refreshed and ready, always.

MAAMA: A man dies without pain only when the gods approve.

CHIEF: I am glad you believe in gods, my daisy.

MAAMA: Don't you believe in gods?

CHIEF: Yes, I do. Very much.

MAAMA: Then why?

CHIEF: Why 'why', my daisy?

MAAMA: Why will you disturb the peace of a god?

CHIEF: What god my daughter?

MAAMA: The tree in your garden. The oak tree. You want to cut down that tree. That tree is a god.

CHIEF: Did your mother send you tell me that?

MAAMA: No.

CHIEF: What is that paper in your hand?

MAAMA: It is a poem.

CHIEF: Let's see. Did you write?

MAAMA: The doctor wrote it.

CHIEF (*reads*): Madame tortoise,
why do you move like you never
ate?
as if you are asleep in that brindled
shell of yours?
Madame tortoise
what is this secret you share with
eternity?
when by such idling you outran the
swiftest hare in that race of life?

MAAMA: Do you like it?

CHIEF: Ataapem, can you see any hidden meaning in these lines? Daughter I forbid you to see that doctor again.

MAAMA: Speak for me Ataapem. You understand, please speak for me.

CHIEF: Daughter, I understand why you and your mother are so keen on preserving that oak tree. Ataapem, go and warn that doctor. There will be no more moonlight embraces under that tree. It will be felled before the sun goes down.

Exit Ataapem.

CHIEF: What do you call this poem?

MAAMA: Do you want to die?

CHIEF: Every man knows he must die.

MAAMA: Why are you so hard on me?

CHIEF: I have shown too much affection.

MAAMA: Ataapem, wait for me. Wait for me, Ataapem.

Exit. Enter Maami Efua.

CHIEF: You are growing too bold, Maami Efua.

EFUA: I have come to plead with you once again not to cut down that tree.

CHIEF: Have you? Well, I have something very interesting to tell you. The tree goes down before nightfall.

Exit.

EFUA: I wish I had never been born.

DOCTOR (*enter*): So you came back.

EFUA: Yes, I came back.

DOCTOR: And with a child.

EFUA: And with a child.

DOCTOR: Very good. Your own child?

EFUA: Of course my own child. Don't you believe me?

DOCTOR: You are not a very good liar, are you?

EFUA: How do you mean?

DOCTOR: I told you you can't have a child.

EFUA: Are you God?

DOCTOR: No, I'm not God. That's why I know you cannot have a child.

EFUA: That child is mine.

DOCTOR: No one has disputed that; but rumours, like birds, have very swift wings. Walk carefully on sodden ground, young lady. Look! I have taken countless pictures with this camera. Nature, after all, is not all that beautiful, though we humans think it is, and we are human. Beauty conceals profound tragedies.

EFUA: You don't know half the things I know.

DOCTOR: No, I don't and I count myself very lucky. It is not easy after all, to come to terms with oneself, is it?

EFUA: I do know myself.

DOCTOR: No man but you can know what you know. How's your husband?

EFUA: The chief?

DOCTOR: Yes, isn't he your husband?

EFUA: Yes, he is my husband.

DOCTOR: Aren't you happy to be his wife?

EFUA: I didn't say that.

DOCTOR: No, you didn't. It would be ridiculous if you said so. You waited ... how many years ... twelve years. That's right, you waited twelve years for him to call you back, didn't you? I must say few women would have had your kind of courage to keep their matrimonial promise: 'for better, for worse'.

EFUA: I was desperate.

DOCTOR: Those twelve years might have been momentous years, years of great change and strange developments. Still, you brought back a child into the bargain.

EFUA: My child.

DOCTOR: Your child, I quite appreciate that. But you see, I have come face to face with a greater part of life's treacheries. I know the hearts of all men, their follies, their ignorance, their lack of foresight and insight. I know that we search for happiness only to destroy ourselves.

EFUA: Do you also think the child is not mine? That I might have stolen it?

DOCTOR: I think the child is yours; but I know too that you are quite incapable of giving birth. And that is that. Goodbye.

EFUA: Don't go yet, doctor.

DOCTOR: What do you want?

EFUA: I'm not a very happy woman.

DOCTOR: You don't have to tell me that.

EFUA: Why?

DOCTOR: It's written in your face.

EFUA: What must I do?

DOCTOR: You must ask the chief that. He is your husband. Good afternoon.(*Exit.*)

EFUA: Goodbye, doctor. (*She breaks into sobs.*)

ATA (*enters*): Maami Efua!

EFUA: What must I do? Ataapem, what must I do?

ATA: Stop weeping, Maami Efua. The world is larger than our minds. When misfortune comes, therefore, we must bear it.

EFUA: Misfortune? Is the tree cut already?

ATA: No, not yet. But stop weeping.

EFUA: When you've known no such suffering as I have, it is easier to console. But I wish I were dead.

ATA: Nonsense. Dead because of an oak tree?

EFUA: You hardly know. Cut that tree and you will destroy everything.

ATA: Stop weeping. Why, will you go on weeping till the crack of doom? Our elders have said: he who has suffered much in life continues a-sorrowing even after death. I can hardly understand this obsession with an oak tree. Obsession with a handsome man, I can understand. But I can't make out what all this is about.

EFUA: Go away! Please, go away.

ATA: What disaster will there be if the tree is cut down?

EFUA: Go away! Go away!

ATA: Go away? Unhappy woman! What life is this? Childless unhappy, are you still unhappy in a child?

EFUA: What must I do? Oh, what must I do? How shall I ever find happiness? Because I married a chief I have thrown myself among people where instead of honour, friendship, and happiness, there is nothing but bitter mockery, such as the heart cannot stand.

Exit Ataapem. Maami Efua continues to cry. Enter Kweku.

KWEKU: Are you not the chief's wife?

EFUA: Who are you?

KWEKU: Why are you crying, madam?

EFUA: I do not know.

KWEKU: Is your daughter dead, or are you crying because you are a noble woman?

EFUA: Who are you?

KWEKU: This place is no good for crying, madam. I know you are a Christian and do not believe in gods; but the gods of this place . . . and there are many here . . . they will be angry with you. They say you disturb their peace on a hot afternoon like this. You must go home, madam. The sun goes down very soon. (*Exit.*)

EFUA: I will go to the chief and make a clean breast of it. Maybe he will have pity when he knows the truth. If not, let me be mistress of my own fate. (*Exit.*)

SCENE FOUR

The Chief's garden

CHIEF: Ataapem, I believe Maami Araba is right. Maami Efua may be deceiving us. You agree yourself that the girl does not resemble any of us. She may be a

daughter of someone ... whom **Maami** Efua has
either stolen or borrowed.

ATA: I don't think you are right, Nana.

CHIEF: But until we know the truth there will be no peace
for me in this house.

ATA: After all, Nana, it's nothing to sacrifice your peace
to her happiness. Remember, you are the chief and all
those who mock her are your subjects. This is the
reward of polygamy: no peace, no rest, continuous
aching of the mind. Nana, it is dangerous to know too
much.

CHIEF: You have been a good advisor to me, Ataapem,
but I want to find out the truth. I must. Maama
behaves so abnormally, though she is obedient and
always proves wise. I watch her all the time and it
seems to me that she has some kind of fit, which is very
unusual in my family. Sometimes she seems quite
incapable of movement. She turns pale like a fairy or
very dark whenever there is thunder and lightning or
rain. We must know the truth. It is better to have
nothing than by having be plagued with an eternal
curse.

ATA: But why don't you believe Maami Efua? When she
didn't have a child your wives mocked her. Now she
has a child you won't allow her peace.

CHIEF: They still mock her.

ATA: After all these years?

CHIEF: After all these years ... It is for her own good that
I want to know the truth. Nature does not overlook
dishonesty. Nature is such a force in our lives we
cannot ignore her so easily.

ATA: Are you thinking of sending her away again?

CHIEF: No! I would like her to be at my bedside on my
day of death. I would like to see her tears at my dying
hour. Our elders have said: lovely tears send the spirit

I

to its proper home of rest quicker and more safely. She has grown so beautiful, Ataapem. Maami Efua has grown so beaut*ful.

ATA: Nature is on her side, Nana.

CHIEF: Fetch your labourers to fell that tree. I will talk with Maami Efua myself.

Exeunt. Enter Maama and the Doctor, meeting.

MAAMA: Ah, doctor, I'm glad you came.

DOCTOR: How's your father?

MAAMA: He's talking to my mother, I fear.

DOCTOR: What do you fear?

MAAMA: The sun goes down very soon.

DOCTOR: Are you afraid of the sun going down?

MAAMA: I have never walked alone in the dark. But I fear for mankind enveloped in darkness.

DOCTOR: The world has always taken care of itself.

MAAMA: It seems so. You know you are my mother's arch-enemy.

DOCTOR: Am I?

MAAMA: You told her she would never have a child. Why did you say that?

DOCTOR: I'm still surprised that she has a daughter.

MAAMA: Human beings can never believe anything.

DOCTOR: We have grown cynical, all of us. And don't blame us. How do you know that she is your mother?

MAAMA: You must go now doctor. You ask too many questions. Goodbye. (*Exit.*)

Enter Kweku and Kodwo.

KWEKU: Is the chief here?

DOCTOR: I am waiting for him, myself.

KWEKU: Have you heard the story, doctor?

DOCTOR: What story?

KWEKU: A stone has turned into a man.

DOCTOR: Where?

KWEKU: In the city.

DOCTOR: Come on, don't tell me fibs.

KWEKU: Yeah, it's not the first time it's happened, it can't be the last.

DOCTOR: Where did you hear this?

KODWO: We saw it, doctor. We saw it.

KWEKU: With our own eyes.

KODWO: That's right. With our own eyes.

KWEKU: Don't like the sound of it, though.

DOCTOR: Sound of what?

KWEKU: I mean cutting that tree down there. Could turn into a man while we're cutting. Could be a nasty experience, you know what I mean.

KODWO: Yeah.

MAAMA (*enters*): What do you want?

KWEKU: Child, we want the chief.

MAAMA: Too late. (*Exit.*)

KWEKU: Why too late?

KODWO: The sun ain't gone down yet.

KWEKU: Yeah, but look at the clouds forming.

KODWO: Seems like it's going to rain, doctor.

DOCTOR: Yes, we need the rain very badly.

CHIEF (*enters*): What do you want?

KWEKU: Nana, we're come to cut down the tree. The advisor told us like.

CHIEF: You won't need to do that job. Thank you. Goodbye.

KWEKU, KODWO: Goodbye, Nana. (*Exeunt Kweku and Kodwo.*)

CHIEF: What are you waiting for?

DOCTOR: You asked me to come.

CHIEF: I never asked you to come. It was the witch doctor I wanted, not you. What am I doing with a doctor who writes poems? Get out. Nothing can save us now. Nothing. I said get out.

DOCTOR: Is there anything I can do for you, Nana? Is anything the matter?

CHIEF: Don't poke your ugly nose too far. I said, go away. Are you defying me?

DOCTOR: No, I'm sorry. (*Exit.*)

EFUA (*enters*): For pity's sake, stop them. Stop your wives shouting that name. It is taboo to mention that name.

CHIEF: It was my fault. I didn't know they were hiding, listening to our conversation. What must we do now? What are we to do? What will become of us?

EFUA: Stop them. For God's sake, stop them.

ARABA (*enters*): Where is she? The witch! Where is she? The daughter? The tree! The tree! (*Exit.*)

EFUA: O, why can't you stop them? (*Exit Chief.*) I have come to live in a house where every source of happiness is turned into bitter mockery. I found happiness in a daughter only to be ungrateful to Nature in the end. How could I have known? Mother Nature, this is what you gave me. This is the happiness you have given me. 'Are you not happy', she said. 'I would be your daughter if only you would not betray me.' And I betrayed her.

Exit Maami Efua. Enter the chief and the doctor meeting.

CHIEF: I told you to go away.

DOCTOR: I went but I could not stay. I felt I had to come back.

CHIEF: What for?

DOCTOR: I don't know.

CHIEF: Then go away. Go away, doctor-poet.

DOCTOR: Yes, I'm sorry. (*Exit.*)

CHIEF: Maami Efua! Maami Efua! (*Exit.*)

Enter Maami Efua and Maama meeting.

EFUA: My daughter! What is it? Look at your helpless mother. Please, don't tear yourself away. Don't desert me, please.

MAAMA: Woman of the world, child of mischief, friend of the serpent, do you so quickly betray me and all my race? Could you not for a moment hold your tongue and thank me for what I have done for you? Have you abused my kindness thus and now turn it to my undoing? I shall go back to where I came from and henceforth may no divine power have mercy on the human race, and may childbearing be a bitter agony to all women. (*Exit.*)

EFUA: Forgive me, my daughter. Please forgive me.

She follows her. Distant drums, increase in tempo and volume and then sound gradually dies away. Enter the chief.

CHIEF: Maami Efua! Maami Efua! (*Enter Ataapem.*)

CHIEF: Ataapem, where is Maami Efua?

ATA: Nana, the most extraordinary and frightening thing on earth has happened. As I came on my way I saw your wife, Maami Efua, following her daughter, and all of a sudden the daughter turned into a tree and her dress vanished. Your wife, screaming, fell down at the foot of the tree and before I could reach her she struck her head against the tree and died. (*Enter Maami Araba.*) She is lying there now, dead. I wanted to carry her here, but as I went near her I was seized with fear. Then a voice cried out: 'Run, son of man, run'. And before I knew what was happening, I found myself running. Is it possible that Nature rules our lives? Did we live with Mother Nature herself and not know it?

CHIEF: Lead me away, Ataapem. Lead me away.

Distant drums increase in tempo and volume and gradually die away.

The Occupation

A script for the camera

ATHOL FUGARD

CHARACTERS

Barend
Koosie
Serge   } 4 *hoboes*
Cappie

THE OCCUPATION

A SCRIPT FOR THE CAMERA

First image: an old house. The camera is moving towards it along the weed-choked path of a neglected garden. Mood of dereliction and decay. The camera moves warily with shots from behind shrubbery and trees to suggest a stealthy approach.
Credits.

The camera reaches the house. A door with the doorknob missing, the paint cracked and peeling. A window either with shutters closed or boarded-up. The camera moves, as would a man, along a wall (shadows of the men?) to another window, then another, then again a door . . . variations on the theme of an old house fallen into desuetude. Sound is natural — footsteps on gravel and cement, vague noises of attempts to prize open shutters, etc. In this opening scene and during the entry into the house the camera functions as a composite eye of the four men, showing us what they see. Our first sight of the men themselves will be, as indicated, in the lounge. Until that moment, all dialogue is off-screen.

K's VOICE (*in the distance*): Ssst! Here. Captain! Over here! *Shot changes abruptly to one of the windows which have already been passed. The shutters have been forced open. A dusty window pane, and through it a dim view of a small room.*

S's VOICE: Go on!

K's VOICE: Captain?

C's VOICE: Okay.

Camera focused on the window pane as it is smashed. Sound. As the glass breaks the shot again changes abruptly to:

Inside the room, which is seen from the position of the men who have just entered through the window. The camera is stationary, but turning in a wide arc so that we see all of the room. Two doors. The room is bare. A few seconds of breathing silence at the start of this sequence, then, muffled by distance, a dove coos. This is also the cue for the following dialogue, which is heard while the camera turns slowly.

K'S VOICE: Captain . . .

C'S VOICE: Sssh!

S'S VOICE: There's no one. I tell you it's empty.

C'S VOICE: Who's in charge here, Sergeant?

S'S VOICE: Sorry, sir.

C'S VOICE (*easier, a little louder*): Okay. It looks all right. You take that door, Sergeant. But watch out for booby-traps. Come on! (*Explosive, neurotic laughter from Sergeant.*)

Camera moves forward to one of the two doors. During this move SERGE's *voice is heard from the other door.*

S'S VOICE: Must have been the kitchen (*pause*). No dice. Water's cut off.

On the last of SERGE's *words the shot changes to The Kitchen. Kitchen sink with taps; snarl of exposed wires where the stove stood against the wall; heap of rubbish — paper, dust, leaves — swept into one corner; on one wall a strip of wood with several nails for hanging up utensils. From one nail hangs an old piece of wire. While the camera is exploring the kitchen we hear the following dialogue from the other room.*

K'S VOICE: It's tight, Captain. But it's not locked. I can see a big room.

C'S VOICE: Mind. Barend!

B'S VOICE: What? (*Sound of a violent blow.*)

C'S VOICE: That's it! (*A second and still more violent blow.*)

On the sound of the second blow the camera cuts abruptly from the

kitchen to the door which the camera approached earlier and which is now swinging open. The camera moves through into:
A very large room, obviously the lounge in the days when the house was occupied. Again the wide swing of the camera, but this time travelling slowly to the centre of the room at the same time. We see: a high, pressed-metal ceiling with two or three broken lengths of chain hanging where the light used to be; cobwebs in corners; somewhere on the floor the remains of a fire — ash and charred pieces of wood; dampstains on the walls with one or two places where the plaster has fallen away; a large marble-sided fireplace; windows and two glass-panelled double-doors, all shuttered. Sunlight is streaming into the room through the latter. They face directly into the setting sun. This room is also bare, but in addition to the remains of the fire the floor is littered with other rubbish indicating occasional and vagrant occupants. There is a second doorway, but in this case the door itself is missing. As previously the following dialogue is heard while the camera establishes the room.

K'S VOICE: Hey!

C'S VOICE: Easy does it, men! Easy does it!

S'S VOICE: Booby traps (*explosive laugh*)!

C'S VOICE: Sergeant!

S'S VOICE: Sorry sir.

K'S VOICE: Whose house is it, Captain?

S'S VOICE: Who cares? It's empty.

K'S VOICE: This was a big room, hey!

C'S VOICE: The lounge. What's the bet? In the good old days.

S'S VOICE: We're not the first.

C'S VOICE: We won't be the last.

B'S VOICE: So what we waiting for?

C'S VOICE: Who's in command here, private?

B'S VOICE: Go to hell.

C'S VOICE: Mark that man, Sergeant.

s's voice: Private Barend, sir.

c's voice: Mark him.

B's VOICE (*suddenly, shouting*): Hullo! HULLO! Anybody home!

On the second 'hullo' an abrupt countershot showing the four men for the first time.

They are hoboes: unshaven, unwashed, with down-at-heel shoes — one of them could have shoes but no socks — shapeless trousers and the same for whatever else they wear — sports coat, lumber jacket, or even just a pullover.

BAREND, *shouting, stands apart from the other three who are watching him. About thirty years old; a dark, brooding man, physically strong, even powerful. But as we see more of him, another impression will form — that of a strength that is inarticulate and lost. His broad shoulders should have been bent under the weight of hard work and those big hands — so empty! — shaping bricks into a wall, or digging. He is an Afrikaner and speaks English with difficulty.*

KOOSIE, *carrying a bundle, is the youngest. About twenty years old. He lives in a schizophrenic world, constantly straining to reconcile illusion and reality. A face, when not wide-eyed and eager, pinched into an anxious frown.*

SERGE *and* CAPPIE *are older men, approximately the same age — between forty-five and fifty.* SERGE *is holding the piece of wire last seen hanging in the kitchen. We have already heard him laugh. We will hear it again — a wild, mirthless sound thrown violently out of an open-mouthed face. More than anything else this expresses the man and his dominant mood: hyper-tension. He sweats a lot.*

CAPPIE *smiles slowly — expressive of his control over himself and the others, the situation. He is fascinated by the transience of all reality. I see him with greying hair and a moustache. He also has a tie — a small knot under a rumpled collar — and has a bottle of wine in each of his trouser pockets.*

CAPPIE: Barend!

BAREND (*facing* CAPPIE): There's no one.

CAPPIE: That's mutiny, Private Barend. Men have been shot for less. (SERGE *laughs*.)

BAREND: Why don't you grow up?

CAPPIE: We're not finished. There's still the rest of the house.

SERGE: It is empty, Cap.

CAPPIE: They might have left something behind. Come on.

Fade to the hall which is beyond the second doorway. A staircase leads to the top floor. There are also a few doors leading off the hall to other rooms and the start of a passage.

KOOSIE: They must have been rich.

SERGE: Stinking rich if you ask me. Hey Cap?

CAPPIE: Wealth doesn't stink, Sergeant. It has a fine cultured aroma. Good cigars and scented bath-water.

As he starts to speak, and followed by SERGE, CAPPIE *moves to the staircase.* KOOSIE *and* BAREND *stand motionless for a few seconds, listening and watching.*

CAPPIE (*moving up the stairs*): Gracious living, my boys. That's what this was. Gracious living in the good old days. They had it good.

KOOSIE *moves to one of the doors in the hallway.* BAREND *is alone for a few seconds.* KOOSIE *comes out.*

KOOSIE (*to* BAREND): Nothing.

KOOSIE *goes into another room.* BAREND *now moves into the passage.*

Here follows a sequence alternating between CAPPIE *and* SERGE *upstairs,* KOOSIE *downstairs and* BAREND *in the passage. The latter image must be established strongly both visually and aurally. There are broken windows along this passage and as a result leaves, now dry and rusty, cover the floor. These and the pieces of glass breaking underfoot when he walks, will create a distinctive sound. But to start with, when* BAREND *moves into this passage we are given a stationary shot of its length. There is a door at the far end. No movement. Shot changes to:*

CAPPIE *and* SERGE *upstairs in an empty room.* CAPPIE *moves to a door in one of the walls, opens it and looks into another room.* SERGE *is drawing a heart with an arrow through it on a dusty window pane.*

CAPPIE: Inter-leading door. Could have been the bed-rooms. Yes. Mr and Mrs.

SERGE: Who?

CAPPIE (*smiles*): Yes.

SERGE: Mr and Mrs Who?

CAPPIE: That's it Serge, Mr and Mrs Who? Don't you get it?

SERGE (*blankly*): Mr and Mrs Who.

CAPPIE: Who were you? (*Walking away from the camera.*) Who were you? Who Were You!

Followed by SERGE, CAPPIE *moves deeper into the house. Shot changes to:*

The passage. The camera is moving down it, steadily and un-hurriedly, centred on the door at the far end. We do not see BAREND, *but we hear his footsteps. Shot changes to:*

Close-up, from inside a room, of KOOSIE *in the doorway. He is intent and watchful. Off-screen we hear the dry, feathered panic of beating wings.* KOOSIE *moves into the room, closing the door behind him. Takes a few steps into the room and then again stands still and watches. Shot changes to:*

CAPPIE *and* SERGE *in another room.*

CAPPIE: And this? Let's see . . . yes. Yes.

SERGE: Well, come on.

CAPPIE: The nursery.

SERGE: How do you know?

CAPPIE: The walls . . . that wall-paper. And it gets the after-noon sun. Just the place for the little mites.

SERGE: Know your way around, hey Cap!

CAPPIE: I'm in tune with the past, Sergeant.

K'S VOICE (*muffled*): Captain! Captain!

CAPPIE: They're most probably still alive.

SERGE: The kids.

CAPPIE: This, Serge, is another man's memory, and what's the bet he hates it.

K'S VOICE (*louder*): Captain!

CAPPIE *and* SERGE *turn and leave in response to* KOOSIE'S *calling. Shot changes to:*

Hallway. Camera at top of stairs, focused on KOOSIE *at the bottom.*

CAPPIE (*off-screen*): Find anything?

KOOSIE: In there, Captain.

Shot changes to:

The passage. BAREND *has reached the door. It opens, but just before we can see what is beyond it there is a change to a countershot of* BAREND'S *face, in close-up. This is held for a few seconds. He is staring at something. Off-screen we hear muffled, indistinct dialogue between* KOOSIE, SERGE *and* CAPPIE. *Without either* BAREND *or the camera moving, this shot changes to:*

Koosie's room. He, CAPPIE *and* SERGE *are all looking up at something. The sound of beating wings. Eyes and heads move.*

KOOSIE: It's wild. It's trying to get out.

SERGE: Cappie! Pigeon pie! (*Laughs.*)

KOOSIE: It's not a pigeon, it's a dove.

SERGE: Just a joke.

KOOSIE: Must I catch it, Captain?

CAPPIE: Yes. Yes, catch it.

KOOSIE *moves forward into the camera. Shot changes to:*

The passage. The camera is positioned outside the door which is now wide open. Through the door, inside a small room, we see BAREND, *his back to the camera, moving towards an old iron bed with a piece of mattress on its sagging springs. When he reaches the bed he moves to the head and looks down at it so that we see him in profile. He holds this position for a few seconds until a mumble of dialogue from the other three makes him look sharply at the door — that is, straight into the camera. The off-screen murmur continues.* BAREND *moves suddenly, straight to the camera which in turn starts backing down the passage.* BAREND *closes the door and hurries furtively down the passage. The camera is backing all the time, but slower so that he eventually moves into it when the shot changes to:* KOOSIE *holding the dove.*

SERGE: Just an old dove.

KOOSIE: What must I do with it, Captain?

SERGE: Why? It's harmless. Eats flies.

KOOSIE: Maybe it carries messages for them.

SERGE: Who?

KOOSIE: The enemy.

CAPPIE *and* SERGE *in close-up while* KOOSIE *talks. They watch him with vacant fascination.*

KOOSIE (*off-screen*): Reinforcements. They need reinforcements. Isn't that so, Captain? And the dove carries the message.

SERGE: Better take it prisoner then (*winking*). Hey, Cap?

KOOSIE: And then?

CAPPIE: We'll decide later. Leave it here.

KOOSIE *releases the dove. They back out of the room;* KOOSIE *closes the door on the camera. Slow fade on the closed door as seen from inside the room. Sound of the bird's wings.*

In the lounge. Shot of the second doorway as SERGE, CAPPIE *and* KOOSIE *enter. They stop and stare. Counter-shot of the room showing* BAREND *sitting on the floor at the far end, his back to the wall, playing with the piece of wire* SERGE *found in the kitchen.*

CAPPIE (*off-screen*): Find anything?

BAREND (*without looking up*): Nothing.

KOOSIE *moves into the frame and sits beside* BAREND.

KOOSIE (*to* BAREND): I found a dove in the other room. It's alive. We've taken it prisoner. We decide its fate later.

CAPPIE (*off-screen*): Nothing?

BAREND (*still not looking up*): Nothing.

Shot changes to CAPPIE *alone at the door.* SERGE *has also moved into the room.*

CAPPIE: Nothing (*slow smile*). How do you like that! Nothing (*moving forward, looking around the room.*) Nothing! Not a fu . . .

Shot changes to SERGE *sitting on the floor, watching* CAPPIE. CAPPIE *will not be seen again until the speech starting 'It was real'.*

SERGE: Remember that one in Italy? Near Monte Casino? (*Speaking across the room to* BAREND) Cappie says it was a palace. Paintings on the ceiling. Life size.

CAPPIE (*off-screen*): . . . last year's leaves and other men's rubbish . . .

SERGE (*still to* BAREND): Did it on his back. Lying down. One of those Italian names. Cappie knows all about it (*Sudden vacancy; to himself*) Monte Casino! Jesus.

Shot changes to BAREND, *still playing with the wire.*

CAPPIE (*off-screen*): Look at it! In rooms like this men . . . men dream! You Dream! The generations to come . . . in the lovely old house that Jack built.

BAREND: I'm hungry . . .

CAPPIE (*off-screen*): Or the future. That's their word. The Future! They sat . . .

BAREND: Let's eat.

KOOSIE (*busy with his bundle*): Fish and chips. There was also enough for cream cakes again. But they got squashed.

BAREND (*betraying a nervousness*): Okay, so let's eat.

KOOSIE: I still got to get water.

CAPPIE (*off-screen*): . . . fat backsides and talked and dreamt . . .

Shot changes back to SERGE.

SERGE (*still in the vacancy of his previous line*): Once is enough. (*Breaking mood*) Hey Barend! Heard this one? 'The cradle of ancient civilization'. (*Laughs.*) Cappie said it.

CAPPIE (*off-screen*): Sergeant! Where's your respect for the dead.

SERGE: Sorry sir.

Shot changes to KOOSIE, *looking up from his bundle at* CAPPIE.

CAPPIE (*off-screen*): Because they're dead. It's finished. Nothing's left. This was the future.

Shot changes to BAREND, *who for the first time in this sequence also looks at* CAPPIE.

CAPPIE (*off-screen*): The four of us. In here. Now! Do you get it? Use your imagination, you nits!

Shot changes to a long shot of the room, taking in all four men – the three sitting on the floor and CAPPIE *standing. A camera angle that will suggest space and emptiness.*

CAPPIE: It was real! Solid! They could touch it. Smell it. See it. Look! Tables and chairs . . . armchairs; pictures on the walls; carpets on the floor! And the noise! The laughing and crying, the whispers wrapped up in these walls! Are you deaf? The air in here was so thick with living it choked them! (*Pause.*) But the clocks were ticking. They were warned. Waking at night, in the neither today, nor yesterday, nor yet tomorrow. A moment in a sleeping house . . . except . . . what is that? You listen hard. Yes. The old clock ticking away on the landing. Ticking. That's all. Ticking away. They never sound quite the same in the light. And then, just for a moment, one seasick little moment, it seems that everything is floating. You, your bed, the walls, the house itself, . . . all gently drifting together . . . for the moment. Because there are no anchors. Nothing is heavier than time, my boys. Everything floats, and one day, maybe just as gently, you and your bed, and the walls . . .

Cut abruptly to BAREND. *He throws away the wire – a strong*

deliberate gesture to break the mood. His next line cuts
CAPPIE's *speech.*

BAREND: I said I'm hungry.

SERGE (*off-screen*): Captain, there's a man here reports he's hungry.

Shot changes to KOOSIE, *anxious-faced as he follows the next few lines of dialogue, all of which is off-screen.*

CAPPIE: Mark him.

SERGE: Private Barend, sir.

CAPPIE: Mark him.

SERGE: Private Barend, step forward!

BAREND: For Christ's sake, grow up.

Shot changes to BAREND, *with* CAPPIE *squatting on his haunches in front of him.*

CAPPIE: What's the matter, Barend? You look worried.

BAREND: Since when?

CAPPIE: Never been in a house like this before? You weren't listening to me. Nobody's left to see your table manners (SERGE *laughs.*)

BAREND: Why don't you drop dead for a change.

CAPPIE: You don't like me. Why Barend? I try my best. Aren't you happy with us? You can always go.

BAREND: You finished?

CAPPIE: Yes (*pause.*) You finished too? (SERGE *laughs.*) All right, chaps. Let's count the kitty.

The four men squat down. KOOSIE *has a cigar box.*

KOOSIE: I think it was a good day.

SERGE (*taking money out of his pocket*): Not so bad.

CAPPIE: Was it a good day, Barend?

BAREND: It was okay.

CAPPIE: Okay? (*Holding a handful of coins under Barend's nose.*) Don't you call that a good day?

SERGE: How do you do it, Cap? Rob them?

CAPPIE: I appeal to their better natures. (*To* BAREND) How did you make out?

BAREND: I did okay. (*Now also has his money out, but he keeps his hand closed.*)

There is a tension between BAREND *and* CAPPIE, *watching each other like players in a poker game.* CAPPIE *is confident;* BAREND *hides fear behind a mask of stubborn indifference.*

CAPPIE: I hope so, because I think it's time we paid dues again. Isn't that so, quartermaster?

KOOSIE: Yes, Captain.

CAPPIE (*placing two half-crowns on the floor in front of* KOOSIE): Come on. Five bob all round. We don't want any bums in this group – do we, Barend?

SERGE *puts down his five shillings, made up of two florins and a shilling.* KOOSIE *puts down a florin, two shillings and two sixpences.* BAREND *counts the money in his hand, holding it so that the others can't see.* CAPPIE *watches him intently. Eventually* BAREND *puts down a collection of coins – a shilling piece, sixpences, tickeys and pennies.*

CAPPIE: Pennies! (*To* KOOSIE, *indicating Barend's contribution*) Count it, quartermaster. (*To* BAREND) Looks like you just made it.

BAREND: I did okay.

SERGE: But you frighten them. He frightens them, Cappie.

CAPPIE: You must smile, Barend. Learn to say 'please'.

BAREND: I did okay.

KOOSIE (*indicating Barend's money*): Five bob, sir.

BAREND (*trying to get away*): Let's eat.

CAPPIE (*enjoying himself*): We're not finished. How we off for stores, quartermaster?

KOOSIE (*putting the money away in a cloth tobacco bag*): I think we need more shoelaces, Captain. (*Opens the cigar box to reveal a few pairs of shoelaces.*) Yes, sir. There's only four left.

CAPPIE (*places two shilling piece on the floor*): You know the rules. Come. (*Watches* BAREND *intently.* SERGE *and* KOOSIE *make their contribution.*) We're waiting, Barend. (BAREND

counts the money in his hand.) What's wrong? (BAREND
opens his hand.) Five pence!

BAREND: I'll give you my share tomorrow . . .

CAPPIE: No, you won't! Nobody stays in the group on
credit. We agreed.

SERGE: You frighten them. That's your trouble.

CAPPIE (*to* BAREND): So?

BAREND: I don't know.

CAPPIE: The rules are that when a man can't make an
equal contribution to stores or pay his dues, then
he must leave the group.

BAREND: I don't care.

SERGE: Hell, Cappie!

CAPPIE (*sudden flash of anger*): What do you mean . . .
'Hell, Cappie!'

SERGE: Just . . . you know . . . hell, man . . .

CAPPIE: If you've got something to say, say it.

SERGE: I'll lend him two bob.

CAPPIE: The rules forbid credit within the group! I didn't
make them. You wanted them. You made them.

SERGE: I'll give him two bob. A present.

CAPPIE: Give! . . . A present! What the hell do you think
you are?

KOOSIE (*consulting a piece of paper*): Captain . . . the shoelaces
left is still all Barend's share. He didn't give any away
since the last lot.

CAPPIE (*looking at* BAREND): He didn't give any away?

KOOSIE: No, sir.

CAPPIE (*to Barend*): Then you're a bum.

BAREND: They don't want to take them.

CAPPIE: You're a bum.

SERGE: Don't frighten them, Barend. Watch Cappie next
time. Smile at them.

CAPPIE: One of these days, Barend . . .

BAREND: So? You think I care?

CAPPIE: Yes! I don't know why. But you care!

The sun is beginning to set outside – a strong dazzle of light through the shutters of the double doors reflecting a pattern of shadows on the walls and ceiling.

KOOSIE: Be dark just now. Must I get things ready, Captain?

CAPPIE: Yes. (*His moment with* BAREND *is past.* CAPPIE *sits back against the wall next to* SERGE.)

SERGE: This could be cosy, you know, Cap.

KOOSIE: I still got to get water.

SERGE: Remember that tank in the yard? And some wood for a fire! Hey, Cap? On the double, Private Koosie.

KOOSIE *leaves the room. During the sequence that now follows* BAREND *will be in focus almost all the time . . . showing increasing restlessness and tension. The effect of the setting sun – light through the shutters and reflections on the wall – will rise to a climax and then fade.*

To start with, while SERGE *is talking (the speech which follows)* BAREND *lights a cigarette and smokes it for a few seconds. Then he stands up and moves halfway across the room to the doorway to the hall, stops, changes direction and goes instead to one of the double doors. He looks out through the shutters at the setting sun. All the time* SERGE'S *voice rambles on off-screen.*

SERGE (*off-screen*): Easily make this cosy, Cap. Set ourselves up for a few days. Remember that place in Doornfontein? Two weeks, Barend. Two whole bloody weeks. The water was turned on and one room had a light. Lavatory, the lot. Old Whitey was still with us. What about it, Cap? Nobody saw us. They wouldn't mind if we kept it clean. H.Q. for future operations (*he laughs*). Old geezer this morning. Did I tell you? Offered me a job. 'No charity my good man, but if you are prepared to do a day's honest work . . . ' 'GO AND DROP DEAD!' Should have seen his

face! 'STUFF YOUR JOB WHERE THE MONKEY STUFFS HIS
NUTS.'

At this point BAREND *sits down on the floor. Change to a
counter-shot of* CAPPIE *and* SERGE *sitting against the opposite
wall.* SERGE *is talking to* CAPPIE. CAPPIE *is watching* BAREND.

SERGE (*mimicking an old man's voice*): 'Tramp . . . a . . . a
vulgar hobo . . . I . . .I'll call the police!' 'You know
what you and the police can do,' I said. You listening,
Cap?

CAPPIE: I'm listening.

SERGE: I told him begging comes from the Bible. Any
case, with the shoelaces it's not begging, hey Cap? The
police can't arrest us. We give something in return.

CAPPIE: That's the whole point.

SERGE: Exactly. That's the whole point. And what about
what they owe us? Hey, Barend! Heard this one.
'Society's debt to the gallant boys with the orange
flash.' (*Violent laugh.*) Smuts. Didn't he say that,
Cappie?

CAPPIE: I was there.

SERGE: What did I tell you? Should have joined up,
Barend. It helps sometimes. Especially old ladies.
They remember.

CAPPIE: He says he was too young.

CAPPIE *and* SERGE *stare silently at* BAREND *for a few seconds.
Camera returns to* BAREND. *In this silence he stands up and
moves to the other double-door where he again stares out at
the sunset. We begin to feel it desolates him. The following
dialogue is again off-screen.*

SERGE: You know something, Cap?

CAPPIE: What?

SERGE: I'm glad we didn't go on the road this winter.
And you? Durban's fine, but the road gets me down,
man. I never liked it, you know. Even Durban's bad
enough, but Cape Town! Split-a-brick! Now, let's

see . . . one . . . two . . . three, with old Hoppy . . .
four . . . five. Five times. It's hell this time of the year.
Those thunderstorms in the Karoo . . .

During this speech another sound is heard – very faint at
first, but growing steadily stronger. It is soon identified
as the sound of BAREND *walking down the passage – the*
dry leaves and broken glass underfoot. As it grows louder,
SERGE'S *voice gets softer until his line 'Thunderstorms in*
the Karoo . . . ' is just audible. For a few seconds after this
SERGE *mumbles on indistinctly while the sound of* BAREND'S
footsteps is heard loud and clear. The camera remains on
BAREND *all the time. The idea, of course, is that* BAREND *is*
hearing those footsteps, that he is re-experiencing his finding of
the bed.

In other words something intensely personal is happening
to him. We sense the contours of a blind and desperate
hope. The function of the camera is to find this and relate
it to the physical reality of the man – the old shoes; the coarse,
calloused, empty hands; the unlovable face.

The sound-illusion and mood are broken by SERGE'S *character-*
istic laugh, following which his voice is heard again at normal
strength.

SERGE (*off-screen*): But it's fact! It could drive a man mad.
Rain on a corrugated iron roof. The Russians use it.
Put a bucket on your head and hit it with broomsticks.
Five minutes and you're loco. The noise does it.
Hoppy read an article. Anyway, I just stood there on
the road and got wet. Jesus, it come down! Hailstones
the lot. Hoppy says I was crying, but I couldn't tell
with the rain running down my face. When it stopped
we went back inside. It was a squeeze. They're only
small you know. Spent the night there . . .

About halfway through the above speech the sound illusion –
the footsteps – starts again. But this time there is also a
visual illusion. As they grow in volume and SERGE'S *voice*

gets softer the shot of BAREND *dissolves slowly into a shot of the bed which he found in the little room at the end of the passage. The bed is seen as* BAREND *must have seen it: first from the door, the camera then travelling up to it and finally moving around to the head.* BAREND *is not seen. Just the bed. There is also no sound – the footsteps fade out with the dissolve.*

This image is going to be shattered by CAPPIE'S *voice. But instead of a simple dissolve or cut back to the reality of* BAREND *at the double-door, the image – the bed – should break up as if it were being seen through a pane of glass which is broken at the appropriate moment, as happened with the window pane at the start of the play. The two moments are parallel in meaning. The change comes on*

CAPPIE'S *second 'Barend!*

CAPPIE (*off-screen*): Barend! Barend!

Shot of BAREND – *a moment of confusion.*

CAPPIE (*off-screen, this time softly; sweetly*): Barend!

As BAREND *turns his head the shot changes to:*

> CAPPIE *and* SERGE: SERGE *is still sitting against the wall, watching* BAREND *and laughing. But* CAPPIE *is now standing – a few steps in front of* SERGE.

CAPPIE: Starting up again, is it?

BAREND: What?

CAPPIE: That's what I'd like to know. (*Moving to* BAREND.) What is it Barend? What happens?

SERGE: Confide in your commanding officer.

BAREND: I don't know what you are talking about.

CAPPIE: Don't you?

BAREND: I . . . I was thinking.

CAPPIE: Thinking. I see. Well, I'm talking about the sunset . . . and you. Always at sunset. I've noticed. You watch it.

BAREND: Why can't I watch it?

CAPPIE: I'm not saying you can't watch it.

BAREND: So what you trying to prove?

CAPPIE: I'm not trying to prove anything.

BAREND: Because if you think I'm scared or something . . .

CAPPIE: Who said anything about being scared? Take Serge now – he's scared. Of the dark. I think he believes in ghosts.

SERGE: Bull dust.

CAPPIE: With you it's . . . it's . . . you know the feeling I get sometimes watching you, Barend? I get the feeling you're lonely.

BAREND: Look, there's nothing. Nothing happens. You're talking a lot of rubbish.

CAPPIE (*quietly*): You know that's a lie. (*To the shutters. He looks out.*) The sun sets. It gets colder . . . darker . . . and shadows. They're different, aren't they Barend? Grey. Old. It's an old world. They come at us like scavengers. (*Changing mood, cheerfully*) You know where you'd be happy, Barend? The land of the midnight sun.

SERGE (*laughing*): You're a bullduster, Cap. Mid . . . night . . . sun!

CAPPIE: Think of it, man. It doesn't set. Twenty-four hours of sunshine.

SERGE: That a fact, Cappie?

CAPPIE: But there's a catch. Six months later the old bastard doesn't come up at all! That would do it, hey! A whole day of night!

KOOSIE (*off-screen and in the distance, but getting louder*): Captain. Captain. Captain!

CAPPIE: That would put the fat in the fire!

Enter KOOSIE *out of breath. At first* CAPPIE *ignores him.*

CAPPIE (*to* BAREND): Got your candle? Use it tonight. Wind doesn't blow in here.

KOOSIE (*agitated*): Captain. Please, sir!

SERGE: O.C.'s busy, Private. What do you want? And Stand To Attention!

KOOSIE: The enemy, Serge. Coming to the house.

SERGE (*urgently*): Cappie!

CAPPIE: What?

KOOSIE: The enemy, please sir, Captain. He's coming to the house.

CAPPIE: Who?

KOOSIE: A native. He's carrying a knob-kierie.

CAPPIE (*moving*): At the back?

KOOSIE: No Captain. There. The front. Where's our guns, Sergeant?

All four to the shutters. They look out. When they speak again it is in whispers.

CAPPIE: Watchman.

KOOSIE: What must we do, Captain? Where's our guns.

SERGE (*note of panic*): Will you shut up about guns! We haven't got . . .

CAPPIE: Easy, easy, easy Serge!

SERGE: I hate this.

BAREND: Maybe he won't come in. (*Pause.*)

SERGE (*rising note of panic; backing away from the double-door*): No. No!! No! He's coming!!

The others also back away, then turn and move.

Now follows a sequence showing their silent, tip-toed panic and flight through the house. To begin with, the lounge; KOOSIE *moves to his bundle and hurriedly collects everything together;* BAREND *makes for the doorway leading to the hall;* SERGE *has backed into a wall and stands rigid.*

CAPPIE (*as* KOOSIE *also moves to the hall*): Not that way! Come back. (*To* SERGE, *whom he gives a violent shove*) Snap out of it! Move. The back window.

SERGE *rushes off through the first door.* CAPPIE, *also at the door, turns around.*

CAPPIE: Koosie! Barend! The back window!

Counter-shot of the empty lounge. A sudden high-pitched scream tears the heavy silence. It is SERGE's *voice imitating a falling* bomb. *Starts on a high note and then slides down the scale, followed by an imitation of the explosion. Again and again.*

CAPPIE: Shit! (*He turns sharply and appears through the door.*)

Series of shots showing the four men in different parts of the house — each shot lasting only a few seconds. KOOSIE *is scampering up the stairs;* BAREND, *in the passage, armed with a heavy stick, turns to face the camera in a defensive attitude:* CAPPIE, *moving through the house looking for* SERGE; *and* SERGE, *in close-up, crouched somewhere, his face twisted, hands protecting his head, screaming. This scream is the only sound; muffled and remote in the shot of* KOOSIE *and* BAREND, *louder with* CAPPIE, *and immediate and real during the shots of* SERGE.

Then, during a shot of KOOSIE, *hiding at the top of the stairs, a silence as sudden as was the start of the screaming. Quick cut to a shot of* BAREND, *stick in his hand, waiting. Then a shot of* CAPPIE *and* SERGE, *now together.* CAPPIE *has his hand over* SERGE'S *mouth.*

Silence. The dove coos.

KOOSIE *and* BAREND *are seen again — so motionless the frames could be stills. Camera returns to* CAPPIE *and* SERGE. *Off-screen a furtive sound (footsteps?). Counter-shot of the door as it opens.* KOOSIE *appears. Camera stays on* KOOSIE *until he leaves.*

KOOSIE: He's gone.

CAPPIE (*off-screen*): What are you staring at?

KOOSIE: Sergeant . . .

CAPPIE: (*off-screen*): Find Barend.

KOOSIE: Is Sergeant . . .?

CAPPIE: I said find Barend!

KOOSIE: Yes, sir.

KOOSIE *turns and leaves. Shot changes to:*

CAPPIE *and* SERGE. CAPPIE *still has his hand over* SERGE'S *mouth.*

CAPPIE: Let go. (SERGE *relaxes.* CAPPIE *takes his hand away.*)

SERGE: They never give you a chance, hey!

CAPPIE: Never.

SERGE: Sudden. Like bombs.

CAPPIE: It's always sudden.

SERGE: Cap, I . . . (*He stops.*) Don't laugh.

CAPPIE: I won't.

SERGE *is limp, damp with sweat, almost on the verge of tears.*
  CAPPIE *plays out this moment with a front of non-committal
  indifference but behind it we feel . . .*

SERGE: I just wanted to be happy. Truly. All my life . . .
  that's all I wanted. (*Pause.*) Do you know what I mean,
  Cap? (*Pause.*) Is that too much?

CAPPIE: No. (*Examines one of his fingers.*)

SERGE: What's that?

CAPPIE: You were biting me.

SERGE: Monte Casino.

CAPPIE: I know.

SERGE: Anyway, he's gone (*starting to laugh*). He's gone,
  Cap!

CAPPIE (*smiling*): And we're still alive.

Shot changes to: The passage. KOOSIE *at one end, the camera
  on* BAREND *at the other.*

KOOSIE: It's okay now. He's gone. (*Pause.*) Come. (*Pause.*)
  Did you hear Serge? He . . . (*stops*). That funny noise.
  It was him. In the kitchen. He . . . he . . . (*Pause.*) Come.
  Captain said you must come.

The camera starts to move to KOOSIE. *Fade.*

  The lounge. SERGE *is sitting on the floor, whistling and playing
  with the piece of wire he found in the kitchen.* CAPPIE *has taken
  out one of his bottles of wine and is drinking. There is a subtle
  change – the excitement has sharpened him, given a keen edge
  to his eyes and smile. This will be heightened by the wine.*
  KOOSIE *comes in from the hall.*

CAPPIE: Where's Barend?

KOOSIE: Coming, Captain.

CAPPIE: What was he doing?

KOOSIE: Waiting.

CAPPIE: Was he frightened?

KOOSIE: He had a stick. If I had a gun, Captain, I could have killed that kaffir. He didn't see me.

BAREND *comes into the lounge. He still has his stick – it comes from a fire which other vagrants had made in the house. One end is charred.*

SERGE: Sa-loo ... oot Arms! All present and accounted for, sir. No casualties.

KOOSIE (*joining* SERGE): I was up top there by the stairs. I could have taken a pot shot at him. Sitting duck.

SERGE: Get the grub. Battle makes a man hungry.

KOOSIE: Must we still bivouac here, Captain?

SERGE: Why not? He didn't see us.

KOOSIE: Maybe he heard us. You were making that noise.

SERGE (*defensive ignorance*): What noise?

KOOSIE: That funny noise.

SERGE: Bull dust.

KOOSIE: And he's gone to call the police! Remember that other place?

SERGE: What do you think, Cappie?

Shot of CAPPIE *with his bottle.*

CAPPIE: He might have heard you.

BAREND (*off-screen*): I'm staying.

Cut to shot of BAREND.

KOOSIE: Captain give the orders.

BAREND: Nobody gives me orders!

KOOSIE: Mustn't fight with me, we're in the same outfit.

BAREND: You can do what you like. I'm staying.

Shot changes to CAPPIE, *watching* BAREND.

CAPPIE: Who's that brave man, Sergeant?

SERGE: Private Barend, sir. A credit to the regiment (*laugh*).

KOOSIE: Captain?

CAPPIE: We'll stay.

KOOSIE: I'll get water.

CAPPIE (*moving to* BAREND): Taken a shine to this spot.
Feeling at home now.

BAREND: Ek is nie bang vir 'n—

CAPPIE: Speak English!

BAREND: I don't run from a kaffir.

CAPPIE: But you did, Barend! We were running. All of us.
Serge had a dose of the jitters. Me too. Koosie. And
you. Yes! You got out of here like all hell was behind
you. We were scared. Fear, Barend, Fear! And then
hate. Them. Theirs. They hate us. Even dead they hate
us. It wasn't that nigger. It's not his house. It's them . . .
witmense like us.

SERGE *is laughing.* CAPPIE, *smiling, takes a drink from his bottle.*
BAREND *is rigid with suppressed emotion. Then he moves
abruptly, crossing the room to the wall with the door through
which they first entered the lounge. With the charred piece
of firewood he starts to scrawl an obscenity on the wall.
Enormous letters.* KOOSIE *appears in the doorway with a bottle
of water.* BAREND *gets as far as . . . when the shot changes to:*
CAPPIE *and* SERGE, *watching him.* CAPPIE *has a detached,
ironic smile.* SERGE *is concentrating, spelling out the letters
under his breath. When he gets the message he starts to laugh,
violently.* KOOSIE *moves into this frame.*

KOOSIE (*to* SERGE): What's he doing?

SERGE: Look!

Shot of BAREND *scrawling another obscenity. Shot changes back
to* SERGE *and* KOOSIE.

KOOSIE: What is it?

SERGE: Can't you read?

Cut back to BAREND. *He has finished and throws away the piece
of wood, then looks defiantly at* CAPPIE.

CAPPIE (*moving up to* BAREND): You also write on lavatory
walls, don't you? Yes. I know your sort. (*Examines the
writing on the wall.*) You've just insulted the dead. Why?
Because they're helpless.

Cut to KOOSIE *and* SERGE.

KOOSIE (*to* SERGE): Who? (SERGE *starts whistling vigorously.*)
Cut back to CAPPIE *and* BAREND.

CAPPIE: Answer me, damn you! Why did you do that?

BAREND: Because I don't care about them or their house.
They're dead. It's empty. Tonight I'm . . .

CAPPIE: No Barend! No! You care! (*The writing on the
wall.*) That proves it. I thought it was empty but you . . .
you feel something in here, don't you?

Shot of KOOSIE *and* SERGE. KOOSIE *is listening seriously to the
dialogue between* CAPPIE *and* BAREND. SERGE *is trying not to
hear it.*

SERGE: Where's the food?

KOOSIE: Is there ghosts here, Serge?

SERGE: Dry up, won't you! Get the grub.

KOOSIE: Captain hasn't said anything . . .

SERGE: Well, I'm second in command and I'm telling you
to get the grub. For Christ's sake!

Shot changes to CAPPIE *and* BAREND.

CAPPIE: A home? Is that it? Can you still smell a home
in here, Barend? You're keen, man. I missed it. Yes,
we're pissing all over the memory of a happy home.
We're not even trespassers. We're defilers. And you're
jealous. That's what that means (*the obscenity*). This
is theirs and you're jealous. Are you that broke? If
we kicked you out, wouldn't you have anywhere to go?

BAREND: You think I'm hard-up for you?

CAPPIE: I hope not. Be hell for you if you were.

BAREND: I'll go my own way anytime. The lot of you can
get . . .

CAPPIE: Yes, yes. You've got it on the wall. We've all read
it. And remember, so have they.

KOOSIE: Is there ghosts here, Captain?

CAPPIE: Do you hear that, Barend? Tell him. I feel them
now.

BAREND: You're talking rubbish. (*Moves away.*)

SERGE: Yes, knock it off, Cap.

CAPPIE: Do you also feel them, Serge? It's worse when they're dead, isn't it? Barend sees them.

SERGE: For the last time, is that food ready, Koosie?

KOOSIE (*correcting him*): Private Koosie.

SERGE: Private be damned!

KOOSIE: Hey!

SERGE: Yes, Private be damned! Wake up for Christ's sake.

CAPPIE: Serge is frightened of ghosts.

SERGE: For crying out aloud . . .!

CAPPIE: Watch it, Serge. Watch it. (*To* BAREND) See what you've done? How many of them, Barend? One? Two? Three? Where? . . . There! Yes? Help me, Barend. A man or a woman? No! It's a little girl. A pretty little girl . . . with her dolly. Don't be frightened girlie. Come to the nice old man. (SERGE *laughs violently.* CAPPIE *pretends suddenly to see someone else.*) Madam! Our humble apologies. Didn't know . . . you'd be home. Ex-servicemen, Lady. Honourable discharge. Down on our luck. Could I interest you in a pair of shoelaces . . . black shoelaces. You see, Lady, we're not beggars. Small matter of shelter though. We'll doss on the floor and piss in the garden. Promise! But you see, Madam, we've forgotten what beds are like, but we do remember roofs. God bless you, Lady. And your little girl . . . God bless you both! (*Turning to the others*) Boys, the lady says we can sleep on the floor.

Three quick close-ups of BAREND, *who says nothing, then* SERGE *and* KOOSIE.

SERGE (*blankly*): Thank you, Ma'am (*then a laugh*).

KOOSIE (*uncertain*): Who . . . who . . .? Thank you, Lady.
Camera back to CAPPIE.

CAPPIE: Barend! Where's your respect! These people were your betters. They've given you shelter for the night.

J

(*Turning to the imaginary presence*) Watch him, Lady. A bad eff. Keep your little girl away from him and lock the door tonight.

BAREND: I wasn't born yesterday you know. There's nothing. This is just an empty old house . . . and I'm going to stay here because I want to . . . and no kaffir chases me away. So, julle kan gaan bars!

CAPPIE (*drinking*): Something's worrying you.

We now see KOOSIE *preparing their supper on a sheet of newspaper. There is a bottle of water, the fish and chips and four cream cakes. The following dialogue is either heard off-screen while* KOOSIE *is busy, or else with* SERGE *also in the frame.* CAPPIE *is not seen. Although* SERGE *speaks easily enough to* CAPPIE, *there are undertones.*

SERGE: Steady on the booze, Cappie.

CAPPIE: Why?

SERGE: Let's make it cosy in here.

KOOSIE (*looking up at the others*): Come and get it.

CAPPIE: What's on your mind, Sergeant?

SERGE: Nothing, Cap. (*he starts whistling.*)

KOOSIE: You can all come and get it now.

Fade.

Later. The four men sitting around the newspaper. It is now quite dark.

SERGE (*pleading*): Just a small fire, Cap?

CAPPIE: No.

SERGE: He's not coming back.

CAPPIE: I said no!

SERGE: I can't see a damn thing. (*Pause.*) This isn't cosy. (*Pause.*) This isn't the way I saw it at all, quite frankly.

KOOSIE: Barend's got a candle.

SERGE: How about it, Barend? Be a sport man. Your smallest piece.

BAREND *takes out a stub of candle from his pocket and throws it on to the newspaper.* KOOSIE *lights it, then holds it on one side so that the molten wax drips on to the floor. He fixes the candle firmly in this. In the light we see:* KOOSIE *and* SERGE *smiling.* BAREND *eating;* CAPPIE *with his bottle, his food still untouched.* CAPPIE *is getting drunk, his self-control beginning to go. He will end up self-indulgent and loose-mouthed. From this point on a shadow of fear behind* SERGE'S *eyes whenever he speaks to* CAPPIE. *He has a premonition of what is coming and tries vainly, clumsily, to prevent it.*

SERGE: Come on, Cap. Eat up.

CAPPIE: Looking after your old Captain, are you, Sergeant?

SERGE: That's the ticket. Eat up.

CAPPIE (*stroking Serge's head*): Faithful as a dog. He'd follow me into hell. Wouldn't you?

SERGE: And back . . . I hope. (*Tries to laugh.*)

KOOSIE *tidies up the newspaper. The dove coos.*

KOOSIE: Listen! We forgotten the dove, Captain. (*To* BAREND) In the other room.

CAPPIE: Let's keep its fate in the balance a little longer.

SERGE (*eating, to Barend*): Not so bad, hey?

CAPPIE: You're happy.

SERGE: Aren't you, Cap?

CAPPIE: If you're happy, I'm happy.

SERGE: One for all and all for one, hey!

CAPPIE: No. *You* for *me*.

SERGE (*trying to ignore this remark*): It's all right when there's a bunch of you . . . like us. What do you say, Barend? What I mean is, we're organized. The shoelaces and all. We've got a scheme. Otherwise it's hell.

CAPPIE: Start a pension fund if you like.

SERGE: If I had a place like this you know what I'd do?

CAPPIE (*total indifference, enunciating each word carefully*): No, we do not know what you would do if you had a place like this.

SERGE: I'd turn it into a sort of boarding house. Holiday

farm style of thing. Select. No nonsense. With a games room. Ping-pong and dominoes. Could make a go of it you know. Grow my own vegetables. That's good soil out there. Cut down costs. Even a cow. Farm butter . . . new-laid eggs. What do you say, Barend?

BAREND (*unexpectedly*): Rhode Island Reds.

SERGE: What's that?

BAREND: They're the best for eggs.

SERGE: That a fact?

SERGE (*excessively grateful*): Rhode Island Reds. Lovely name. I'll remember that, Barend. (*Pause.*) Thanks.

BAREND: Two hundred eggs a year average.

SERGE (*encouraging*): Is that so!

BAREND: But you got to watch with the feeding. Bonemeal – for the egg shells.

SERGE (*hanging on to the moment*): Well, I'll be . . . goes to show, you, hey! How come you know all about poultry, Barend?

BAREND: We had a . . . hok.

SERGE: Run, fowl run.

BAREND: In the backyard.

SERGE: That must have been okay.

BAREND: Yes. It was. But I don't mind too much. You forget. Only sometimes, you know. And my hands also. They feel empty. It feels like I don't know what to do with them sometimes. I worked you see . . . (*He stops, suddenly aware of the three faces watching him.*)

CAPPIE: Go on, Barend. This is getting nice and chummy.

SERGE: Knock it off, Cap.

CAPPIE: Serge is trying to be friendly, Barend. He's extending a hand of friendship.

SERGE: Don't spoil everything, Cap!

CAPPIE: You'll make me jealous, Serge! Take my hand instead. (*Pause.*) Sergeant, that's an order.

SERGE *takes* CAPPIE'*s hand and shakes it, trying to turn the incident into a harmless joke. But when he wants to withdraw his hand,* CAPPIE *holds on to it.*

CAPPIE: Don't be afraid.

SERGE: I'm not afraid.

CAPPIE: I won't eat you.

SERGE *starts whistling. With a smile,* CAPPIE *lets go of his hand.*

KOOSIE: Once upon a time we had pigeons. Homers and racers.

SERGE: And then?

KOOSIE: We had races. Beaufort West and back.

SERGE: Where's back?

KOOSIE: Cape Town.

SERGE: You can keep it.

KOOSIE: Three hundred miles one way.

SERGE: Did you gamble?

KOOSIE: You don't gamble with pigeons. It's for the sport of the thing.

SERGE: Poultry is a paying proposition. Hey, Barend? Is it true that they get lice?

KOOSIE: But sometimes they never came back. They get lost. Or hawks eat them.

SERGE: Sounds stupid to me. How could you deal with lice, Barend?

KOOSIE: Mountain View Road, Woodstock. We was number nine. Poensie was seventeen.

SERGE: Poensie?

KOOSIE: Poensie Grobbelaar. He also kept pigeons. When we going to Cape Town, Captain?

CAPPIE: Tomorrow.

SERGE (*worried*): You're just joking.

KOOSIE: Captain promised. My father would give us food and we could all share my room.

CAPPIE: What would your mother give us?

KOOSIE: She's dead. Sometime you must also write me another letter to my father, Captain.

CAPPIE: Tomorrow.

KOOSIE: Explaining.

CAPPIE: I'll tell him you're dead.

KOOSIE: Me?

CAPPIE: Killed in action. How's that? I'll give you a medal. Make him proud. Dear Mr . . .

KOOSIE: Rossouw. Jacobus Rossouw.

CAPPIE: Dear Mr Rossouw, it is my painful duty to inform you that your son . . .

KOOSIE: Koosie Rossouw. Aged nineteen. Brown eyes.

CAPPIE: . . . is dead. Killed in action. As his commanding officer, I can say without hesitation that he died like a man. He was wounded. Badly wounded. But he faced the end without flinching.

KOOSIE: Go on.

CAPPIE: Reconnaissance patrol. Four of us. Myself, Sergeant Atkins, Private Barend and your son with his brown eyes. Bivouacked for the night in an old house. Thought it was empty. But Barend . . . correction, Private Barend . . . made us realise that we were not alone. The enemy, Mr Rossouw . . . Them. A presence, something hard and bitter, resenting us, in the shadows. We sat. Waiting. Talked, bluffed each other with brave noises. Because, you see, we were helpless. That is war, Mr Rossouw – time and helplessness. And ruins. At the end of it all – ruins. Man is a builder of ruins. I remember Rome. Went up there when it was over. Rome! The Glory that was Greece and the Grandeur that was Rome. I stood and stared, Mr Rossouw. Broken corners, spaces, fallen walls, pieces . . . it was in pieces . . . the glory, the grandeur was . . . and I recognised It . . . Time . . . realised . . . Time. A thousand years of it in one shell. Eternity at the end of a bayonet.

I've seen it! Smashed, and wrecked and falling! (*Pause*.) Then the guns were silent. They said we had won. Won! I walked through a ruin . . . been a house I think. The dust was settling. It was finished. Broken. That house was dead. But such a peace, Mr Rossouw! Nothing. Silence. Emptiness . . . and it was such a peace.

'It's all over', they said. 'We won,' And then, 'Go home.' Just like that. God, Home! 'What?' I asked. 'What must go home?' Are you blind? We're also ruins. The guns have left our hearts in ruins! (*Pointing to* SERGE.) Look at him. We went to war! 'To defend', they said. To protect. Justice, dignity, freedom! But *that* came back. That! (*Indicates* SERGE.) His laugh is the sound of it falling to pieces! You want to know what the dead hate most of all about us here tonight? His laugh! When Serge laughs they know they're dead. And me? Once upon a time I was a man living happily ever after. But when I came out of that ruin . . . 'you're going home', they said. Just like that. I went mad. Fear! I picked up pieces – a million lives were lying around me in pieces . . . I picked up pieces. But nothing fits! My smile doesn't belong to my face, or my face to my fear, or that to me . . . Me! Nothing fits! And you, Barend?

SERGE: He never went to war.

CAPPIE: He's a ruin.

KOOSIE: Captain . . .

CAPPIE: And him.

KOOSIE: You didn't get to my medal.

CAPPIE: Medal?

KOOSIE: Killed in action – in the ruins. Bravery in battle.

CAPPIE: What the hell! I'll give you the V.C.

SERGE: And me? (*Laughing*) I was there too.

CAPPIE: Degenerate Soldier's Order.

SERGE: And yourself?

CAPPIE: Iron Cross and the Star of David. How's that?

BAREND *stands up and leaves the room through the doorway to the hall.*

CAPPIE (*to* BAREND *as he leaves*): We promised the lady we'd do it outside.

Cut from the lounge to the passage and BAREND. *He is standing quite still. In the distance the voices of* CAPPIE *and* SERGE. *Though we cannot hear what they are saying the noise becomes strident and angry.* BAREND *turns and walks back to the lounge. The voices get clearer. The following dialogue is off-screen.*

SERGE (*emphatic*): No. No. (*There is an indistinct mumble from* CAPPIE.) I know what's coming and I say no. Just cut it out. That's all. Why must you always spoil everything?

CAPPIE (*a military bark*): Sergeant!

SERGE: Cut-it-out, Cappie!

BAREND *reaches the doorway to the lounge. As he moves through it and quick change to a shot of* CAPPIE, SERGE *and* KOOSIE. CAPPIE *is still sitting, still has his bottle.* SERGE *is now standing. He is agitated and at first does not see* BAREND. KOOSIE *is huddled up against a wall, fingers in his ears, eyes tightly closed, trying not to hear what is being said.*

SERGE: I'm not sleeping in here if you're going to start that. This time I mean it. (*He sees* BAREND.) It's nothing. Just . . . it's nothing.

CAPPIE (*to* BAREND): What you up to? Hey? Where you been? Visiting the little girl in her room?

SERGE: Leave him alone, Cappie.

CAPPIE: He's up to something.

SERGE: Can't we just for once go to sleep quietly! All of us?

KOOSIE *opens his eyes and takes his fingers away from his ears.*

KOOSIE: I'll clear up.

During the following dialogue KOOSIE *will drift in and out of the scene. His last exit will be through the doorway leading to the hall and when he returns it will be with the news that he has found the bed.*

SERGE: This could have been cosy. Lay off the booze, Cap. Make a resolution.

CAPPIE: I want to know what Barend's up to. Look at him! Barend! Look us in the eye and say you're not up to something.

SERGE: Knock It Off!

CAPPIE: I'm suspicious of him.

SERGE: Go to bed.

CAPPIE: Bed! Poor old Serge. Faithful as a dog. What bed?

SERGE: All right, then the floor. Lie down and sleep it off.

CAPPIE (*to* BAREND, *aggressively*): I'm suspicious of you.

BAREND *sits down near what remains of the candle, watching the flame and his hands while* CAPPIE *speaks.*

CAPPIE: I've always been. An' you know why? You stink of wages. And dreaming. You dream, don't you Barend? The way you write on lavatory walls – on the sly! You don't fool me. Nobody pulls the wool over Cappie's eyes. What do you dream about?

KOOSIE *returns to the lounge through the second doorway. He goes straight to* CAPPIE.

KOOSIE: Captain . . .

CAPPIE: I'll find that dream, Barend . . . and then I'll piss on it.

KOOSIE: Captain, guess what?

CAPPIE: Roses are red, violets are blue, lilies are white and I love you.

KOOSIE: I found a bed, Captain. A real bed.

CAPPIE: A bed.

KOOSIE: A real one. It's even got a mattress.

SERGE: Where?

KOOSIE: In the little room down there. Must I show you?

KOOSIE *leads* CAPPIE *and* SERGE *out of the lounge, carrying what is left of the candle on a piece of plank.* BAREND *doesn't move. He sits alone, his back to the other three as they leave. Shot changes to:*

The passage. KOOSIE *leading* CAPPIE *and* SERGE. *Shadows. Sound of the leaves and glass as they walk.*

KOOSIE: I was just looking around when I found it. First I went to the dove and then I came down here and found it. It's in there.

They reach the door. Shot changes to:

The room. The bed. KOOSIE, CAPPIE *and* SERGE.

KOOSIE: There. How's that, Captain?

SERGE: It's a bed all right.

KOOSIE: Definitely.

CAPPIE: How did we miss it?

SERGE: What's the odds? We've found it. Try it for size, Cappie.

KOOSIE: Yes, you must have it Captain.

BAREND (*off-screen*): No! Leave it alone.

KOOSIE, SERGE *and* CAPPIE *turn in response.* BAREND *comes through the door into the light.*

BAREND: I found it first. It's mine.

SERGE: What do you mean?

KOOSIE: I found it first.

CAPPIE: You knew about it!

BAREND: This is my room. You can have all the others. This is mine.

CAPPIE: All the time! You knew it was here!

BAREND: Get away from it.

BAREND *moves forward and sits on the bed. The other three move back to the wall where they stand and watch him.*

BAREND: I'm warning you. It's mine.

CAPPIE: So that's it.

BAREND: Get out!

CAPPIE: Home.

BAREND: Get out!

CAPPIE: Your dream is Home.

SERGE: Come, Cap.

KOOSIE: What's going on?

SERGE: Let's move.

CAPPIE: He wants a Home.

KOOSIE: Who's got a home?

BAREND: I'm warning you: Get out! This is my room. My bed. MINE!

SERGE: Let's move, soldier.

SERGE *starts pulling* CAPPIE *to the door.*

CAPPIE: You're not one of us. You're one of them. You're a ghost. You're dead, Barend. Dead.

BAREND *jumps up and pushes the three out of the room, then forces the door closed. The camera stays on* BAREND. *Outside in the passage* CAPPIE *starts hammering on the door. The following dialogue is all heard off-screen through the door.*

CAPPIE (*hammering*): Barend! Barend! Are you there? (*Pause.*) Listen! Barend, listen to me. (*Slowly, very carefully*) The nigger slept in the bed, Barend. Smell the room. His stink is still in the room. You've got a nigger's bed, Dutchman. (*Pause.*) Barend (*starting to shout.*) Barend!

SERGE: Come on, Cap.

KOOSIE: Let's go, Captain.

CAPPIE: We're finished with you. D'you hear. You're out. Tomorrow you'll crawl around like a lost dog. We don't want you. (*Getting fainter.*) Nobody wants you. You've had it. Barend you're . . . (*words muffled and indistinct.*)

BAREND *listens for a few more seconds, then moves back to the bed.* CAPPIE's *voice is still heard from time to time – an indistinct jeering sound. Then silence.* BAREND *prepares for bed. From his pocket three stubs of candle, one of which he lights and places beside the bed on the floor. Rolls up his coat to use as a pillow. He is still busy when the shot changes to:*

The lounge. KOOSIE *holding their candle. It is just about finished.*

KOOSIE (*watching the candle*): Captain . . .

CAPPIE *and* SERGE. SERGE *now has the bottle.* CAPPIE *is forcing him to drink.*

SERGE (*desperate*): I knew it. (*He drinks.*) I saw it coming.

CAPPIE: More. All of it.

SERGE: I'm still sore, Cappie (*He drinks – the wine spilling out of his mouth.*) S'true's Christ. I'm still as sore as hell.

KOOSIE (*off-screen*): Captain!

CAPPIE *and* SERGE *look in* KOOSIE's *direction. Shot changes just in time for us to see the candle guttering and then going out. Silence.*

KOOSIE: Finished.

CAPPIE (*to Serge*): Bottoms up.

KOOSIE: Captain, there is still the dove.

CAPPIE: Kill it.

KOOSIE: Death sentence! I'll do it at dawn.

SERGE: Just remember it hurts. Not so rough this time. Try and be gentle.

KOOSIE: And sentry duty, Captain? He might come again. What's the password?

CAPPIE: Ravioli.

KOOSIE: Ravioli. You haven't got a gun for me, Captain? Captain, you . . .

SERGE (*singing*): Roll me over, in the clover, roll me over, lay me down and do it again.

KOOSIE *leaves the room. Slow fade to:*

BAREND. *He is ready for bed. His shoes and socks are placed neatly on the floor beside the candle. He goes to the door, listens, then opens it and looks out. He closes it and then goes to the windows where he tries to look out through the shutters. Finally to his bed.*

BAREND (*sitting on the edge of the bed*): It's late! Tomorrow . . . ?

The last word is said with emphasis, as if a statement is to follow, but then cannot be found. For a few seconds BAREND *stares at the inscrutable surface of the word. This one word, followed by a silence which turns statement into question, can be repeated by* BAREND *once or twice off-screen, between this moment and the end.*

He lies down. Camera comes in close. Shot changes to:

The lounge. Close-up of CAPPIE. *He is awake, curled up in a corner. More than anything else we see his eyes — open, alert, listening, like an animal whose only defence is to lie quiet and hope it will not be seen. Then a shot of* SERGE, *sprawled out on the floor, asleep. Finally a shot, the camera again close up, of* KOOSIE. *The camera starts to move back. We see that* KOOSIE *is holding the dove, still alive, and* BAREND'S *stick . . . that he is sitting on the front verandah of the house. The camera keeps moving back. We see the whole house.*

Notes on the Plays

1. ENCOUNTER

The 'encounter' of the title of this play carries the many meanings of its theme. It signifies a verb and a noun, it means 'come up against one another' – 'being face to face', 'meeting', 'making contact', 'clashing', 'fighting'. It is the encounter of two opposite outlooks that the playwright spotlights.

Encounter stages the dramatic conflict between two groups of people by showing it both as a physical and mental struggle, and highlights this by centreing around one, as it were, 'neutral' person. This person at different times sees the fight of the Mau-Mau as a 'war of independence' and as a 'rebellion'. But always, despite this ambivalence in the background, in the forefront of the action the playwright skilfully counterbalances two opposite and opposing points of view.

The play opens in the middle of a clash between John Dewey and Paddy. Their long, tense discussion anticipates and contains the excitement of the meeting with 'General' Nyati. In the camp of the terrorists of guerrillas there is also tension, generated again by the unrevealed presence of the General whose personality exudes an influence that is pervasive, alive, constant. When the General is uncovered, the clash in situation and character, and the quick changes of position (between him and John Dewey) recall Scene 1. Dewey and Paddy were locked in an intellectual, verbal combat; Dewey's views then were distinctly different from, even opposite to, his present. Why?

This is the kind of question (and, with it, the kind of irony and suspense) which informs the play. The play is committed; it involves us; yet it is refreshingly open in its outlook. But it is sharp in its insights, and tightly constructed.

For instance, under the apparently relaxed surface of the scene of the jungle fighters there lurk tension and irony, menace and question, fear, hope and solace. The scene is laden with echoes from Scene 1; so it is vibrant with urgency and a sense of the sinister. The scarcely hidden suspicion nerves the entire scene with dramatic double irony: speeches are double-edged, and the audience can interpret them as they wish. In fact, double irony becomes multiple irony.

While still in the second scene, there is also inherent interest in the interplay of the unnamed, but clearly differentiated characters: the first guerrilla is choleric, fervent, emotional; the second is innocent, idealistic, rational, a person of sentiment, sympathy and balance; no. 3 is an evasive irritant, cynically sceptical; no. 4 seems young, is questing, unsurely probing, anxious, sentimental; and the sixth is practical, observant.

Quick action, sudden climaxes and surprise load into the internal ironies of Scene 3. The ironies are chiefly in the attitudes of and changing relationships between Lieut. John Dewey and General Nyati; these ironies are expressed against a background of muted bitterness and are expressed in a dialogue of fine shadings.

Glossary

shauri (*p. 18*): Swahili for 'plan', 'advice', 'strategy'; here skirmish, revolt, rebellion

bwana (*p. 18*): Sir, master, mister, gentleman
ser-(i)-kali (*p. 19*): government
jamaa (*p. 19*): fellow(s), friend(s), comrade(s); men
mzungu (*p. 20*): white man, European
panga (*p. 24*): broad, flat-bladed knife; scimitar-like sword-axe
Ngai (*p. 26*): the Creator, the Almighty, God
kwa-heri (*p. 55*): Goodbye

2. YON KON

The apparent indefiniteness of *Yon Kon* belies its actual structure. Basically this is a comedy, but a comedy of menace set in a kind of shut-in world. The play has a very moral groundwork, and it deals with the meaning, value and purpose of individual existence: but, again, out of the personal ethic that is expressed through Yon Kon, a social pathos and a tenderness are expressed. These survive the suggestions of 'Life is absurd!', 'Life is cruel!' that seem basic to the play. Finally, the fundamental structure of the play is on the lines of: Right-left-left-right, yes-no-no-yes.

Glossary

gumbay (*p. 67*): practice; dance with singing; drum music. 'Gumbay' itself is a drum
lappa (*p. 67*): cloth
agbakra (*p. 69*): intoxicant
'*see to see*' (*p. 74*): reference to bribery; distrust bred by dishonesty

3. THE GAME

The light, amoral little play is carried forward by its vital gusto in life and the energy of its expansiveness. Its style and movement recall the Roman satyr-plays with their central slave-instructor 'side-kicks', classical French comedy, Italian Commedia del Arte and Restoration light drama. *The Game* is wholly in the picaresque tradition, with the big-hearted scoundrel as hero.

An interesting comparison can be made of *The Game* and *Blind Cyclos* (in this volume), and with both these and *The Lion and the Jewel* by Wole Soyinka.

4. BLIND CYCLOS

This swift-moving, fluid, Brechtian satire exposes social evils ranging from election-trickery and rent-racketeering, to bribery and corruption and hypocrisy. It achieves a beautiful fusion of scenes and of the various textures in its dialogue, its rhythm and its style.

One thinks of Akoneddi as an Ariel, a Puck, or Fate or Poetic (Dramatic) Justice, that is both magically and logically responsible for the delirium, blindness and wounding of Olemu. Then again, Akoneddi is very like a chorus that reminds us, and remarks for us that

> . . . the earth that takes round ours and us
>
> Is deep and unclean as a refuse pit.

Such a central personage could be interestingly used in adapting this play (written for the convention of the radio) for production on stage.

It is with a series of deft strokes of construction that the playwright engineers his scenes, people, events and issues into place, not least being Nkem, who appears late but was introduced quite early. It is all smooth-oiled cogs and sharp-toothed combs sliding and slipping meticulously into co-ordinated movement.

Glossary

kola (*p. 118*): bribe

cowries, manillas, toròs, sisi (*p. 122*): traditional currency
cunny (*p. 125*): cunning

5. WITH STRINGS

Although Sondhi's theme and treatment are so different here from those in *Encounter*, his strengths are the same. At first sight this drawing-room drama may seem almost pedestrian: its domestic naturalism is leisurely; there is a none-too-startling plot, slight character development and little style. And yet the delineation of character, and the establishment of character, is steady and in the true drawing-room manner: we can nearly predict the behaviour of the characters, but there is surprise and development in the central character. And as he is revealed, there is a good, slow-paced development of the situation, and we find ourselves involved in it, and in its growing ramifications. There is humour – mild, quiet, smiling, sympathetic; and there is also mystery around the gradual deployment of the theme: a morally sound personal choice is possible to a person even where racial and social (monetary) factors obtrude openly and most directly on the individual life.

Although the dialogue sometimes sounds stilted, bookish and studied, there are always hidden openings for irony. The irony is sometimes suggested, sometimes stated. Thus in Scene 1 we seem to tune in to high-school debate, but in Scene 2 there is a discovering of various ironies and a revelation of interesting situations.

Throughout the play we are conscious of the central dilemma: there are situations when one is faced with a choice between alternatives, either of which entails loss or deprivation of some kind; yet one *must* choose.

A comparison between *With Strings* and *The Deviant*, or another between *With Strings* and *The Opportunity*, may prove interesting.

Glossary

masala (p. 144): spicy Indian condiment

saried (p. 148): from sari – long, ankle-length, graceful draped female garment generally worn by conventional Indians

samaj (p. 151): religio-cultural meeting-place (Hindu)

6. THE DEVIANT

In the single scene of this play and around its one, fairly simple setting, a lot happens. It is a play mainly of the intellect, but it touches the heart.

In parts, especially at the beginning, *The Deviant* strikes a mannered, cynical note, like an Oscar Wilde comedy. In others it becomes a verbal farce, like the plays of Eugene Ionesco. Its dialogue is often witty: funny, clever, and significant: then it is sharp, biting, sardonic, mordant. Often again it uses the double-take, or paradox and epigram, or repetition, to achieve comic effects. Or else speeches run from a poetic form into a rhetorical style into pure bombast, then back to natural speech and realism. Some jokes sound forced, but the over-all effect is of a fast, well-played game, especially with its wealth of quotations and allusions and its apparent reference, in plot and situation, to two of Shaw's plays.

What can be regarded as the preface and introduction of the action are like a skirmish between a fool and a clown in which the thick-skinned yes-man is battered with insults. Here the bookish conversation of the intellectual cynic is quite in character with his thought, and it sounds right. On the other hand there is the naïveté of the simpleton.

But there is soon a sharpening of feeling and a heightening of atmosphere. Midway through the play nerves are exposed and, with the coming of the third person onto the scene, the plot broadens and deepens. We even begin to wonder now who is protagonist and who is antagonist. The theme widens.

Now we are in a sphere where public causes are set beside private lives: how do they mix? do they ever square?

We are to be involved in physical and intellectual conflict: should we opt for the rôle of Don Quixote? Or that of Falstaff?

There are universal and general causes! But life is mine. I am individual. How are these causes specific to me? Are they applicable?

Finally we have the humour and pathos of the concluding talk which is a conversation and dialogue of cross-purposes.

Glossary

sari (p. 169): long, draped dress; a female garment

choli (p. 169): garment worn with sari

buddu chairs (p. 169): low, comfortable seats, generally of cane

Karl Marx (p. 174): author and founder of Communism

Marx Brothers (p. 174): famous film comedians

Divine Comedy (p. 174): long allegorical poem by Dante

Moslem (= Muslim) (p. 177): a believer in Islam; one of the Mohammedan faith

Kashmir (p. 177): a state in the Indian sub-continent, bone of contention between Pakistan and Republic of India

Antigone and Creon (p. 179): in classical legend and drama, rebellious loyalty and harsh authority in ancient Thebes

John Collins (p. 182): a 'cocktail' for 'he-men'

Angola, Sharpeville,
Algiers, Bizerta, Congo, } in recent history, scenes of
Little Rock (p. 183): } wars and civil clashes

Hiroshima, Nagasaki (p. 184): Japanese cities struck by
first atomic bombs loosed over an enemy

7. FUSANE'S TRIAL

This is a quick-moving, trenchant play that seems episodic
only because it was originally written for the radio.

It is comparable in style, treatment and structure with
this playwright's published full-length stage play, *The
Rain-Killers.* Interesting similarities and differences
are revealed when one reads these two Hutchinsons side
by side.

Glossary

Ma- (Magwaza, Mtetwa) (p. 192): the wife of, Mrs; literally,
mother of

La- (Ngwenya, Mkize, etc.) (p. 192): indicative of con-
cubinage; literally, child of

Mfundisi (p. 193): Reverend

Lobola (p. 194): bride-price, dowry (paid in livestock –
cattle – or money to the bride's family)

kraal (p. 197): settlement; family or clan home; (tribal)
village

dudu s'thandwa sami (p. 200): sleep, my beloved; be still, my
dear; sweet sleep of mine

Ntsefestefestefe (p. 201): spring-mattress (Onomatopaeic
word, echoing sound of springs in rhythmic motion)

Production Notes

For production purposes, Scenes 7 and 8 may be made
continuations of Scene 6, following short blackouts.

At the start of Scene 6, the slow fade may be achieved
by any one or different combinations of several devices:

rostra (for varying levels), taped voices, screens (very light and mobile), moving pools of light.

8. THE OPPORTUNITY

This is a play that boldly faces the perils and ably releases the potentials of the setting and the subject. It takes personal and political themes and draws on them mutually, showing how they interact. It exposes a stock-in-trade theme in an amazingly new manner.

The tale that is told is remorseless; the telling is frank, clear, open. This is because the dramatist has a mind that is open for objective irony and a heart equally open to sympathetic humour. The themes are finely perceived, and so are the characters, and they are sharply drawn, cunningly drawn together. Maimane's dialogue lives, his plot grows, his relationships continuously expand. Because of a rising line of artfully achieved climaxes in a context of reality and within a realistic style, the play is vitally rhythmical, paced and incisive.

The construction of the play is crisp; the introduction leads straight into the middle of things, and right through the motivation of action is beautifully clear, though subtle; hence both characters and characterisation are 'apt'—especially because Maimane's ear is there to tune in to simplicity, passionate rhetoric, to 'proverbialism' that never becomes 'proverbialese', and to the dramatic, meaningful scream or silence. What is more, there is a fully achieved balance of expression.

The dramatic acrobatics of *The Opportunity* make for a complex involved richness that is also remarkably simple. In production it calls for finesse in pace and delivery: conviction, clarity, the right tempo and good timing are always necessary for a play to live, but the more especially so with a finely and variously textured product of realism like *The Opportunity*.

Production Note

Scene 2 may, for economy's sake, be placed in the Dining-room or the Kitchen of Scene 3.

9. MAAMA

This charming play owes much of its attractiveness to the appealing, almost classical simplicity of its form and style. There are no airs and graces about it, and yet it is more than a naïve drama about the old-new theatrical theme of civilization versus barbarism; medicine versus superstition and witchcraft.

Some of this 'more' is due to the light and easy alternation between courtly or royal scenes and domestic ones; yet more is attributable to the grace and ease with which scenes change and faintly remind us, not only of earlier or other scenes in the present play, but of notes and tones, images and symbols in other plays from many different places and times.

Different times or eras quite removed from each other, in fact, often seem to co-exist in this play. Nor does it disturb the tenor of a quite memorable little drama; in fact this seeming anachronistic tendency is only one of the quite numerous, rather subtle 'African' features about *Maama*.

10. THE OCCUPATION

The play in its present (and original) form is meant for television. It would probably not be very easy to present it on stage unless it were fully adapted for performance in the theatre. A possible way out may be to use filmed and projected images, or a device such as rapidly changeable backdrops and lighting effects to do some of the work of the T.V. camera.

The television script provides us with a play of wide significance, possibly because it is the only T.V. script in our anthology. This apart, its meaning in terms of the three ex-soldiers (Koosie seems the rookie, the raw recruit to the new army of tramps that the others have mobilised themselves into) as particular individuals and Koosie as a specific young man, is second only to what it says in terms of war and its effects. More probably these meanings run side by side: these shell-shocked, perverted, de-normalised men are what they are because of their make-up and their history, and their history includes war. Each of the men is individualised by his authority, his history and his distinct personality.

Along with these meanings, there also seems to run the further allegorical meaning of life and the social situation in South Africa, perhaps that of a world in which life is existence, and existence is 'the occupation' of a derelict house, a one-time home now occupied only by tramps and desires and haunted by ghostly memories and fears.

Glossary

tickeys (*p. 268*): threepenny bits

orange flash (*p. 271*): the tab of the South African soldier during World War II

Smuts (*p. 271*): South African Prime Minister during World War II

Karoo (*p. 272*): wide, arid area in the centre of Cape Province, South Africa

native (*p. 275*): slighting term for South African aboriginal

knob-kierie (*p. 275*): cudgel, club; stick with knobbed end *kaffir (p. 278)*: highly derogatory term for African in South Africa

ek is nie bang vir 'n . . . (p. 279): I'm not afraid of a . . . (Afrikaans)

witmense (p. 279): white people

so, julle kan gaan bars (p. 282): Afrikaans for: and so you can go to hell

hok (p. 284): Afrikaans for: (fowl) run, (dove) cote

Woodstock (p. 285): a (relatively) poor suburb of Cape Town, South Africa

BIOGRAPHICAL NOTES

GANESH BAGCHI born 1926 in India. He read English at the University of Calcutta. After teaching in Uganda, he spent a year at the Institute of Education, London University. Before returning to Calcutta, he was first a headmaster in Uganda and then principal of a government teacher training college in Kampala. He started writing one-act plays in 1958 and has won a number of awards at the Uganda Drama Festivals.

FEMI EUBA born and educated in Nigeria. He trained at a London drama school and now lives and works in England. He has played leading parts in the London productions of Wole Soyinka's plays, as well as participating in many broadcast plays for the B.B.C. Some of his work, including *The Game*, has been broadcast by the B.B.C.

ATHOL FUGARD born in South Africa, his play *The Blood Knot* took him first to England and then to the United States, where he had considerable success in one of the two parts. The play has also been televised by the B.B.C. He first organized a theatre group in Port Elizabeth and subsequently worked with new groups in Johannesburg and London. *The Occupation* was first published in South Africa, by *Contrast*.

ALFRED HUTCHINSON born in 1924 in South Africa. He graduated from Fort Hare University College and then taught in Johannesburg. While there he started writing articles and short stories, but was involved in the South African Treason Trial and had to flee the country. On reaching Ghana, he published *Road to Ghana*, a vivid account of his escape. Now resident in England, he has had a number of plays (including *Fusane's Trial*) broadcast, as well as having *The Rain-Killers* published.

IME IKIDDEH born in Eastern Nigeria in 1938, he later went to Ghana, where he graduated in English. He then read for a post-graduate degree at the University of Leeds and was appointed lecturer in English at the University of Ghana in October 1966. One of several plays he has written, *Blind Cyclos* was first broadcast by the B.B.C.

KWESI KAY born and educated in Ghana. As an actor he has appeared in repertory, television, films and on the radio since going to England in 1963. *Maama* is his second play, written in 1961. In addition he has written reviews and poems which have been broadcast by the B.B.C.

PAT MADDY born in 1936 in Sierra Leone, where he was educated. After working briefly for Sierra Leone Railways, he went to Europe and is now living in Denmark. He was the first African to go to Denmark and lecture on contemporary African literature. His plays have been televised in England and Denmark and his poems published there as well as in East and West Africa.

ARTHUR MAIMANE born in South Africa in 1932. He trained

as a journalist in South Africa and then became Reuter's correspondent in East Africa. After working for a time in Ghana he went to England and now works as a current affairs commentator for the B.B.C. In addition to having several plays broadcast, he has published a number of short stories in such magazines as *Transition*, *The New African* and *Drum*.

COSMO PIETERSE born in 1930 in South West Africa. After graduating from Cape Town University, he taught in South Africa for ten years before taking up a teaching appointment in London. Besides writing scripts, poems and reviews, he produces and acts in plays both on stage and for radio.

KULDIP SONDHI born in Lahore in 1924, was educated in Kenya before gaining an M.Sc. in aeronautical engineering in U.S.A. He has always written as a hobby. Another play, *Undesignated* has recently been published in *Short East African Plays* (Heinemann Educational Books).